Contents

Silverlight 2 Visual Essentials

by Matthew MacDonald

Microsoft Silverlight is a cross-browser, cross-platform plug-in, similar to Flash, that delivers rich interactive applications for the Web. Silverlight offers a flexible programming model based largely on Windows Presentation Foundation (WPF); it supports a number of different programming languages and techniques (making it cross-platform) and all major browsers (providing cross-browser support). There is lots of interest in Microsoft's Flash killer, and several conferences have seen heavy support for this exciting technology.

Little published information on this technology is available on the market now, and so this introduction to the visual features and capabilities of Silverlight will hopefully get you going quickly.

This concise book is meant to give you a sense of what you, as a programmer, can expect from Silverlight in terms of what the user is going to see. The emphasis here is on understanding what Silverlight has to offer. While there is some code given, that is not the point of the book. The point is to be able to quickly understand what functionality is available to you and what options you might have without getting bogged down in much code.

The text assumes that you are a programmer and that you have an understanding of XAML. However, if you ignore the code that exists in the book, then any layperson, or even an administrator, can come to grips with the visual element of Silverlight.

The text that follows is largely adapted from Matthew MacDonald's Pro Silverlight 2 in C# 2008, *Berkeley, CA: Apress, 2008 (http://apress.com/ book/view/1590599497).*

Chapter 1: Introducing Silverlight

Silverlight is a framework for building rich, browser-hosted applications that run on a variety of operating systems. Silverlight works its magic through a *browser plug-in*. When you surf to a web page that includes some Silverlight content, this browser plug-in runs, executes the code, and renders that content in a specifically designated region of the page. The important part is that the Silverlight plug-in provides a far richer environment than the traditional blend of HTML and JavaScript that powers ordinary web pages. Used carefully and artfully, you can create Silverlight pages that have interactive graphics, use vector animations, and play video and sound files.

If this all sounds familiar, it's because the same trick has been tried before. Several other technologies use a plug-in to stretch the bounds of the browser, including Java, ActiveX, Shockwave, and (most successfully) Adobe Flash. Although all these alternatives are still in use, none of them has become the dominant platform for rich web development. Many of them suffer from a number of problems, including installation headaches, poor development tools, and insufficient compatibility with the full range of browsers and operating systems. The only technology that's been able to avoid these pitfalls is Flash, which boasts excellent cross-platform support and widespread adoption. However, Flash has only recently evolved from a spunky multimedia player into a set of dynamic programming tools. It still offers far less than a modern programming environment like .NET.

That's where Silverlight fits into the picture. Silverlight aims to combine the raw power and cross-platform support of Flash with a first-class programming platform that incorporates the fundamental concepts of .NET. At the moment, Flash has the edge over Silverlight because of its widespread adoption and its maturity. However, Silverlight boasts a few architectural features that Flash can't match—most importantly, the fact that it's based on a scaled-down version of .NET's common language runtime (CLR) and allows developers to write client-side code using pure C#.

In this chapter, you'll take your first tour of the Silverlight world. You'll see how Silverlight applications are structured, and you'll learn to create one in Visual Studio. Lastly, you'll peer under the covers to see how Silverlight applications are compiled and deployed to the Web.

Understanding Silverlight

Silverlight uses a familiar technique to go beyond the capabilities of standard web pages: a lightweight browser plug-in.

The advantage of the plug-in model is that the user needs to install just a single component to see content created by a range of different people and companies. Installing the plug-in requires a small download and forces the user to confirm the operation in at least one security dialog box (and usually more). It takes a short but definite amount of time, so it's an obvious inconvenience. However, once the plug-in is installed, the browser can process any content that uses the plug-in seamlessly, with no further prompting.

Note   Silverlight is designed to overcome the limitations of ordinary HTML to allow developers to create more graphical and interactive applications. However, Silverlight isn't a way for developers to break out of the browser's security sandbox. For the most part, Silverlight applications are limited in equivalent ways to ordinary web pages. For example, a Silverlight application is allowed to create and access files, but only those files that are stored in a special walled-off *isolated storage* area. Conceptually, isolated storage works like the cookies in an ordinary web page. Files are separated by web site and the current user, and size is severely limited.

Figure 1-1 shows two views of a page with Silverlight content. On the top is the page you'll see if you *don't* have the Silverlight plug-in installed. At this point, you can click the Get Microsoft Silverlight picture to be taken to Microsoft's web site, where you'll be prompted to install the plug-in and then sent back to the original page. On the bottom is the page you'll see once the Silverlight plug-in is installed.

Figure 1-1. Installing the Silverlight plug-in

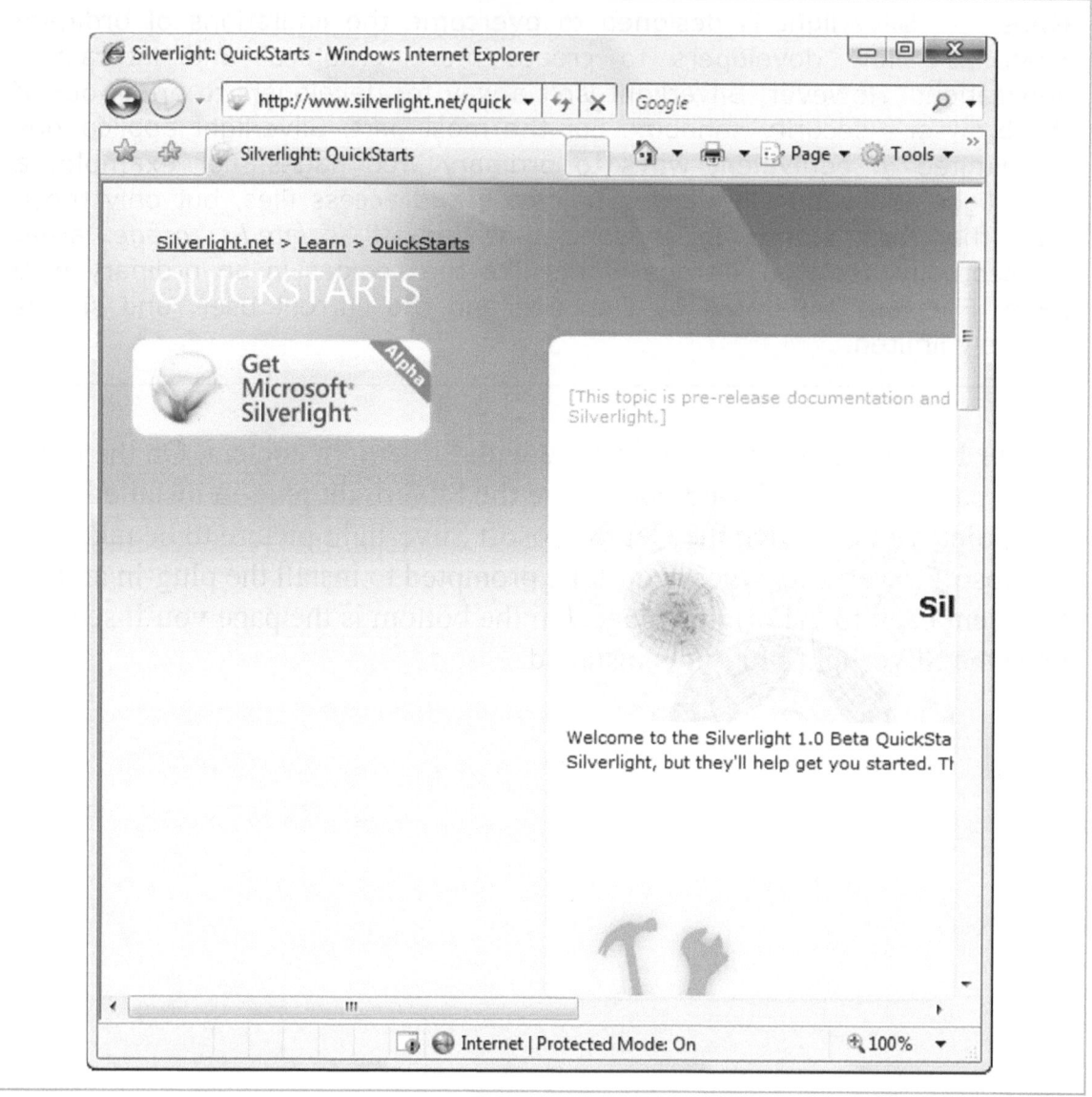

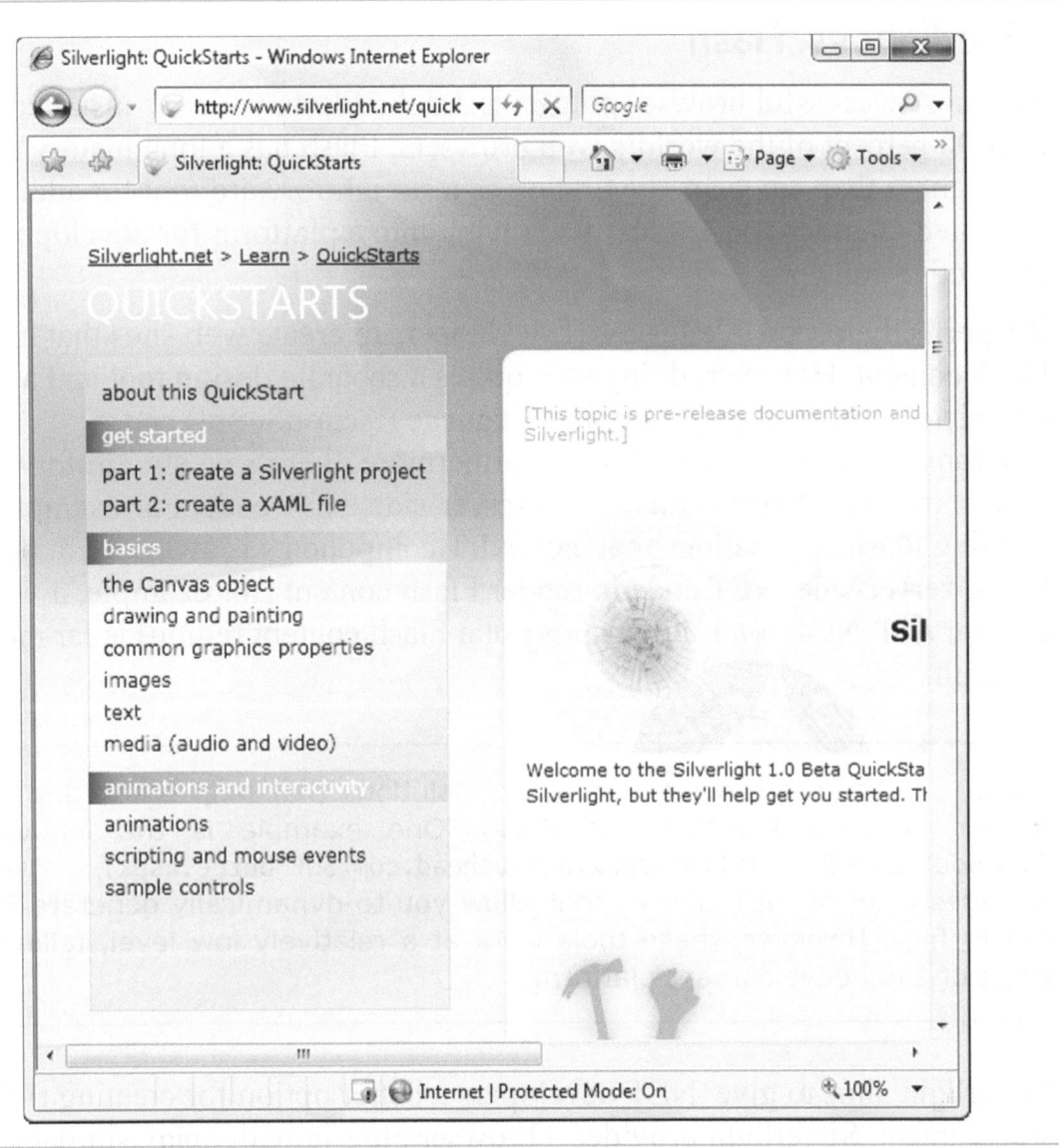

Silverlight vs. Flash

The most successful browser plug-in is Adobe Flash, which is installed on over 90 percent of the world's web browsers. Flash has a long history that spans more than ten years, beginning as a straightforward tool for adding animated graphics and gradually evolving into a platform for developing interactive content.

It's perfectly reasonable for .NET developers to create web sites that use Flash content. However, doing so requires a separate design tool and a completely different programming language (ActionScript) and programming environment (Flex). Furthermore, there's no straightforward way to integrate Flash content with server-side .NET code. For example, creating Flash applications that call .NET components is awkward at best. Using server-side .NET code to render Flash content (for example, a custom ASP.NET control that spits out a Flash content region) is far more difficult.

Note There are some third-party solutions that help break down the barrier between ASP.NET and Flash. One example is the innovative SWFSource.NET (http://www.activehead.com/SWFSource.aspx), which provides a set of .NET classes that allow you to dynamically generate Flash (SWF) files. However, these tools work at a relatively low level, falling far short of a full development platform.

Silverlight aims to give .NET developers a better option for creating rich web content. Silverlight provides a browser plug-in with many similar features to Flash, but one that's designed from the ground up for .NET. Silverlight natively supports the C# language and embraces a range of .NET concepts. As a result, developers can write client-side code for Silverlight in the same language they use for server-side code (such as C#

and VB) and use many of the same abstractions (including streams, controls, collections, generics, and LINQ).

The Silverlight plug-in has an impressive list of features, some of which are shared in common with Flash, and a few of which are entirely new and even revolutionary. Here are some highlights:

- **Widespread browser support**: It's too early to tell how well the Silverlight browser works on different platforms. Currently, the beta builds of Silverlight 2.0 work on Windows Vista and Windows XP (in the PC universe) and OS X 10.4.8 or later (in the Mac world). The minimum browser versions that Silverlight 2.0 supports are Internet Explorer 6, Firefox 1.5.0.8, and Safari 2.0.4. Although Silverlight 2.0 doesn't currently work on Linux, the Mono team is creating an open source Linux implementation of Silverlight 1.0 and Silverlight 2.0. This project is known as Moonlight, and it's being developed with key support from Microsoft. To learn more, visit `http://www.mono-project.com/Moonlight`.

- **Lightweight download**: In order to encourage adoption, Silverlight is installed with a small-size setup (about 4MB) that's easy to download. That allows it to provide an all-important "frictionless" setup experience, much like Flash (but quite different from Java).

- **2D drawing**: Silverlight provides a rich model for 2D drawing. Best of all, the content you draw is defined as shapes and paths, so you can manipulate this content on the client side. You can even respond to events (like a mouse click on a portion of a graphic), which makes it easy to add interactivity to anything you draw.

- **Controls**: Developers don't want to reinvent the wheel, so Silverlight is stocked with a few essentials, including buttons, text boxes, lists, and a grid. Best of all, these basic building blocks can be restyled with custom visuals if you want all of the functionality but none of the stock look.

- **Animation**: Silverlight has a time-based animation model that lets you define what should happen and how long it should take. The Silverlight plug-in handles the sticky details, like interpolating intermediary values and calculating the frame rate.

- **Media**: Silverlight provides playback of Windows Media Audio (WMA), Windows Media Video (WMV7 through WMV9), MP3 audio, and VC-1 (which supports high definition). You aren't tied to the Windows Media Player ActiveX control or browser plug-in—instead, you can create any front end you want, and you can even show video in full-screen mode. Microsoft also provides a free companion hosting service (at `http://silverlight.live.com`) that gives you space to store media files. Currently, it offers a generous 10GB.

- **The CLR**: Most impressively, Silverlight includes a scaled-down version of the CLR, complete with an essential set of core classes, a garbage collector, a just-in-time (JIT) compiler, support for generics, threading, and so on. In many cases, developers can take code written for the full .NET CLR and use it in a Silverlight application with only moderate changes.

- **Networking**: Silverlight applications can call old-style ASP.NET web services (ASMX) or Windows Communication Foundation (WCF) web services. They can also send manually created XML requests over HTTP. This gives developers a great way to combine rich client-side code with secure server-side routines.

- **Data binding**: Although it's not as capable as in its big brother, Windows Presentation Foundation (WPF), Silverlight data binding provides a convenient way to display large amounts of data with minimal code. You can pull your data from XML or in-memory objects, giving you the ability to call a web service, receive a collection of objects, and display their data in a web page—often with just a couple of lines of code.

Of course, it's just as important to note what Silverlight *doesn't* include. Silverlight is a new technology that's evolving rapidly, and it's full of stumbling blocks for developers who are used to relying on .NET's rich libraries of prebuilt functionality. Prominent gaps include lack of database support (there's no ADO.NET), no support for 3D drawing, no printing, no command model, and few rich controls like trees and menus (although many developers and component companies are building their own). All of these features are available in Windows-centric WPF applications, and they may someday migrate to the Silverlight universe—or not.

Silverlight 1.0 and 2.0

Silverlight exists in two versions:

- The first version, Silverlight 1.0, is a relatively modest technology. It includes the 2D drawing features and the media playback features. However, it doesn't include the CLR engine or support for .NET languages, so any code you write must use JavaScript.

- The second version, Silverlight 2.0, adds the .NET-powered features that have generated the most developer excitement. It includes the CLR, a subset of .NET Framework classes, and a user interface model based on WPF (as described in the next section, "Silverlight and WPF").

Many developers consider Silverlight 2.0 to be the *real* first release of the Silverlight platform. It's the only version you'll consider in this book.

Note   At present, Silverlight is only on a fraction of computers. However, Microsoft is convinced that if compelling content exists for Silverlight, users will download the plug-in. A number of factors support this argument. Flash grew dramatically in a short space of time, and Microsoft has obvious experience with other web-based applications that have started small and eventually gained wide adoption. (Windows Messenger comes to mind, along with numerous ActiveX plug-ins for tasks ranging from multiuser coordination on MSN Games to Windows verification on MSDN.)

Silverlight and WPF

One of the most interesting aspects of Silverlight is the fact that it borrows the model WPF uses for rich, client-side user interfaces.

WPF is a next-generation technology for creating Windows applications. It was introduced in .NET 3.0 as the successor to Windows Forms. WPF is notable because it not only simplifies development with a powerful set of high-level features, but also increases performance by rendering everything through the DirectX pipeline. To learn about WPF, you can refer to another of my books, *Pro WPF in C# 2008: Windows Presentation Foundation with .NET 3.5, Second Edition* (Apress, 2008).

Silverlight obviously can't duplicate the features of WPF, because many of them rely deeply on the capabilities of the operating system, including Windows-specific display drivers and DirectX technology. However, rather than invent an entirely new set of controls and classes for client-side development, Silverlight uses a subset of the WPF model. If you've had any experience with WPF, you'll be surprised to see how closely Silverlight resembles its bigger brother. Here are a few common details:

- To define a Silverlight user interface (the collection of elements that makes up a Silverlight content region), you use XAML markup, just as you do with WPF. You can even map data to your display using the same data binding syntax.

- Silverlight borrows many of the same basic controls from WPF, along with the same styling system (for standardizing and reusing formatting) and a similar templating mechanism (for changing the appearance of standard controls).

- To draw 2D graphics in Silverlight, you use shapes, paths, transforms, geometries, and brushes, all of which closely match their WPF equivalents.

- Silverlight provides a declarative animation model that's based on storyboards and works in the same way as WPF's animation system.

- To show video or play audio files, you use the `MediaElement` class, as you do in WPF.

Microsoft has made no secret about its intention to continue to expand the capabilities of Silverlight by drawing from the full WPF model. In future Silverlight releases, you're likely to find that Silverlight borrows more and more features from WPF. This trend is already on display with the shift from Silverlight 1.0 to Silverlight 2.0.

In other words, Silverlight is a .NET-based Flash competitor. It aims to compete with Flash today, but provide a path to far more features in the future. Unlike the Flash development model, which is limited in several ways due to the way it's evolved over the years, Silverlight is a starting-from-scratch attempt that's thoroughly based on .NET and WPF, and will therefore allow .NET developers to be far more productive. In many ways, Silverlight is the culmination of two trends: the drive to extend web pages to incorporate more and more rich-client features, and the drive to give the .NET Framework a broader reach.

Note Understanding XAML is critical to Silverlight application design, as it will help you learn key Silverlight concepts and ensure that you get the markup you really want. More importantly, a host of tasks are only possible—or are far easier to accomplish—with handwritten XAML, including wiring up event handlers, defining resources, creating control templates, writing data binding expressions, and defining animations. In the future, most Silverlight developers will probably use a combination of techniques, laying out some of their user interface with a design tool (Visual Studio or Expression Blend) and then fine-tuning it by editing the XAML markup by hand. However, the support for Silverlight in the current generation of design tools is limited and changing rapidly. As a result, you'll probably find yourself shouldering using tools to create key content (for example, complex graphics), while adding most of the controls by hand.

Note WPF is not completely cut off from the easy deployment world of the Web. WPF allows developers to create browser-hosted applications called XAML Browser Applications (XBAPs). These applications download seamlessly, cache locally, and run directly inside the browser window, all without security prompts. However, although XBAPs run in Internet Explorer and Firefox, they are still a Windows-only technology, unlike Silverlight.

Silverlight and Visual Studio

Although it's technically possible to create the files you need for a Silverlight application by hand, professional developers always use a development tool. If you're a graphic designer, that tool is likely to be Microsoft Expression Blend 2.5, a graphically rich design package. If you're a developer, you'll probably start with Visual Studio 2008 instead. Because both tools are equally at home with the Silverlight 2.0 application model, you can easily create a workflow that incorporates both of them. For example, a developer could create a basic user interface with Visual Studio and then hand it off to a crack design team, which would then polish it up with custom graphics in Expression Blend. When the facelift is finished, they'd deliver the project back to the developer, who could then continue writing and refining code in Visual Studio.

Note Before you can use Visual Studio 2008 to create Silverlight applications, you need to install a set of extensions for Silverlight development.

Understanding Silverlight Web Sites

There are two types of Silverlight web sites that you can create in Visual Studio:

- **Ordinary HTML web site**: In this case, the entry point to your Silverlight application is a basic HTML file that includes a Silverlight content region.

- **ASP.NET web site**: In this case, Visual Studio creates two projects—one to contain the Silverlight application files, and one to hold the server-side ASP.NET web site that will be deployed alongside your Silverlight files. The entry point to your Silverlight application can be an ordinary HTML file or an ASP.NET web form that also includes server-generated content.

No matter which option you choose, your Silverlight application will run the same way—the client browser will receive an HTML web page, that HTML page will include a Silverlight content region, and the Silverlight code will run on the local computer, *not* the web server. However, the ASP.NET web approach makes it easier to mix ASP.NET and Silverlight content. This is usually a better approach in the following cases:

- You want to create a web application that combines ASP.NET web pages with Silverlight-enhanced pages.

- You want to generate Silverlight content indirectly, using ASP.NET web controls.

- You want to create a Silverlight application that calls a web service, and you want to design the web service at the same time (and deploy it to the same web server).

If you decide to create an ASP.NET web site, your application's requirements will change. Silverlight content can be served by any web server, because it's sent directly to the web browser and processed on the client side. ASP.NET content runs on the web server, which must have the ASP.NET engine installed.

ADDING SILVERLIGHT CONTENT TO AN EXISTING WEB SITE

A key point to keep in mind when considering the Silverlight development model is that in many cases you'll use Silverlight to *augment* the existing content of your web site, which will still include generous amounts of HTML, CSS, and JavaScript. For example, you might add Silverlight content that shows an advertisement or allows an enhanced experience for a portion of a web site (such as playing a game, completing a survey, interacting with a product, taking a virtual tour, and so on). Your Silverlight pages may present content that's already available in your web site in a more engaging way, or they may represent a value-added feature for users who have the Silverlight plug-in.

Of course, it's also possible to create a Silverlight-only web site, which is a somewhat more daring approach. The key drawback is that Silverlight is still relatively new, and it doesn't support legacy clients (most notably, it currently has no support for users of Windows ME and Windows 98, and Internet Explorer–only support for Windows 2000). As a result, it doesn't have nearly the same reach as ordinary HTML. Many businesses that are adopting Silverlight are using it to distinguish themselves from other online competitors with cutting-edge content.

Creating a Silverlight Project

Now that you understand the two types of Silverlight web sites, you're ready to create a new Silverlight application by following these steps:

1. Select File ➤ New ➤ Project in Visual Studio, choose the Visual C# group of project types, and select the Silverlight Application template. As usual, you need to pick a project name and a location on your hard drive before clicking OK to create the project.

2. At this point, Visual Studio will prompt you to choose whether you want to create an ordinary HTML web site or a full-fledged ASP.NET web site that can run server-side code (see Figure 1-2). For now, choose the second option to create an ordinary web site and click OK.

Figure 1-2. Choosing the type of web site

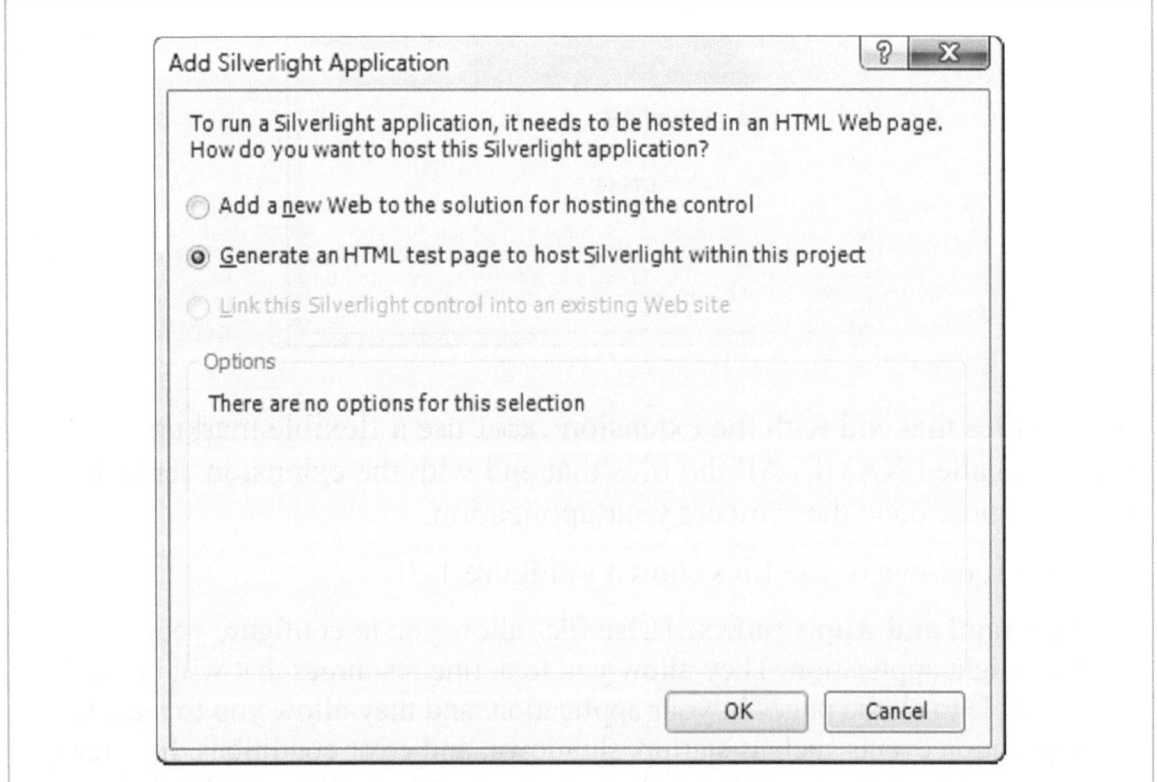

The Anatomy of a Silverlight Application

Every Silverlight project starts with a small set of essential files, as shown in Figure 1-3.

Figure 1-3. A Silverlight project

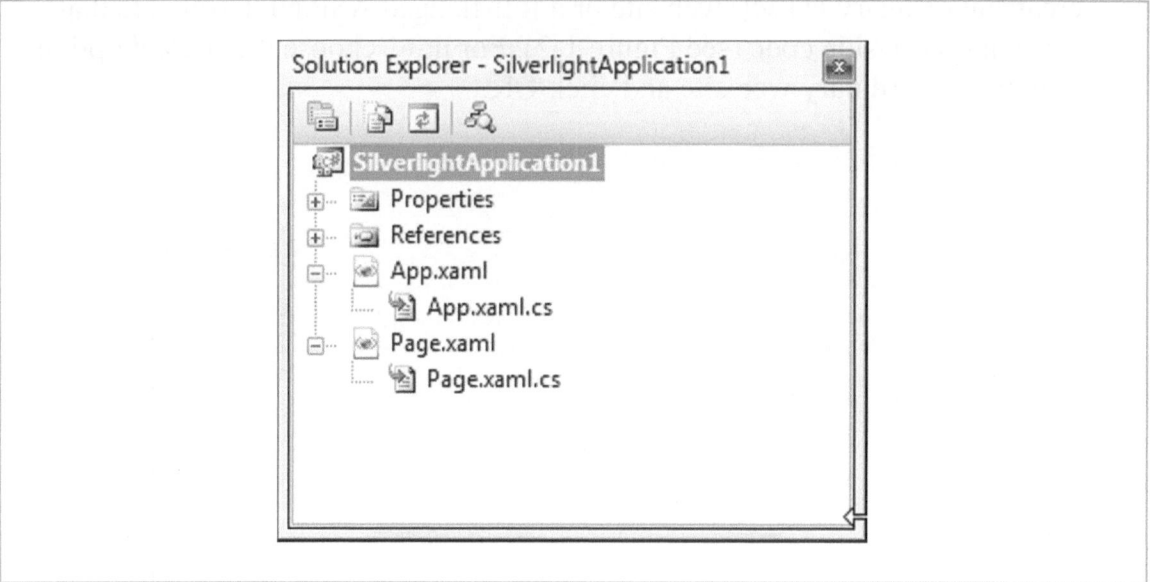

All the files that end with the extension `.xaml` use a flexible markup standard called XAML. All the files that end with the extension `.cs` hold the C# source code that powers your application.

Here's a rundown of the files shown in Figure 1-3:

- **App.xaml and App.xaml.cs**: These files allow you to configure your Silverlight application. They allow you to define resources that will be made available to all the pages in your application, and they allow you to react to application events such as startup, shutdown, and error conditions. In a newly generated project, the startup code in the `App.xaml.cs` file specifies that your application should begin by showing `Page.xaml`.

- **Page.xaml**: This file defines the user interface (the collection of controls, images, and text) that will be shown for your first page. Technically, Silverlight pages are user controls. A Silverlight application can contain as many pages as you need—to add more, simply choose Project ➤ Add New Item, pick the Silverlight User Control template, choose a file name, and click Add.

- **Page.xaml.cs**: This file includes the code that underpins your first page, including the event handlers that react to user actions

---

Tip   Unlike `App.xaml`, the name of your pages is not important. However, if you simply renaming a XAML file in Solution Explorer, you'll still keep the old class name. (For example, if you rename `Page.xaml` to `Page1.xaml`, you'll end up with a file named `Page1.xaml` that defines a class named `Page.xaml`.) To correct this discrepancy and make sure your file names and code are consistent, you can change the class name by hand (using XAML), or you can simply delete the existing file and add a new one with the right name.

Along with these four essential files, there are a few more ingredients that you'll only find if you dig around. Under the Properties node in Solution Explorer, you'll find a file named `AppManifest.xml`, which lists the assemblies that your application uses. You'll also find a file named `AssemblyInfo.cs` that contains information about your project (such as its name, version, and publisher), which is embedded into your Silverlight assembly when it's compiled. Neither of these files should be edited by hand—instead, they're modified by Visual Studio when you add references or set projects properties.

Lastly, the gateway to your Silverlight application is an automatically generated but hidden HTML file named `TestPage.html` (see Figure 1-4). To see this file, click the Show All Files icon at the top of the Solution Explorer window, and expand the `ClientBin` folder (which is where your application is compiled). You'll take a closer look at the content of the `TestPage.html` file a bit later in this chapter.

Figure 1-4. The HTML entry page

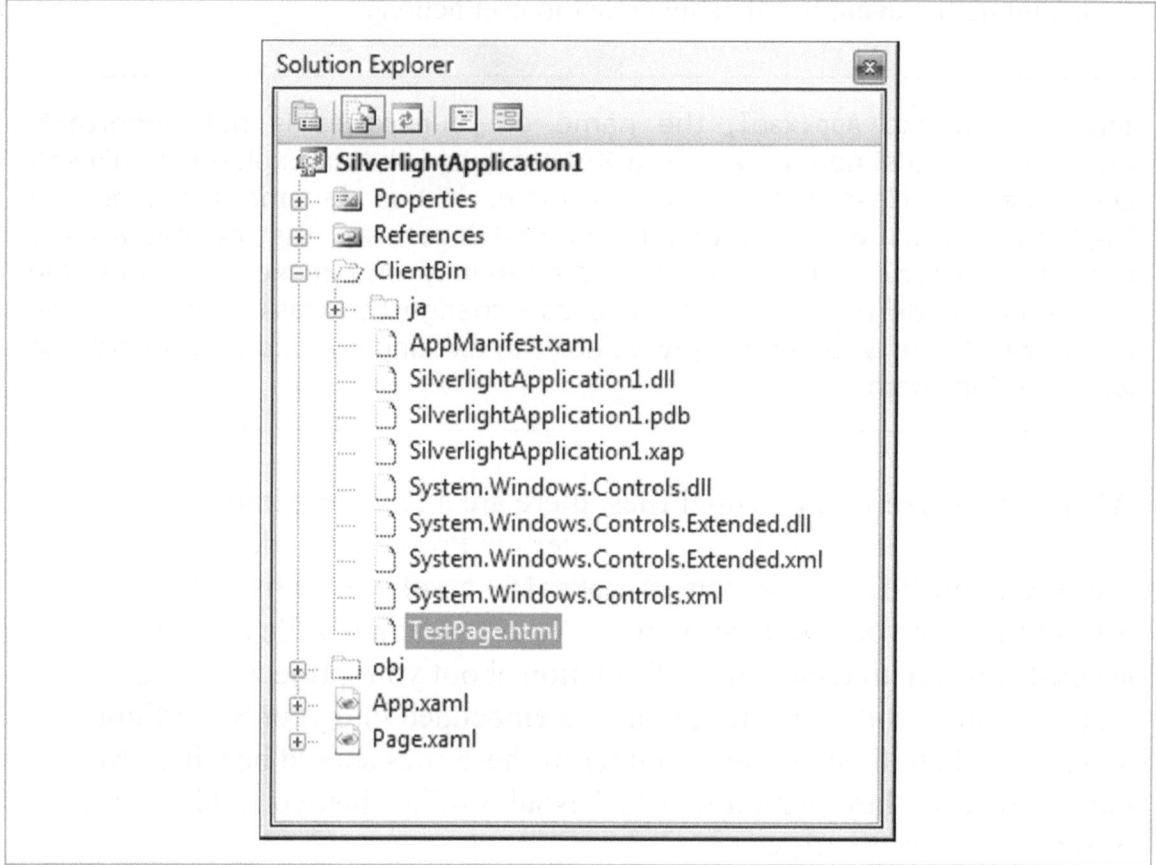

Creating a Simple Silverlight Page

As you've already learned, every Silverlight page includes a markup portion that defines the visual appearance (the XAML file) and a source code file that contains event handlers. To customize your first Silverlight application, you simply need to open the `Page.xaml` file and begin adding markup.

Visual Studio gives you two ways to look at every XAML file—it displays a visual preview (known as the *design surface*) or the underlying markup (known as the *source view*). By default, Visual Studio shows both parts, stacked one atop the other. Figure 1-5 shows this view and points out the buttons you can use to change your vantage point.

Figure 1-5. Viewing XAML pages

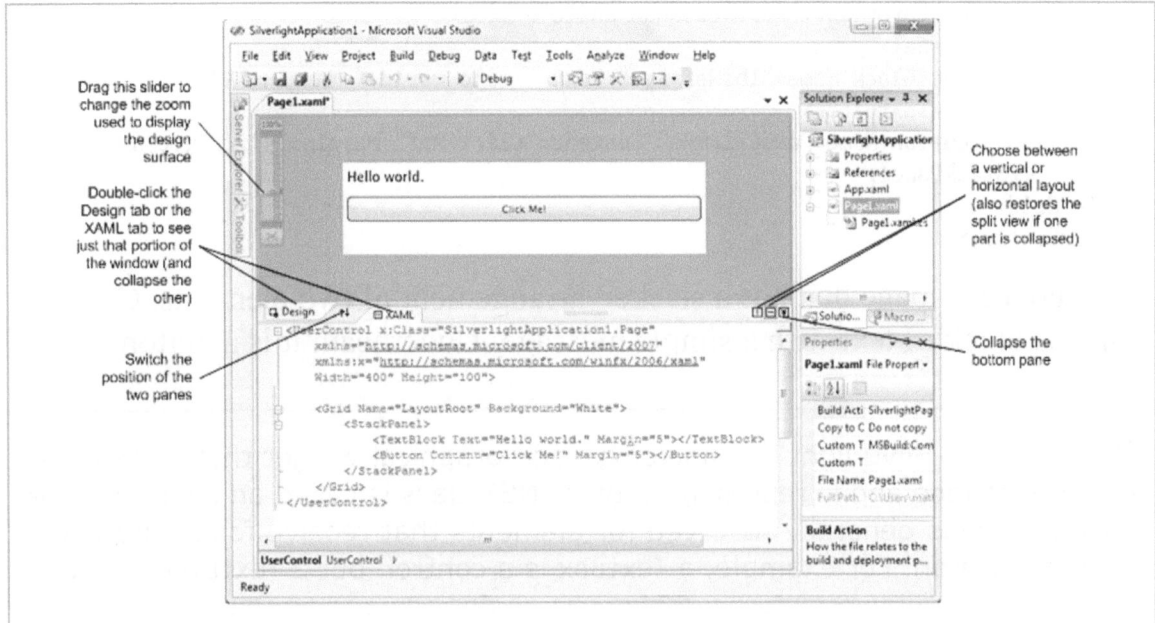

As you've no doubt guessed, you can start designing your XAML page by dragging controls from the Toolbox and dropping them onto the design surface. However, this convenience won't save you from learning the full intricacies of XAML. In order to organize your elements into the right layout containers, change their properties, wire up event handlers, and use Silverlight features like animation, styles, templates, and data binding, you'll need to edit the XAML markup by hand.

To get started, you can try creating the page shown here, which defines a block of text and a button. The portions in bold have been added to the basic page template that Visual Studio generated when you created the project.

```
<UserControl x:Class="SilverlightApplication1.Page"
    xmlns="http://schemas.microsoft.com/client/2007"
    xmlns:x="http://schemas.microsoft.com/winfx/2006/xaml"
    Width="400" Height="100">

    <Grid Name="LayoutRoot" Background="White">
        <StackPanel>
            <TextBlock Name="lblMessage" Text="Hello world." Margin="5">
              </TextBlock>
            <Button Name="cmdClickMe" Content="Click Me!" Margin="5"></Button>
        </StackPanel>
    </Grid>
</UserControl>
```

This creates a page that has a stacked arrangement of two elements. On the top is a block of text with a simple message. Underneath it is a button.

Note   In Silverlight terminology, each graphical widget that appears in a user interface and is represented by a .NET class is called an *element*. The term *control* is generally reserved for elements that receive focus and allow user interaction. For example, a TextBox is a control, but a TextBlock is not.

Adding Event Handling Code

You attach event handlers to the elements in your page using attributes, which is the same approach that developers take in WPF, ASP.NET, and JavaScript. For example, the Button element exposes an event named Click that fires when the button is triggered with the mouse or keyboard. To react to this event, you add the Click attribute to the Button element, and set it to the name of a method in your code:

```
<Button Name="cmdClickMe" Click="cmdClickMe_Click" Content="Click Me!"
 Margin="5"></Button>
```

This example assumes that you've created an event handling method named `cmd_ClickMe`. Here's what it looks like in the `Page.xaml.cs` file:

```
private void cmdClickMe_Click(object sender, RoutedEventArgs e)
{
    lblMessage.Text = "Goodbye, cruel world.";
}
```

You can't coax Visual Studio into creating an event handler by double-clicking an element or using the Properties window (as you can in other types of projects). However, once you've added the event handler, you can use IntelliSense to quickly assign it to the right event. Begin by typing in the attribute name, followed by the equal sign. At this point, Visual Studio will pop up a menu that lists all the methods that have the right syntax to handle this event and currently exist in your code-behind class, as shown in Figure 1-6. Simply choose the right event handling method.

Figure 1-6. Attaching an event handler

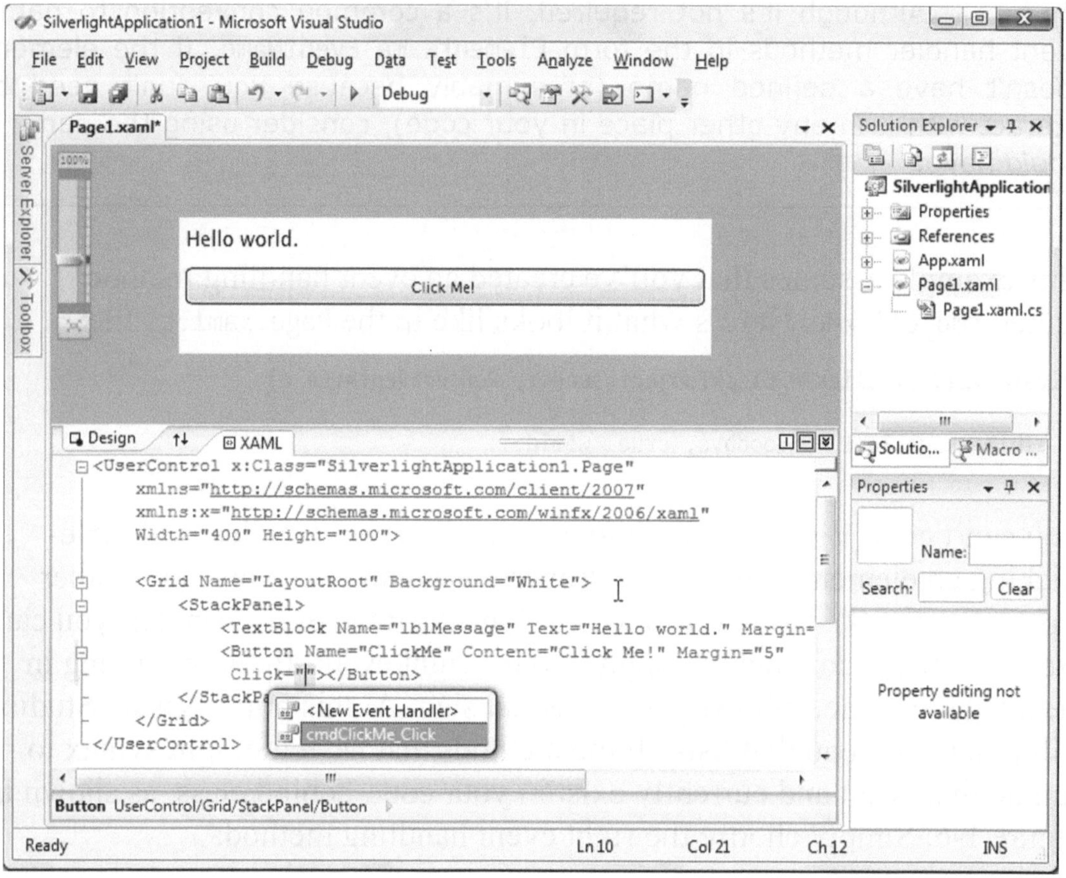

It's possible to use Visual Studio to create and assign an event handler in one step by adding an event attribute and choosing the <New Event Handler> option in the menu.

Tip　　To jump quickly from the XAML to your event handling code, right-click the appropriate event attribute and choose Navigate to Event Handler.

You can also connect an event with code. The place to do it is the constructor for your page, after the call to `InitializeComponent()`, which initializes all your controls. Here's the code equivalent of the XAML markup shown previously:

```
public Page()
{
    InitializeComponent();
    cmdClickMe.Click += cmdClickMe_Click;
}
```

The code approach is useful if you need to dynamically create a control and attach an event handler at some point during the lifetime of your window. By comparison, the events you hook up in XAML are always attached when the window object is first instantiated. The code approach also allows you to keep your XAML simpler and more streamlined, which is perfect if you plan to share it with nonprogrammers, such as a design artist. The drawback is a significant amount of boilerplate code that will clutter up your code files.

If you want to detach an event handler, code is your only option. You can use the `-=` operator, as shown here:

```
cmdClickMe.Click -= cmdClickMe_Click;
```

It is technically possible to connect the same event handler to the same event more than once. This is usually the result of a coding mistake. (In this case, the event handler will be triggered multiple times.) If you attempt to remove an event handler that's been connected twice, the event will still trigger the event handler, but just once.

Browsing the Silverlight Class Libraries

In order to write practical code, you need to know quite a bit about the classes you have to work with. That means acquiring a thorough knowledge of the core class libraries that ship with Silverlight.

Silverlight includes a subset of the classes from the full .NET Framework. Although it would be impossible to cram the entire .NET Framework into Silverlight—after all, it's a 4MB download that needs to support a variety of browsers and operating systems—Silverlight includes a remarkable amount of functionality.

The Silverlight version of the .NET Framework is simplified in two ways. First, it doesn't provide the sheer number of types you'll find in the full .NET Framework. Second, the classes that it does include often don't provide the full complement of constructors, methods, properties, and events. Instead, Silverlight keeps only the most practical members of the most important classes, which leaves it with enough functionality to create surprisingly compelling code.

Note   The Silverlight classes are designed to have public interfaces that resemble their full-fledged counterparts in the .NET Framework. However, the actual plumbing of these classes is quite different. All the Silverlight classes have been rewritten from the ground up to be as streamlined and efficient as possible.

Before you start doing any serious Silverlight programming, you might like to browse the Silverlight version of the .NET Framework. One way to do so is to open a Silverlight project, and then show the Object Browser in Visual Studio (choose View ➤ Object Browser). Along with the assembly for the code in your project, you'll see the following Silverlight assemblies (shown in Figure 1-7):

- **mscorlib.dll**: This assembly is the Silverlight equivalent of the `mscorlib.dll` assembly that includes the most fundamental parts of the .NET Framework. The Silverlight version includes core data types, exceptions, and interfaces in the `System` namespace, ordinary and generic collections, file management classes, and support for globalization, reflection, resources, debugging, and multithreading.

- **System.dll**: This assembly contains additional generic collections, classes for dealing with URIs, and classes for dealing with regular expressions.

- **System.Core.dll**: This assembly contains support for LINQ. The name of the assembly matches the full .NET Framework, which implements new .NET 3.5 features in an assembly named `System.Core.dll`.

- **System.Windows.dll**: This assembly includes many of the classes for building Silverlight user interfaces, including basic elements, shapes and brushes, classes that support animation and data binding, and a version of the `OpenFileDialog` that works with isolated storage.

- **System.Windows.Controls.dll**: This assembly defines the Silverlight controls—elements that have support user interaction and use a flexible template model, which allows you to supply new visuals without rewriting a control's built-in functionality.

- **System.Windows.Controls.Extended.dll**: This assembly defines controls that are specialized for Silverlight or aren't based on WPF at all. For example, this assembly includes Silverlight's `Calendar` and `WatermarkedTextBox` controls, neither of which is present in WPF.

- **System.Windows.Browser.dll**: This assembly contains classes for interacting with HTML elements.

- **System.Xml.core.dll**: This assembly includes the bare minimum classes you need for XML processing: `XmlReader` and `XmlWriter`.

Figure 1-7. Silverlight assemblies in the Object Browser

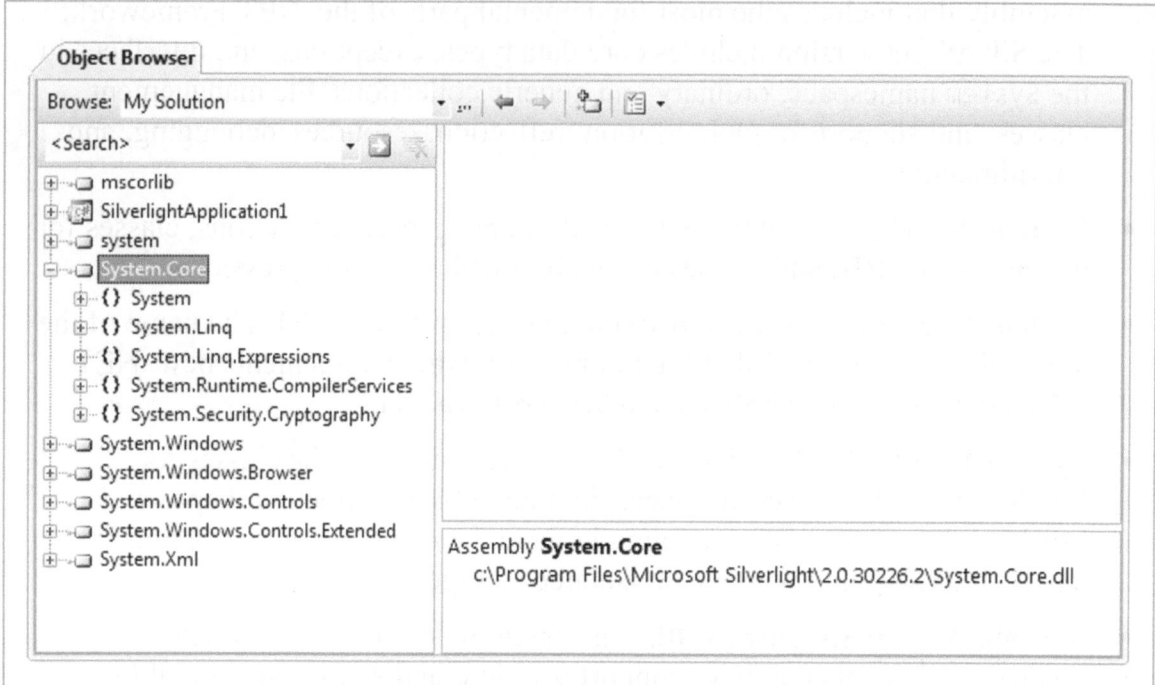

Note   Some of the members in the Silverlight assemblies are only available to .NET Framework code, and aren't callable from your code. These members are marked with the **SecurityCritical** attribute. However, this attribute does not appear in the Object Browser, so you won't be able to determine whether a specific feature is usable in a Silverlight application until you try to use it. (If you attempt to use a member that has the **SecurityCritical** attribute, you'll get a **SecurityException**.) For example, Silverlight applications are only allowed to access the file system through the isolated storage API. For that reason, the constructor for the **FileStream** class is decorated with the **SecurityCritical** attribute.

Testing a Silverlight Application

You now have enough to test your Silverlight project. When you run a Silverlight application, Visual Studio launches your default web browser and navigates to the hidden browser entry page, named `TestPage.html`. The test page creates a new Silverlight control and initializes it using the markup in `Page.xaml`.

Note   Visual Studio sets `TestPage.html` to be the start page for your project. As a result, when you launch your project, this page will be loaded in the browser. You can choose a different start page by right-clicking an HTML file in Solution Explorer and choosing Set As Start Page.

Figure 1-8 shows the previous example at work. When you click the button, the event handling code runs and the text changes. This process happens entirely on the client—there is no need to contact the server or post back the page, as there is in a server-side programming framework like ASP.NET. All the Silverlight code is executed on the client side by the scaled down version of .NET that's embedded in the Silverlight plug-in.

Figure 1-8. Running a Silverlight application (in Firefox)

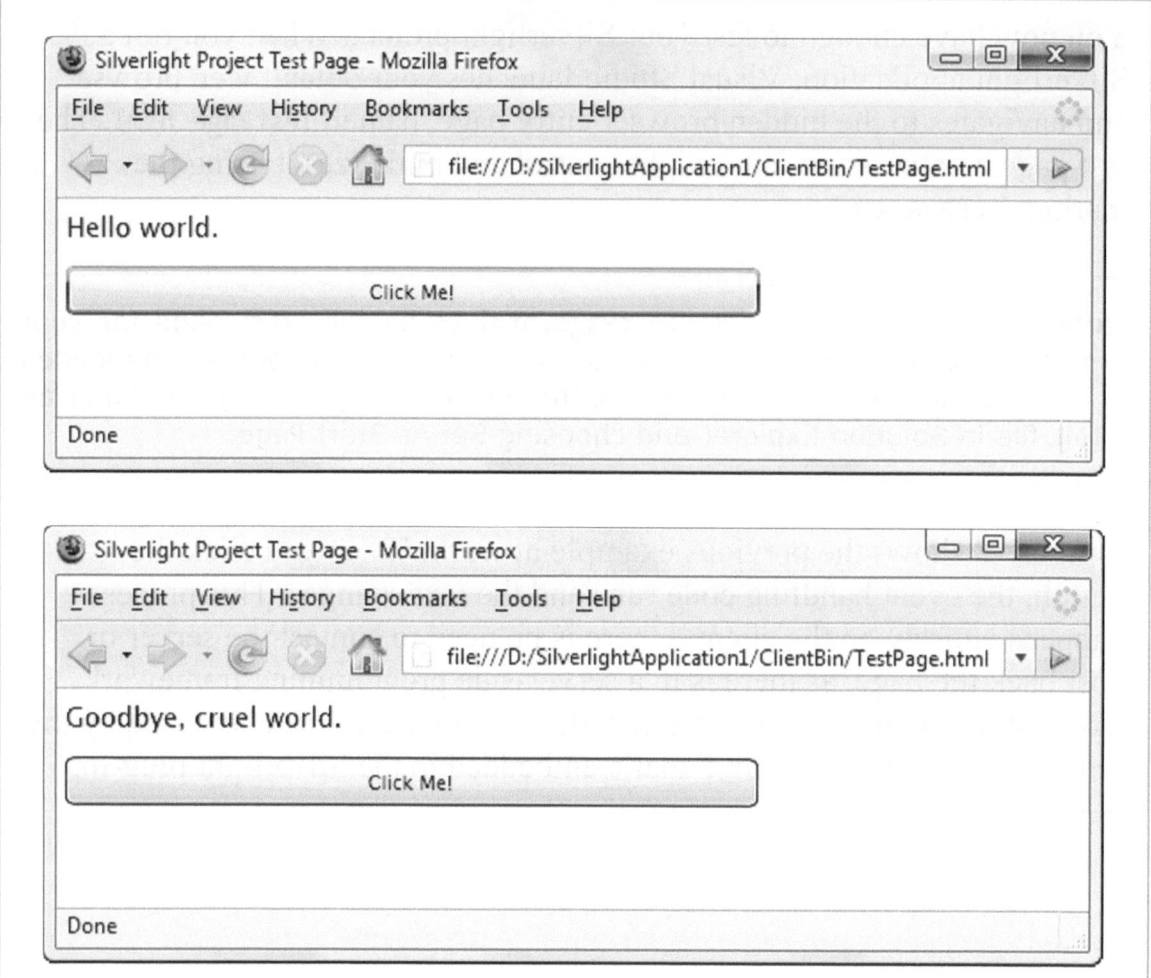

If you're hosting your host Silverlight content in an ordinary web site (with no server-side ASP.NET), Visual Studio won't use its integrated web server during the testing process. Instead, it simply opens the HTML entry page for your Silverlight project in your browser. (You can see this in the address bar in Figure 1-7.)

In some situations, this behavior could cause discrepancies between your test environment and your deployed environment, which will use a full-fledged web server that serves pages over HTTP. The most obvious difference is the security context—in other words, you could configure your web browser to allow local web pages to perform actions that remote web content can't. In practice, this isn't often a problem, because Silverlight always executes in a stripped-down security context and doesn't include any extra functionality for trusted locations. This simplifies the Silverlight development model and ensures that features won't work in certain environments and break in others. However, when production testing a Silverlight application, it's best to create an ASP.NET test web site (as described in the next section) or—even better—deploy your Silverlight application to a test web server.

Creating an ASP.NET Web Site with Silverlight Content

Although Silverlight does perfectly well on its own, you can also develop, test, and deploy it as part of an ASP.NET web site. Here's how to create a Silverlight project and an ASP.NET web site that uses it in the same solution:

1. Select File ➤ New ➤ Project in Visual Studio, choose the Visual C# group of project types, and select the Silverlight Application template. It's a good idea to use the Create directory for solution option, so you can group together the two projects that Visual Studio will create—one for the Silverlight assembly and one for ASP.NET web site.

2. Once you've picked the solution name and project name, click OK to create it.

3. When asked whether you want to create a test web, choose the first option, Add a new Web. You'll also need to supply a project name for the ASP.NET web site. By default, it's your project name with the added text _Web, as shown in Figure 1-9. Finally, click OK to create the solution.

Figure 1-9. Creating an ASP.NET web site to host Silverlight content

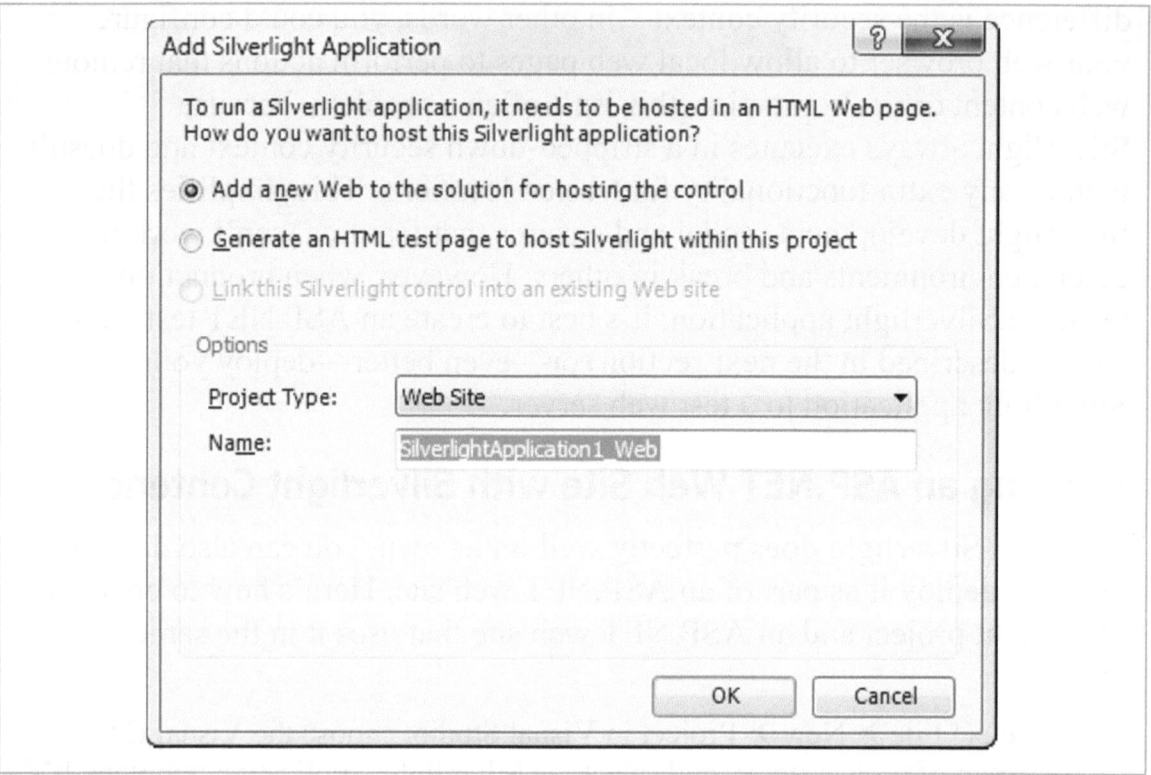

There are two ways to integrate Silverlight content into an ASP.NET application:

- **Create HTML files with Silverlight content**: You place these files in your ASP.NET web site folder, just as you would with any other ordinary HTML file. The only limitation of this approach is that your HTML file obviously can't include ASP.NET controls, because it won't be processed on the server.

- **Place Silverlight content inside an ASP.NET web form**: To pull this trick off, you need the help of the `Xaml` web control. You can also add other ASP.NET controls to different regions of the page. The only disadvantage to this approach is that the page is always processed on the server. If you aren't actually using any server-side ASP.NET content, this creates an extra bit of overhead that you don't need when the page is first requested.

Of course, you're also free to mingle both of these approaches, and use Silverlight content in dedicated HTML pages and inside ASP.NET web pages in the same site. When you create a Silverlight project with an ASP.NET web site, you'll start with both. For example, if your Silverlight project is named SilverlightApplication1, you can use `SilverlightApplication1TestPage.html` or `SilverlightApplication1TestPage.aspx`. The HTML file is identical to the test page in the ordinary Silverlight-only solution you saw earlier. The `.aspx` file is an ASP.NET web form that uses ASP.NET's `Xaml` web control to show your Silverlight application. The end result is the same, but the Silverlight control creates the test page markup dynamically, when it's processed on the server. (This extra step gives you a chance to use your own server-side code to perform other tasks when the page is initially requested, before the Silverlight application is downloaded and launched.)

Figure 1-10 shows how a Silverlight and ASP.NET solution starts out. Along with the two test pages, the ASP.NET web site also includes a `Default.aspx` page (which can be used as the entry point to your ASP.NET web site) and `web.config` (which allows you to configure various web site settings).

Figure 1-10. Creating an ASP.NET web site to host Silverlight content

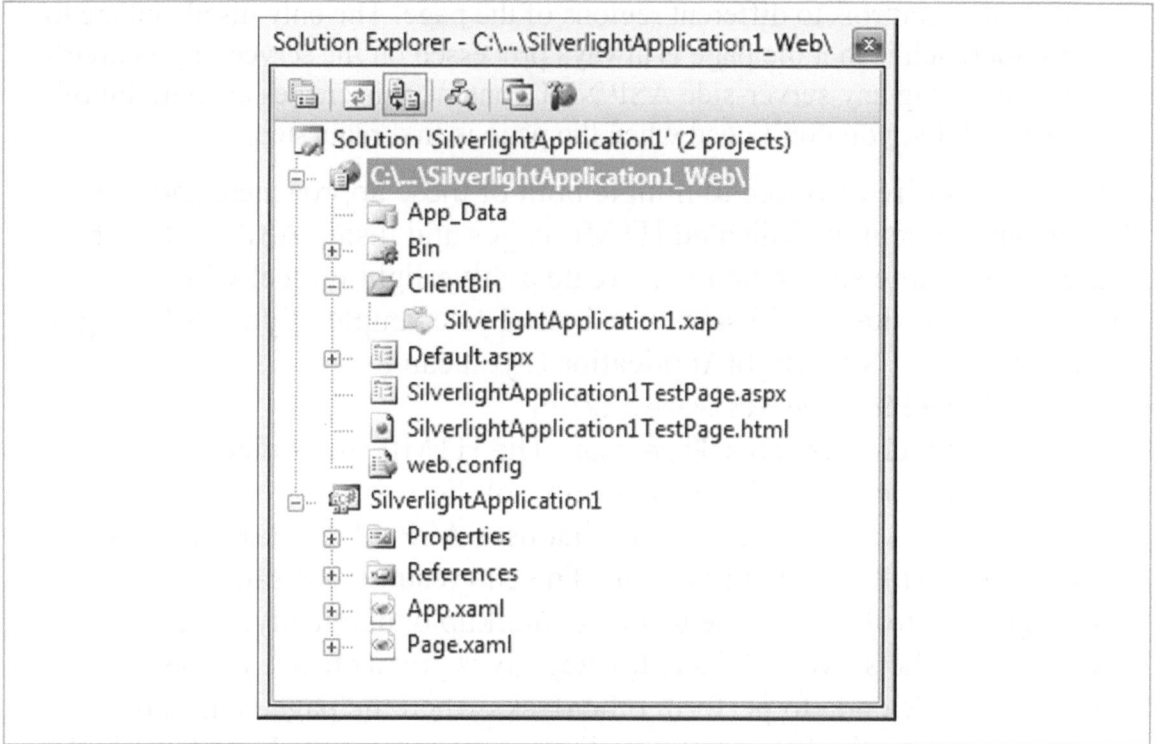

Silverlight and ASP.NET provide essentially the same debugging experience as a Silverlight-only solution. When you run the solution, Visual Studio compiles both projects and copies the Silverlight assembly to the ClientBin folder in the ASP.NET web site. (This is similar to assembly references—if an ASP.NET web site references a private DLL, Visual Studio automatically copies this DLL to the Bin folder.) Once both projects are compiled, Visual Studio looks to the startup project (which is the ASP.NET web site) and looks for the start page (which is SilverlightApplication1TestPage.aspx). It then launches the default browser and navigates to the start page.

The difference is that it doesn't request the start page directly from the file system. Instead, it communicates with its built-in test web server. This web server automatically loads up on a randomly chosen port. It acts like a scaled-down version of IIS, but accepts requests only from the local computer. This gives you the ease of debugging without needing to configure IIS virtual directories. Figure 1-11 shows the same Silverlight application you considered earlier, but hosted by ASP.NET.

Figure 1-11. An ASP.NET page

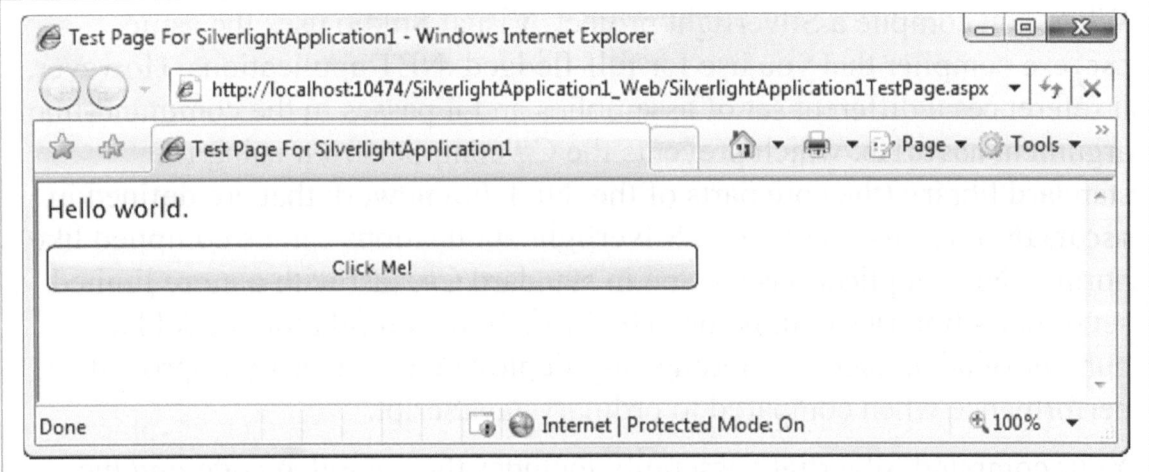

To navigate to a different page from the ASP.NET project, you can type in the address bar of the browser. Or, you can change the startup page by right-clicking the page you want to use and choosing Set As Start Page.

Note   Remember, when building a Silverlight and ASP.NET solution, you add all your Silverlight files and code to the Silverlight project. The ASP.NET web site consumes the final, compiled Silverlight assembly and makes it available through one or more of its web pages.

Silverlight Compilation and Deployment

Now that you've seen how to create a basic Silverlight project, add a page with elements and code, and run your application, it's time to dig a bit deeper. In this section, you'll see how your Silverlight is transformed from a collection of XAML files and source code into a rich browser-based application.

Compiling a Silverlight Assembly

When you compile a Silverlight project, Visual Studio uses the same `csc.exe` compiler that you use for full-fledged .NET applications. However, it references a different set of assemblies and it passes in the command-line argument `nostdlib`, which prevents the C# compiler from using the standard library (the core parts of the .NET Framework that are defined in `mscorlib.dll`). In other words, Silverlight applications can be compiled like normal .NET applications written in standard C#, just with a more limited set of class libraries to draw on. The Silverlight compilation model has a number of advantages, including easy deployment and vastly improved performance when compared to ordinary JavaScript.

Your compiled Silverlight assembly includes the compiled code *and* the XAML documents for every page in your application, which are embedded in the assembly as resources. This ensures that there's no way for your event handling code to become separated from the user interface markup it needs. Incidentally, the XAML is not compiled in any way (unlike WPF, which converts it into a more optimized format called BAML).

Your Silverlight project is compiled into a DLL file named after your project. For example, if you have a project named `SilverlightApplication1`, the `csc.exe` compiler will create the file `SilverlightApplication1.dll`. The project assembly is dumped into a `ClientBin` folder in your project directory, along with a few other important files:

- **A PDB file**: This file contains information required for Visual Studio debugging. It's named after your project assembly (for example, `SilverlightApplication1.pdb`).

- **AppManifest.xaml**: This file lists assembly dependencies.

- **Dependent assemblies**: The `ClientBin` folder contains the assemblies that your Silverlight project uses, provided these assemblies have the Copy Local property set to true. Assemblies that are a core part of Silverlight have Copy Local set to False, because they don't need to deployed with your application. (You can change the Copy Local setting by expanding the References node in Solution Explorer, selecting the assembly, and using the Properties window.).

- **TestPage.html**: This is the entry page that the user requests to start your Silverlight application.

- **A XAP file**: This is a Silverlight package that contains everything you need to deploy your Silverlight application, including the application manifest, the project assembly, and any other assemblies that your application uses.

Of course, you can change the assembly name, the default namespace (which is used when you add new code files), and the XAP file name using the Visual Studio project properties (see Figure 1-12). Just double-click the Properties node in Solution Explorer.

Figure 1-12. Project properties in Visual Studio

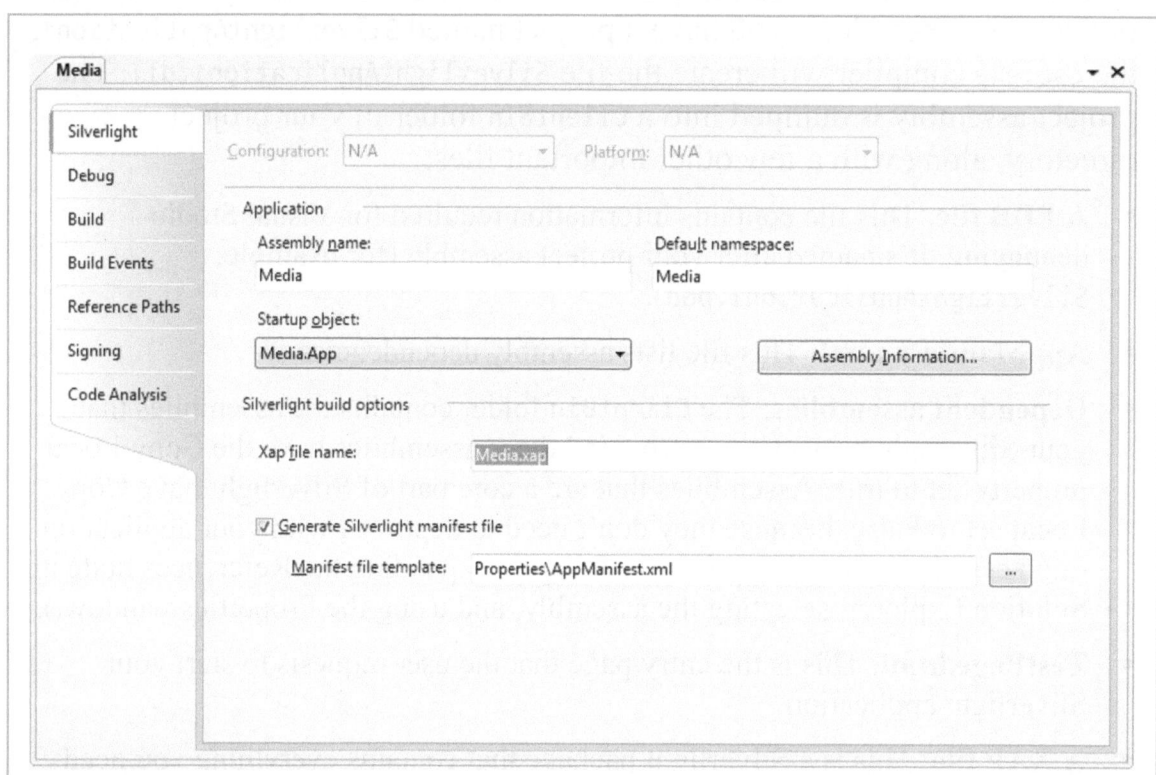

Deploying a Silverlight Assembly

Once you understand the Silverlight compilation model, it's a short step to understanding the deployment model. The XAP file is the key piece. It wraps the units of your application (the application manifest and the assemblies) into one neat container.

Technically, the XAP file is a ZIP archive. To verify this, rename a XAP file like `SilverlightApplication1.xap` to `SilverlightApplication1.xap.zip`. You can then open the archive and view the files inside. Figure 1-13 shows the contents of the XAP file for the simple example shown earlier in this chapter.

Figure 1-13. The contents of a XAP file

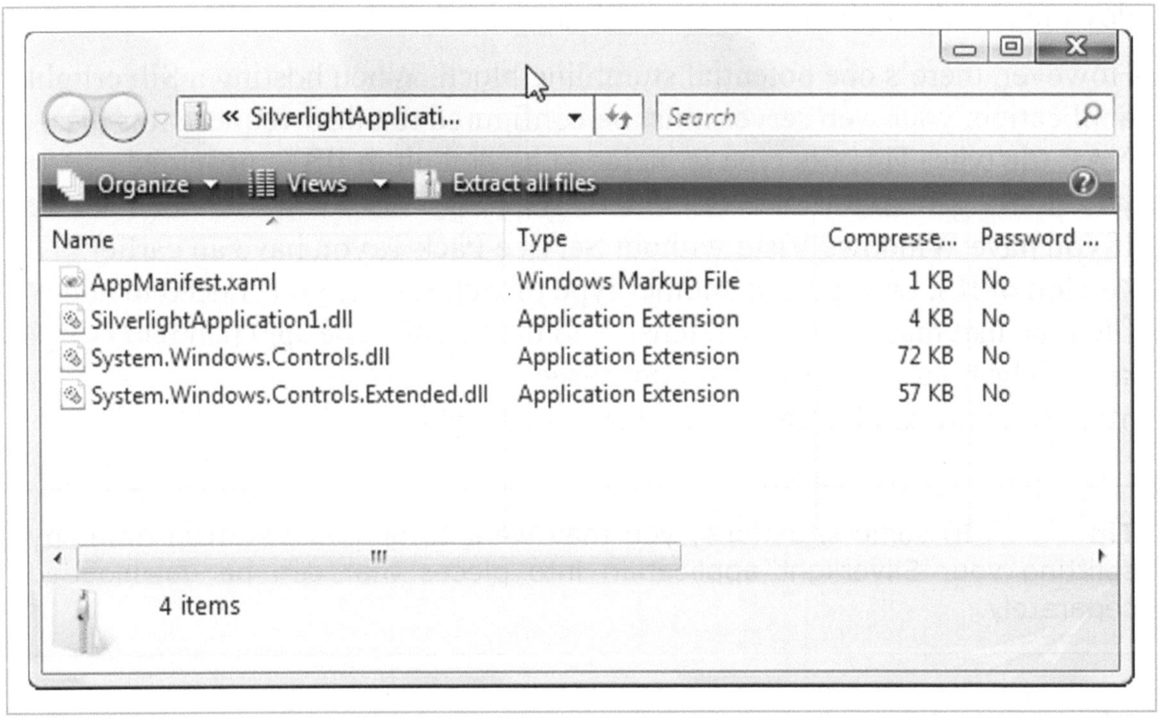

The XAP file system has two obvious benefits:

- **It compresses your content**: Because this content isn't decompressed until it reaches the client, it reduces the time required to download your application. This is particularly important if your application contains large static resources , like images or blocks of text.

- **It simplifies deployment**: When you're ready to take your Silverlight application live, you simply need to copy the XAP file to the web server, along with `TestPage.html` or a similar HTML file that includes a Silverlight content region. You don't need to worry about keeping track of the assemblies and resources.

Thanks to the XAP model, there's not much to think about when deploying a simple Silverlight application. Hosting a Silverlight application simply involves making the appropriate XAP file available, so the clients can download it through the browser and run it on their local machines.

However, there's one potential stumbling block. When hosting a Silverlight application, your web server must be configured to allow requests for the XAP file type. This file type is included by default in IIS 7, provided you're using Windows Server 2008 or Windows Vista with Service Pack 1. If you have Windows Vista without Service Pack 1, you have an earlier version of IIS, or you have another type of web server, you'll need to add a file type that maps the `.xap` extension to the MIME type `application/x-silverlight-app`. For IIS instructions, see `http://learn.iis.net/page.aspx/262/silverlight`.

Tip   In some situations, you may want to optimize startup times by splitting your Silverlight application into pieces that can be downloaded separately.

The HTML Entry Page

The last ingredient in the deployment picture is the HTML entry page. This page is the entry point into your Silverlight content—in other words, the page the user requests in the web browser. Visual Studio names this file `TestPage.html` (in a Silverlight-only solution), although you'll probably want to rename it to something more appropriate.

The HTML entry page doesn't actually contain Silverlight markup or code. Instead, it simply sets up the content region for the Silverlight plug-in, using a small amount of JavaScript. (For this reason, browsers that have JavaScript disabled won't be able to see Silverlight content.) Here's a slightly shortened version of the HTML entry page that preserves the key details:

```html
<html xmlns="http://www.w3.org/1999/xhtml" >
<head>
    <title>Silverlight Project Test Page</title>

    <style type="text/css">
        ...
    </style>

    <script type="text/javascript">
        ...
    </script>
</head>

<body>
    <!-- Runtime errors from Silverlight will be displayed here. -->
    <div id='errorLocation' style="font-size: small;color: Gray;"></div>

    <!-- Silverlight content will be displayed here. -->
    <div id="silverlightControlHost">
        <object data="data:application/x-silverlight,"
          type="application/x-silverlight-2" width="100%" height="100%">
            <param name="source" value="SilverlightApplication1.xap"/>
            <param name="onerror" value="onSilverlightError" />
            <param name="background" value="white" />

            <a href="http://go.microsoft.com/fwlink/?LinkID=108182">
              <img src="http://go.microsoft.com/fwlink/?LinkId=108181"
               alt="Get Microsoft Silverlight" style="border-style: none"/>
            </a>
        </object>
        <iframe style='visibility:hidden;height:0;width:0;border:0px'></iframe>
    </div>
</body>
</html>
```

The key details in this markup are the two highlighted <div> elements. Both of these <div> elements are placeholders that are initially left empty. The first <div> element is reserved for error messages. If the Silverlight plug-in is launched but the Silverlight assembly fails to load successfully, an error message will be shown here, thanks to this JavaScript code, which is featured earlier in the page:

```
<script type="text/javascript">
    function onSilverlightError(sender, args) {
        if (args.errorType == "InitializeError")  {
            var errorDiv = document.getElementById("errorLocation");
            if (errorDiv != null)
                errorDiv.innerHTML = args.errorType + "- " + args.errorMessage;
        }
    }
</script>
```

Tip   The error display is a debugging convenience. When you're ready to deploy the application, you should remove the <div> element so sensitive information won't be shown to the user (who isn't in a position to correct the problem anyway).

This second <div> element is more interesting. It represents the Silverlight content region. It contains an <object> element that loads the Silverlight plug-in and an <iframe> element that's used to display it in certain browsers. The <object> element includes four key attributes: data (which indentifies it as a Silverlight content region), type (which indicates the required Silverlight version), and height and width (which determine the dimensions of the Silverlight content region).

```
<object data="data:application/x-silverlight,"
  type="application/x-silverlight-2" width="100%" height="100%">
    ...
</object>
```

Sizing the Silverlight Content Region

By default, the Silverlight content region is given a width and height of 100%, so the Silverlight content can consume all the available space in the browser window. You can constrain the size of the Silverlight content region by hard-coding pixel sizes for the height and width attributes (which is limiting and usually avoided). Or, you can place the <div> element that holds the Silverlight content region in a more restrictive place on the page—for example, in a cell in a table, in another fixed-sized element, or between other `<div>` elements in a multicolumn layout.

Even though the default entry page allows Silverlight content to take as much size as it wants, your XAML pages may include hard-coded dimensions. By default, Visual Studio gives every new page a width of 400 pixels and a height of 300 pixels, and the example you saw earlier in this chapter limited the page to 400×100 pixels. If the browser window is larger than the hard-coded page size, the extra space won't be used. If the browser window is smaller than the hard-coded page size, part of the page may fall outside the visible area of the window.

Hard-coded sizes make sense when you have a graphically rich layout with absolute positioning and little flexibility. If you don't, you might prefer to remove the `Width` and `Height` attributes from the `<UserControl>` start tag. That way, the page will be sized to match the browser window, and your Silverlight content will fit itself into the currently available space.

To get a better understanding of the actual dimensions of the Silverlight content region, you can add a border around it by adding a simple style rule to the `<div>`, like this:

```
<div id="silverlightControlHost" style="border: 1px red solid">
```

Configuring the Silverlight Content Region

The `<object>` element contains a series of `<param>` elements that specify additional options to the Silverlight plug-in. Here are the options in the standard entry page that Visual Studio generates:

```
<param name="source" value="SilverlightApplication1.xap"/>
<param name="onerror" value="onSilverlightError" />
<param name="background" value="white" />
```

Table 1-1 lists all the parameters that you can use.

Table 1-1. Parameters for the Silverlight Plug-In

NAME	VALUE
source	A URI that points to the XAP file for your Silverlight application. This parameter is required.
background	The color that's used to paint the background of the Silverlight content region, behind any content that you display (but in front of any HTML content that occupies the same space). If you set the Background property of a page, it's painted over this background.
enableHtmlAccess	A Boolean that specifies whether the Silverlight plug-in has access to the HTML object model. Use true if you want to be able to interact with the HTML elements on the entry page through your Silverlight code
initParams	A string that you can use to pass custom initialization information. This technique is useful if you plan to use the same Silverlight application in different ways on different pages.

NAME	VALUE
maxFramerate	The desired frame rate for animations. Higher frame rates result in smoother animations, but the system load and processing power of the current computer may mean that a high frame rate can't be honored. The value is 60 (for 60 frames per second). Animation is discussed briefly in Chapter 8.
splashScreenSource	The location of a XAML splash screen to show while the XAP file is downloading.
windowless	A Boolean that specifies whether the plug-in renders in windowed mode (the default) or windowless mode. If you set this to true, the HTML content underneath your Silverlight content region can show through. This is ideal if you're planning to create a shaped Silverlight control that integrates with HTML content.
onSourceDownloadProgressChanged	A JavaScript event handler that's triggered when a piece of the XAP file has been downloaded. You can use this event handler to build a startup progress bar.

Table 1-1. continued

NAME	VALUE
onSourceDownloadComplete	A JavaScript event handler that's triggered when the entire XAP file has been downloaded.
onLoad	A JavaScript event handler that's triggered when the markup in the XAP file has been processed and your startup page has been loaded.
onResize	A JavaScript event handler that's triggered when the size of Silverlight content region has changed.
onError	A JavaScript event handler that's triggered when an unhandled error occurs in the Silverlight plug-in or in your code.

Note By convention, all of these parameter names should be written completely in lowercase (for example, **splashscreensource** rather than **splashScreenSource**). However, they're shown with mixed case here for better readability.

Displaying Alternative Content

The <div> element also has some HTML markup that will be shown if the <object> tag isn't understood or the plug-in isn't available. In the standard entry page, this markup consists of a "Get Silverlight" picture, which is wrapped in a hyperlink that, when clicked, takes the user to the Silverlight download page.

```
<a href="http://go.microsoft.com/fwlink/?LinkID=108182">
  <img src="http://go.microsoft.com/fwlink/?LinkId=108181"
  alt="Get Microsoft Silverlight" style="border-style: none"/>
</a>
```

CHANGING THE TEST PAGE

If you're creating a combined Silverlight and ASP.NET solution, the test page is generated when the project is first created. As a result, it's easy to change it. However, if you're using a Silverlight-only project, you need to go to a bit more work. That's because the test page is generated each time you run the project, and so any changes you make to it will be discarded.

The easiest solution is to create a new test page for your project. Here's how:

1. Run your project at least once to create the test page.

2. Click the Show All Files icon at the top of Solution Explorer.

3. Expand the **ClientBin** folder in Solution Explorer.

4. Find the **TestPage.html** file, right click it, and choose Copy. Then right-click the **ClientBin** folder and choose Paste. This duplicate will be your custom test page. Right-click the new file and choose Rename to give it a better name.

5. To make the custom test page a part of your project, right-click it and choose Include in Project.

6. To tell Visual Studio to navigate to your test page when you run the project, right-click your test page and choose Set As Start Page.

The Application Manifest

As you've seen, the Silverlight execution model is quite straightforward. First, the client requests the HTML entry page (such as `TestPage.html`). At this point, the browser downloads the HTML file and processes its markup. When it reaches the `<object>` element, it loads the Silverlight plug-in and creates the Silverlight content region. After this step, the client-side plug-in takes over. First, it downloads the linked XAP file (which is identified by the source parameter inside the `<object>` element). Then, it looks at the `AppManifest.xaml` file to decide what to do next.

Here's the content of the `AppManifest.xaml` for a newly generated Visual Studio project, which also matches the `AppManifest.xaml` in the simple example you saw earlier in this chapter:

```
<Deployment xmlns="http://schemas.microsoft.com/client/2007/deployment"
 xmlns:x="http://schemas.microsoft.com/winfx/2006/xaml"
 EntryPointAssembly="SilverlightApplication1"
 EntryPointType="SilverlightApplication1.App"
 RuntimeVersion="2.0.30226.2">
  <Deployment.Parts>
    <AssemblyPart x:Name="SilverlightApplication1"
     Source="SilverlightApplication1.dll" />
    <AssemblyPart x:Name="System.Windows.Controls"
     Source="System.Windows.Controls.dll" />
    <AssemblyPart x:Name="System.Windows.Controls.Extended"
     Source="System.Windows.Controls.Extended.dll" />
  </Deployment.Parts>
</Deployment>
```

The `EntryPointAssembly` and `EntryPointType` attributes are the key details that determine what code the Silverlight plug-in will execute next. `EntryPointAssembly` indicates the name of the DLL that has your compiled Silverlight code (without the `.dll` extension). `EntryPointType` indicates the name of the application class in that assembly. When the Silverlight plug-in sees the `AppManifest.xaml` shown here, it loads the `SilverlightApplication1.dll` assembly, and then creates the `App` object inside. The **App** object triggers a **Startup** event, which runs this code, creating the first page:

```
private void Application_Startup(object sender, StartupEventArgs e)
{
    // Load the main control.
    this.RootVisual = new Page();
}
```

If you've added a different user control to your application, and you want to show it as the first page, simply edit the **App.xaml.cs** file, and replace the **Page** class with the name of your custom class:

```
this.RootVisual = new CustomPage();
```

SILVERLIGHT DECOMPILATION

Now that you understand the infrastructure that underpins a Silverlight 2.0 project, it's easy to see how you can decompile any existing application to learn more about how it works. Here's how:

1. Surf to the entry page.

2. View the source for the web page, and look for the `<param>` element that points to the XAP file.

3. Type a request for the XAP file into your browser's address bar. (Keep the same domain, but replace the page name with the partial path that points to the XAP file.)

4. Choose Save As to save the XAP file locally.

5. Rename the XAP file to add the `.zip` extension. Then, open it and extract the project assembly. This assembly is essentially the same as the assemblies you build for ordinary .NET applications. Like ordinary .NET assemblies, it contains Intermediate Language (IL) code.

6. Open the project assembly in a tool like Reflector (http://www.aisto.com/roeder/dotnet) to view the IL and embedded resources. Using the right plug-in, you can even decompile the IL to C# syntax.

Of course, many Silverlight developers don't condone this sort of behavior (much as many .NET developers don't encourage end users to decompile their rich client applications). However, it's an unavoidable side effect of the Silverlight compilation model.

Because IL code can be easily decompiled or reverse engineered, it's not an appropriate place to store secrets (like encryption keys, proprietary algorithms, and so on). If you need to perform a task that uses sensitive code, consider calling a web service from your Silverlight application. If you just want to prevent other hotshots from reading your code and copying your style, you may be interested in raising the bar with an *obfuscation* tool that uses a number of tricks to scramble the structure and names in your compiled code without changing its behavior. Visual Studio ships with a scaled-down obfuscation tool named Dotfuscator, and many more are available commercially.

The Last Word

In this chapter, you took your first look at the Silverlight application model. You saw how to create a Silverlight project in Visual Studio, add a simple event handler, and test it. You also peered behind the scenes to explore how a Silverlight application is compiled and deployed.

In the following chapters, you'll learn much more about the full capabilities of the Silverlight platform. Sometimes, you might need to remind yourself that you're coding inside a lightweight browser-hosted framework, because much of Silverlight coding feels like the full .NET platform, despite the fact that it's built on only a few megabytes of compressed code. Out of all of Silverlight's many features, its ability to pack a miniature modern programming framework into a slim 4MB download is surely its most impressive.

Chapter 2: Layout

Half the battle in user interface design is organizing the content in a way that's attractive, practical, and flexible. In a browser-hosted application, this is a particularly tricky task, because your application may be used on a wide range of different computers and devices (all with different display hardware), and you have no control over the size of the browser window in which your Silverlight content is placed.

Fortunately, Silverlight inherits the most important part of WPF's extremely flexible layout model. Using the layout model, you organize your content in a set of different layout *containers*. Each container has its own layout logic—one stacks elements, another arranges them in a grid of invisible cells, and another uses a hard-coded coordinate system. If you're ambitious, you can even create your own containers with custom layout logic.

The Layout Containers

A Silverlight window can hold only a single element. To fit in more than one element and create a more practical user interface, you need to place a container in your page and then add other elements to that container. Your layout is determined by the container that you use.

All the Silverlight layout containers are panels that derive from the abstract `System.Windows.Controls.Panel` class (see Figure 2-1).

Figure 2-1. The hierarchy of the Panel class

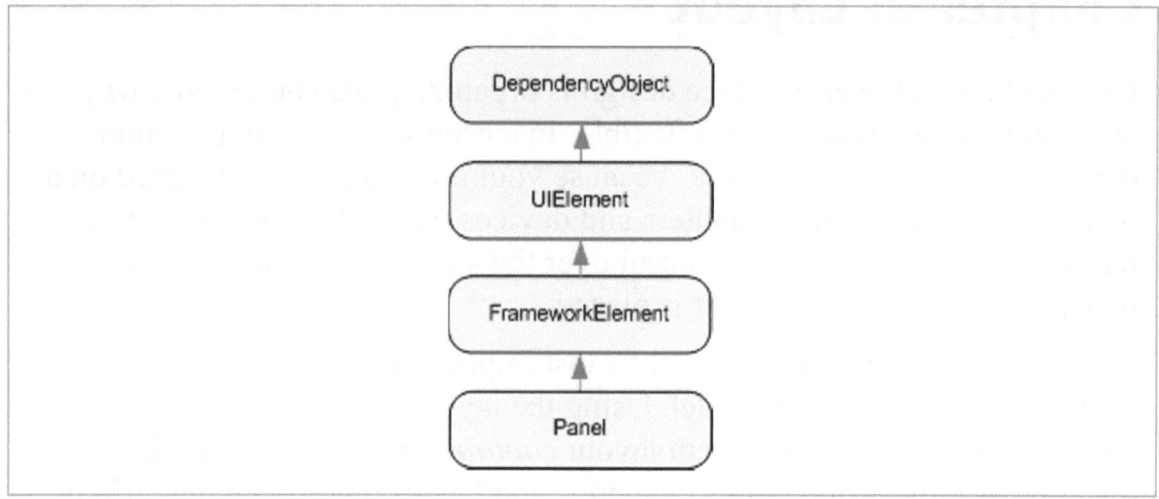

The **Panel** class adds two public properties: **Background** and **Children**.
Background is the brush that's used to paint the panel background. (You'll
learn more about brushes in Chapter 7.) **Children** is the collection of items
that's stored in the panel. This is the first level of elements—in other
words, these elements may themselves contain more elements.

Note   The **Panel** class also has a bit of internal plumbing you can use if
you want to create your own layout container. You'll learn how it works
when you learn how to create a custom layout container later in this
chapter.

On its own, the base **Panel** class is nothing but a starting point for other
more specialized classes. Silverlight provides three **Panel**-derived classes
that you can use to arrange layout, which are listed in Table 2-1. As with
all Silverlight controls and most visual elements, these classes are found in
the **System.Windows.Controls** namespace.

Table 2-1. Core Layout Panels

NAME	DESCRIPTION
StackPanel	Places elements in a horizontal or vertical stack. This layout container is typically used for small sections of a larger, more complex page.
Grid	Arranges elements in rows and columns according to an invisible table. This is one of the most flexible and commonly used layout containers.
Canvas	Allows elements to be positioned absolutely using fixed coordinates. This layout container is the simplest but least flexible.

Layout containers can be nested. A typical user interface begins with the Grid, Silverlight's most capable container, and contains other layout containers that arrange smaller groups of elements, such as captioned text boxes, items in a list, icons on a toolbar, a column of buttons, and so on.

The Panel Background

All Panel elements introduce the concept of a background by adding a Background property. It's natural to expect that the Background property would use some sort of color object. However, this property actually uses something much more versatile: a Brush object. That gives you the flexibility to fill your background and foreground content with a solid color (by using the SolidColorBrush) or something more exotic (for example, by using a LinearGradientBrush or TileBrush). In this section, you'll consider only the simple solid-color fills provided by the SolidColorBrush (I will mention other options later on in the book).

Note   All Brush classes are found in the System.Windows.Media namespace.

For example, if you want to give your entire page a light blue background, you could adjust the background of the root panel. Here's the code that does the trick:

```
layoutRoot.Background = new SolidColorBrush(Colors.AliceBlue);
```

This code creates a new **SolidColorBrush** using a ready-made color via a static property of the handy **Colors** class. (The names are based on the color names supported by most web browsers.) It then sets the brush as the background brush for the button, which causes its background to be painted a light shade of blue.

The **Colors** class offers handy shortcuts, but it's not the only way to set a color. You can also create a **Color** object by supplying the R, G, B values (red, green, and blue). Each one of these values is a number from 0 to 255:

```
int red = 0; int green = 255; int blue = 0;
layoutRoot.Background = new SolidColorBrush(Color.FromRgb(red, green, blue));
```

You can also make a color partly transparent by supplying an alpha value when calling the **Color.FromArgb()** method. An alpha value of 255 is completely opaque, while 0 is completely transparent.

Often, you'll set colors in XAML rather than in code. Here, you can use a helpful shortcut. Rather than define a **Brush** object, you can supply a color name or color value. The type converter for the **Background** property will automatically create a **SolidColorBrush** object using the color you specify. Here's an example that uses a color name:

```
<Grid x:Name="layoutRoot" Background="Red">
```

It's equivalent to this more verbose syntax:

```
<Grid x:Name="layoutRoot">
  <Grid.Background>
    <SolidColorBrush Color="Red" />
  </Grid.Background>
</Grid>
```

You need to use the longer form if you want to create a different type of brush, such as a `LinearGradientBrush`, and use that to paint the background.

If you want to use a color code, you need to use a slightly less convenient syntax that puts the R, G, and B values in hexadecimal notation. You can use one of two formats—either #rrggbb or #aarrggbb (the difference being that the latter includes the alpha value). You need only two digits to supply the A, R, G, and B values because they're all in hexadecimal notation. Here's an example that creates the same color as in the previous code snippets using #aarrggbb notation:

```
<Grid x:Name="layoutRoot" Background="#FFFF0000">
```

Here the alpha value is FF (255), the red value is FF (255), and the green and blue values are 0.

Note   Brushes support automatic change notification. In other words, if you attach a brush to a control and change the brush, the control updates itself accordingly.

The `Background` isn't the only drawing detail you can set with a brush. You can also paint foreground text color in many controls using the `Foreground` property, and paint a border around some using the `BorderBrush` and `BorderThickness` properties. `BorderBrush` takes a brush of your choosing, and `BorderThickness` takes the width of the border in device-independent units. You need to set both properties before you'll see the border.

By default, the `Background` of a layout panel is set to a null reference, which is equivalent to this:

```
<Grid x:Name="layoutRoot" Background="{x:Null}">
```

When your panel has a null background, any content underneath will show through (similar to setting a fully transparent background color). However, there's an important difference—the layout container won't be able to receive mouse events.

Borders

The layout containers allow you to paint a background, but not a border outline. However, there's an element that fills in the gap—the Border.

The Border class is pure simplicity. It takes a single piece of nested content (which is often a layout panel) and adds a background or border around it. To master the Border, you need nothing more than the properties listed in Table 2-2.

Table 2-2. Properties of the Border Class

NAME	DESCRIPTION
Background	Sets a background that appears behind all the content in the border using a Brush object. You can use a solid color or something more exotic.
BorderBrush and BorderThickness	Sets the color of the border that appears at the edge of the Border object, using a Brush object, and sets the width of the border, respectively. To show a border, you must set both properties.
CornerRadius	Allows you to gracefully round the corners of your border. The greater the CornerRadius, the more dramatic the rounding effect is.
Padding	Adds spacing between the border and the content inside. (By contrast, margin adds spacing outside the border.)

Here's a straightforward, slightly rounded border around a button in a
StackPanel:

```
<Border Margin="25" Padding="8" Background="LightYellow"
 BorderBrush="SteelBlue" BorderThickness="8" CornerRadius="15">
  <Button Margin="3" Content="Click Me"></Button>
</Border>
```

Figure 2-2 shows the result.

Figure 2-2. A basic border

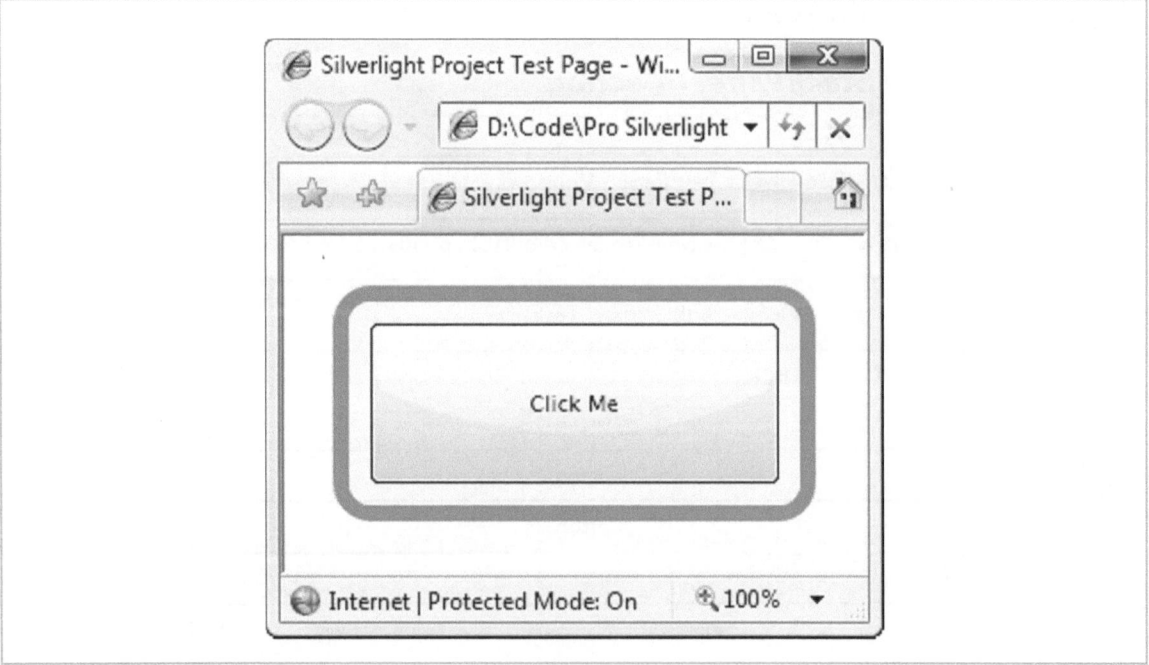

Simple Layout with the StackPanel

The StackPanel is one of the simplest layout containers. It simply stacks its
children in a single row or column. These elements are arranged based on
their order.

For example, consider this page, which contains a stack with one TextBlock
and four buttons:

```
<UserControl x:Class="Layout.SimpleStack"
 xmlns="http://schemas.microsoft.com/client/2007"
 xmlns:x="http://schemas.microsoft.com/winfx/2006/xaml">
  <StackPanel Background="White">
    <TextBlock Text="A Button Stack"></TextBlock>
    <Button Content="Button 1"></Button>
    <Button Content="Button 2"></Button>
    <Button Content="Button 3"></Button>
    <Button Content="Button 4"></Button>
  </StackPanel>
</UserControl>
```

Figure 2-3 shows the result.

Figure 2-3. The StackPanel in action

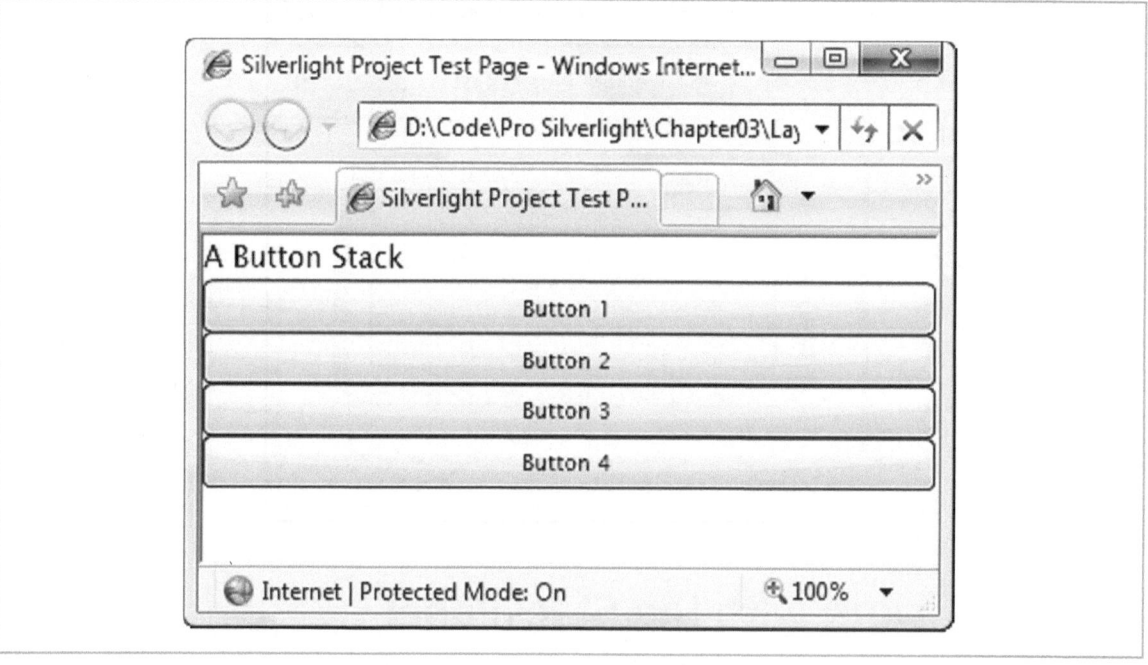

By default, a StackPanel arranges elements from top to bottom, making each one as tall as is necessary to display its content. In this example, that means the TextBlock and buttons are sized just large enough to comfortably accommodate the text inside. All the elements are then stretched to the full width of the StackPanel, which is the width of your page.

In this example, the Height and Width properties of the page are not set. As a result, the page grows to fit the full the Silverlight content region (in this case, the complete browser window). Most of the examples in this chapter use this approach, because it makes it easier to experiment with the different layout containers and see how they resize themselves to fit different sizes.

Note   Once you've examined all the layout containers, you'll take a closer look at the issue of page sizes, and you'll learn about your different options for dealing content that doesn't fit. For more information, see the section "The Page" later in this chapter.

The StackPanel can also be used to arrange elements horizontally by setting the Orientation property:

```
<StackPanel Orientation="Horizontal" Background="White">
```

Now elements are given their minimum width (wide enough to fit their text) and are stretched to the full height of the containing panel (see Figure 2-4).

Figure 2-4. The StackPanel with horizontal orientation

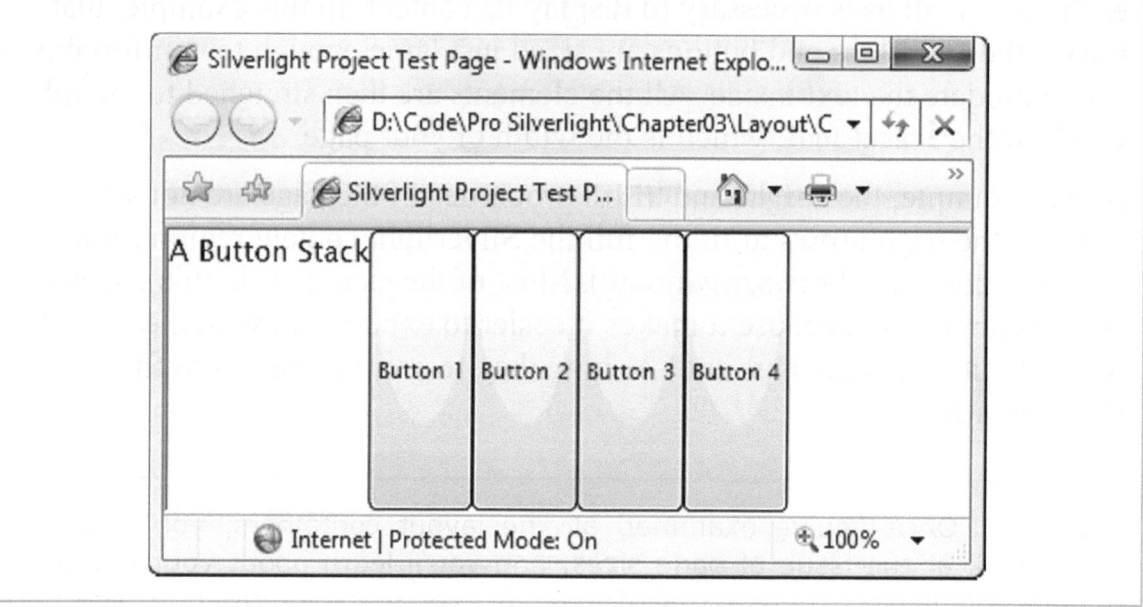

Clearly, this doesn't provide the flexibility real applications need. Fortunately, you can fine-tune the way the StackPanel and other layout containers work using layout properties, as described next.

Layout Properties

Although layout is determined by the container, the child elements can still get their say. In fact, layout panels work in concert with their children by respecting a small set of layout properties, as listed in Table 2-3.

Table 2-3. Layout Properties

NAME	DESCRIPTION
HorizontalAlignment	Determines how a child is positioned inside a layout container when there's extra horizontal space available. You can choose Center, Left, Right, or Stretch.

NAME	DESCRIPTION
VerticalAlignment	Determines how a child is positioned inside a layout container when there's extra vertical space available. You can choose Center, Top, Bottom, or Stretch.
Margin	Adds a bit of breathing room around an element. The Margin property is an instance of the System.Windows.Thickness structure, with separate components for the top, bottom, left, and right edges.
MinWidth and MinHeight	Set the minimum dimensions of an element. If an element is too large for its layout container, it will be cropped to fit.
MaxWidth and MaxHeight	Set the maximum dimensions of an element. If the container has more room available, the element won't be enlarged beyond these bounds, even if the HorizontalAlignment and VerticalAlignment properties are set to Stretch.
Width and Height	Explicitly set the size of an element. This setting overrides a Stretch value for the HorizontalAlignment or VerticalAlignment properties. However, this size won't be honored if it's outside of the bounds set by the MinWidth, MinHeight, MaxWidth, and MaxHeight.

All of these properties are inherited from the base FrameworkElement class and are therefore supported by all the graphical widgets you can use in a Silverlight page.

Note   As you learned in Chapter 2, different layout containers can provide *attached properties* to their children. For example, all the children of a `Grid` object gain `Row` and `Column` properties that allow them to choose the cell where they're placed. Attached properties allow you to set information that's specific to a particular layout container. However, the layout properties in Table 2-3 are generic enough that they apply to many layout panels. Thus, these properties are defined as part of the base `FrameworkElement` class.

Alignment

To understand how these properties work, take another look at the simple `StackPanel` shown in Figure 2-3. In this example—a `StackPanel` with vertical orientation—the `VerticalAlignment` property has no effect because each element is given as much height as it needs and no more. However, the `HorizontalAlignment` *is* important. It determines where each element is placed in its row.

Ordinarily, the default `HorizontalAlignment` is `Left` for a label and `Stretch` for a button. That's why every button takes the full column width. However, you can change these details:

```
<StackPanel Background="White">
  <TextBlock HorizontalAlignment="Center" Text="A Button Stack"></TextBlock>
  <Button HorizontalAlignment="Left" Content="Button 1"></Button>
  <Button HorizontalAlignment="Right" Content="Button 2"></Button>
  <Button Content="Button 3"></Button>
  <Button Content="Button 4"></Button>
</StackPanel>
```

The first two buttons are given their minimum sizes and aligned accordingly, while the bottom two buttons are stretched over the entire `StackPanel`. If you resize the page, you'll see that the label remains in the middle and the first two buttons stay stuck to either side.

Margin

There's an obvious problem with the `StackPanel` example in its current form. A well-designed page doesn't just contain elements—it also includes a bit of extra space in between the elements. To introduce this extra space and make the `StackPanel` example less cramped, you can set control margins.

When setting margins, you can set a single width for all sides, like this:

```
<Button Margin="5" Content="Button 3"></Button>
```

Alternatively, you can set different margins for each side of a control in the order *left, top, right, bottom*:

```
<Button Margin="5,10,5,10" Content="Button 3"></Button>
```

In code, you can set margins using the `Thickness` structure:

```
cmd.Margin = new Thickness(5);
```

Getting the right control margins is a bit of an art because you need to consider how the margin settings of adjacent controls influence one another. For example, if you have two buttons stacked on top of each other, and the topmost button has a bottom margin of 5, and the bottommost button has a top margin of 5, you have a total of 10 pixels of space between the two buttons.

Ideally, you'll be able to keep different margin settings as consistent as possible and avoid setting distinct values for the different margin sides. For instance, in the StackPanel example, it makes sense to use the same margins on the buttons and on the panel itself, as shown here:

```
<StackPanel Margin="3" Background="White">
  <TextBlock Margin="3" HorizontalAlignment="Center"
   Text="A Button Stack"></TextBlock>
  <Button Margin="3" HorizontalAlignment="Left" Content="Button 1"></Button>
  <Button Margin="3" HorizontalAlignment="Right" Content="Button 2"></Button>
  <Button Margin="3" Content="Button 3"></Button>
  <Button Margin="3" Content="Button 4"></Button>
</StackPanel>
```

This way, the total space between two buttons (the sum of the two button margins) is the same as the total space between the button at the edge of the page (the sum of the button margin and the StackPanel margin). Figure 2-5 shows this more respectable page, and Figure 2-6 shows how the margin settings break down.

Figure 2-5. Adding margins between elements

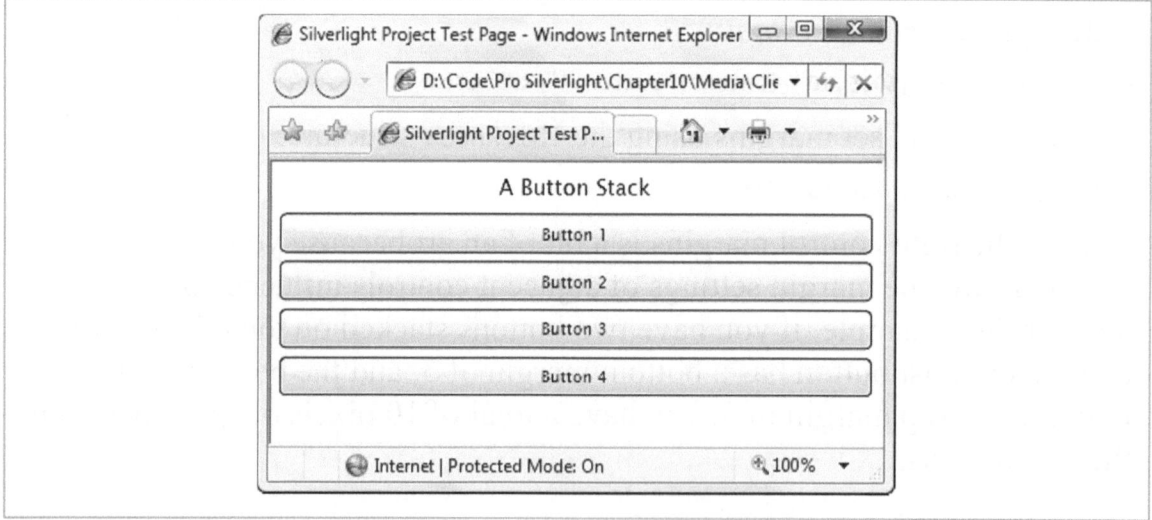

Figure 2-6. How margins are combined

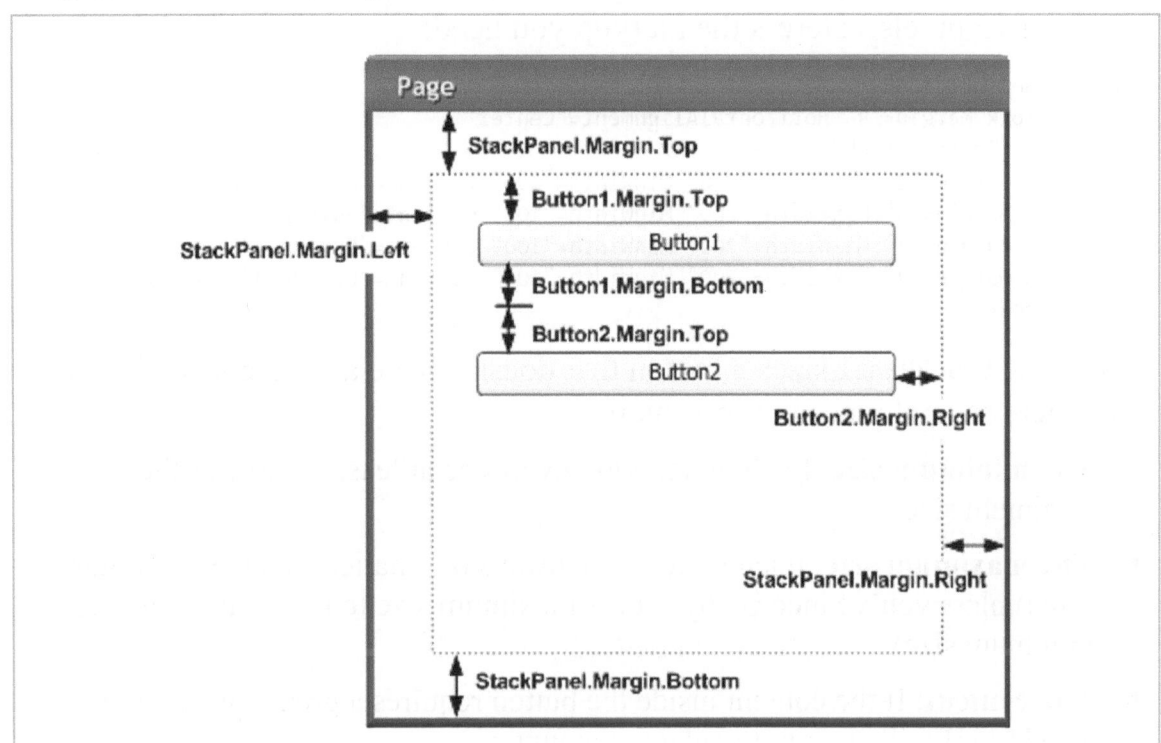

Minimum, Maximum, and Explicit Sizes

Finally, every element includes `Height` and `Width` properties that allow you to give it an explicit size. However, just because you can set explicit sizes doesn't mean you *should*. In most cases, it's better to let elements grow to fit their content. For example, a button expands as you add more text. You can lock your elements into a range of acceptable sizes by setting a maximum and minimum size, if necessary. If you do add size information, you risk creating a more brittle layout that can't adapt to changes and (at worst) truncates content that doesn't fit.

For example, you might decide that the buttons in your `StackPanel` should stretch to fit the `StackPanel` but be made no larger than 200 pixels wide and no smaller than 100 pixels wide. (By default, buttons start with a minimum width of 75 pixels.) Here's the markup you need:

```
<StackPanel Margin="3">
  <TextBlock Margin="3" HorizontalAlignment="Center"
   Text="A Button Stack"></TextBlock>
  <Button Margin="3" MaxWidth="200" MinWidth="100" Content="Button 1"></Button>
  <Button Margin="3" MaxWidth="200" MinWidth="100" Content="Button 2"></Button>
  <Button Margin="3" MaxWidth="200" MinWidth="100" Content="Button 3"></Button>
  <Button Margin="3" MaxWidth="200" MinWidth="100" Content="Button 4"></Button>
</StackPanel>
```

When the StackPanel sizes a button that doesn't have a hard-coded size, it considers several pieces of information:

- **The minimum size**: Each button will always be at least as large as the minimum size.

- **The maximum size**: Each button will always be smaller than the maximum size (unless you've incorrectly set the maximum size to be smaller than the minimum size).

- **The content**: If the content inside the button requires a greater width, the StackPanel will attempt to enlarge the button.

- **The size of the container**: If the minimum width is larger than the width of the StackPanel, a portion of the button will be cut off. Otherwise, the button will not be allowed to grow wider than the StackPanel, even if it can't fit all its text on the button surface.

- **The horizontal alignment**: Because the button uses a HorizontalAlignment of Stretch (the default), the StackPanel will attempt to enlarge the button to fill the full width of the StackPanel.

The trick to understanding this process is to realize that the minimum and maximum size set the absolute bounds. Within those bounds, the StackPanel tries to respect the button's desired size (to fit its content) and its alignment settings.

Figure 2-7 sheds some light on how this works with the StackPanel. On the top is the page at its minimum size. The buttons are 100 pixels each, and the page cannot be resized to be narrower. If you shrink the page from this point, the right side of each button will be clipped off. (You can deal with this situation using scrolling, as discussed later in this chapter.)

Figure 2-7. Constrained button sizing

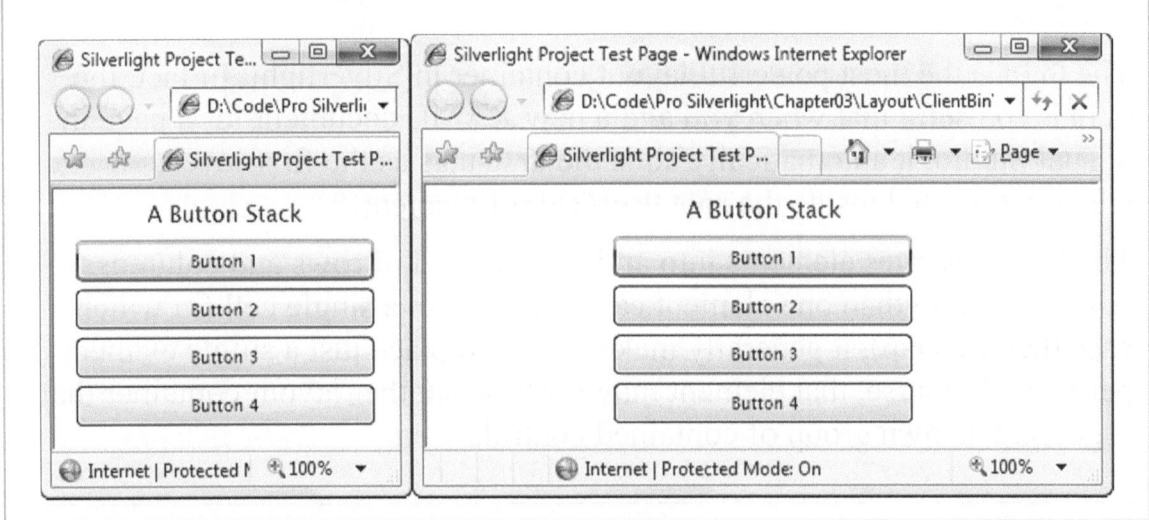

As you enlarge the page, the buttons grow with it until they reach their maximum of 200 pixels. From this point on, if you make the page any larger, the extra space is added to either side of the button (as shown on the right).

Note   In some situations, you might want to use code that checks how large an element is in a page. The `Height` and `Width` properties are no help because they indicate your desired size settings, which might not correspond to the actual rendered size. In an ideal scenario, you'll let your elements size to fit their content, and the `Height` and `Width` properties won't be set at all. However, you can find out the actual size used to render an element by reading the `ActualHeight` and `ActualWidth` properties. But remember, these values may change when the page is resized or the content inside it changes.

The Grid

The `Grid` is the most powerful layout container in Silverlight. In fact, the `Grid` is so useful that when you add a new XAML document for a page in Visual Studio, it automatically adds the `Grid` tags as the first-level container, nested inside the root `UserControl` element.

The `Grid` separates elements into an invisible grid of rows and columns. Although more than one element can be placed in a single cell (in which case they overlap), it generally makes sense to place just a single element per cell. Of course, that element may itself be another layout container that organizes its own group of contained controls.

Tip   Although the `Grid` is designed to be invisible, you can set the `Grid.ShowGridLines` property to true to take a closer look. This feature isn't really intended for prettying up a page. Instead, it's a debugging convenience that's designed to help you understand how the `Grid` has subdivided itself into smaller regions. This feature is important because you have the ability to control exactly how the `Grid` chooses column widths and row heights.

Creating a Grid-based layout is a two-step process. First, you choose the number of columns and rows that you want. Next, you assign the appropriate row and column to each contained element, thereby placing it in just the right spot.

You create grids and rows by filling the Grid.ColumnDefinitions and Grid.RowDefinitions collections with objects. For example, if you decide you need two rows and three columns, you'd add the following tags:

```
<Grid ShowGridLines="True" Background="White">
  <Grid.RowDefinitions>
    <RowDefinition></RowDefinition>
    <RowDefinition></RowDefinition>
  </Grid.RowDefinitions>
  <Grid.ColumnDefinitions>
    <ColumnDefinition></ColumnDefinition>
    <ColumnDefinition></ColumnDefinition>
    <ColumnDefinition></ColumnDefinition>
  </Grid.ColumnDefinitions>

  ...
</Grid>
```

As this example shows, it's not necessary to supply any information in a RowDefinition or ColumnDefinition element. If you leave these elements empty (as shown here), the Grid will share the space evenly between all rows and columns. In this example, each cell will be exactly the same size, depending on the size of the containing page.

To place individual elements into a cell, you use the attached Row and Column properties. Both these properties take 0-based index numbers. For example, here's how you could create a partially filled grid of buttons:

```
<Grid ShowGridLines="True" Background="White">
  ...

  <Button Grid.Row="0" Grid.Column="0" Content="Top Left"></Button>
  <Button Grid.Row="0" Grid.Column="1" Content="Middle Left"></Button>
  <Button Grid.Row="1" Grid.Column="2" Content="Bottom Right"></Button>
```

```
  <Button Grid.Row="1" Grid.Column="1" Content="Bottom Middle"></Button>
</Grid>
```

Each element must be placed into its cell explicitly. This allows you to place more than one element into a cell (which rarely makes sense) or leave certain cells blank (which is often useful). It also means you can declare your elements out of order, as with the final two buttons in this example. However, it makes for clearer markup if you define your controls row by row, and from right to left in each row.

There is one exception. If you don't specify the Grid.Row property, the Grid assumes that it's 0. The same behavior applies to the Grid.Column property. Thus, you leave both attributes off of an element to place it in the first cell of the Grid.

Figure 2-8 shows how this simple grid appears at two different sizes. Notice that the ShowGridLines property is set to true so that you can see the separation between each column and row.

Figure 2-8. A simple grid

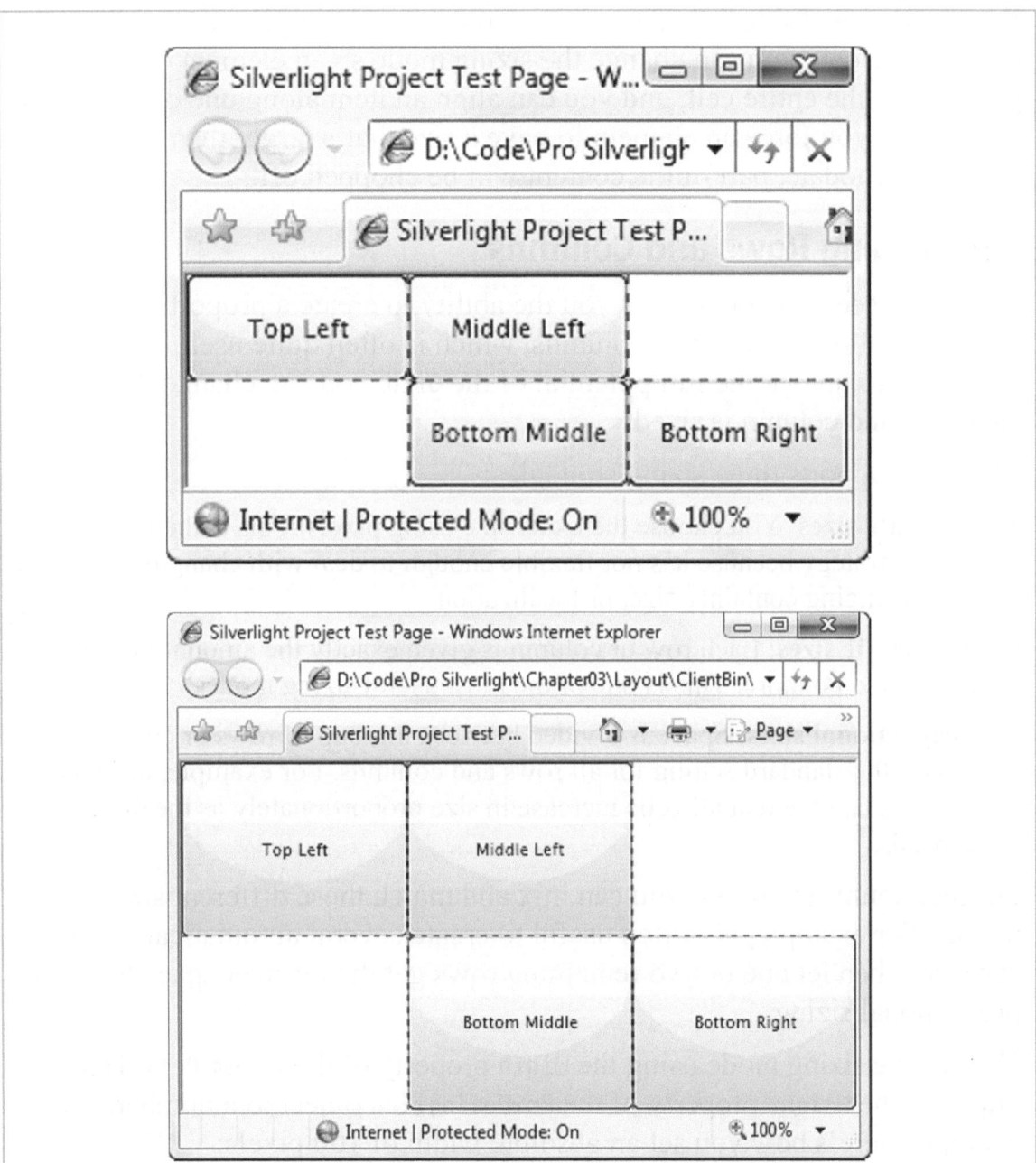

As you would expect, the `Grid` honors the basic set of layout properties listed earlier in Table 2-3. That means you can add margins around the content in a cell, you can change the sizing mode so an element doesn't grow to fill the entire cell, and you can align an item along one of the edges of a cell. If you force an element to have a size that's larger than the cell can accommodate, part of the content will be chopped off.

Fine-Tuning Rows and Columns

As you've seen, the `Grid` gives you the ability to create a proportionately sized collection of rows and columns, which is often quite useful. However, to unlock the full potential of the `Grid`, you can change the way each row and column is sized.

The `Grid` supports three sizing strategies:

- **Absolute sizes**: You choose the exact size using pixels. This is the least useful strategy because it's not flexible enough to deal with changing content size, changing container size, or localization.

- **Automatic sizes**: Each row or column is given exactly the amount of space it needs, and no more. This is one of the most useful sizing modes.

- **Proportional sizes**: Space is divided between a group of rows or columns. This is the standard setting for all rows and columns. For example, in Figure 2-8, you can see that all cells increase in size proportionately as the `Grid` expands.

For maximum flexibility, you can mix and match these different sizing modes. For example, it's often useful to create several automatically sized rows and then let one or two remaining rows get the leftover space through proportional sizing.

You set the sizing mode using the `Width` property of the `ColumnDefinition` object or the `Height` property of the `RowDefinition` object to a number. For example, here's how you set an absolute width of 100 pixels:

```
<ColumnDefinition Width="100"></ColumnDefinition>
```

To use automatic sizing, you use a value of Auto:

```
<ColumnDefinition Width="Auto"></ColumnDefinition>
```

Finally, to use proportional sizing, you use an asterisk (*):

```
<ColumnDefinition Width="*"></ColumnDefinition>
```

This syntax stems from the world of the Web, where it's used with HTML frames pages. If you use a mix of proportional sizing and other sizing modes, the proportionally sized rows or columns get whatever space is left over.

If you want to divide the remaining space unequally, you can assign a *weight*, which you must place before the asterisk. For example, if you have two proportionately sized rows and you want the first to be half as high as the second, you could share the remaining space like this:

```
<RowDefinition Height="*"></RowDefinition>
<RowDefinition Height="2*"></RowDefinition>
```

This tells the **Grid** that the height of the second row should be twice the height of the first row. You can use whatever numbers you like to portion out the extra space.

Note   It's easy to interact with **ColumnDefinition** and **RowDefinition** objects programmatically. You simply need to know that the **Width** and **Height** properties are **GridLength** objects. To create a **GridLength** that represents a specific size, just pass the appropriate value to the **GridLength** constructor. To create a **GridLength** that represents a proportional (*) size, pass the number to the **GridLength** constructor, and pass **GridUnitType.Star** as the second constructor argument. To indicate automatic sizing, use the static property **GridLength.Auto**.

Nesting Layout Containers

The Grid is impressive on its own, but most realistic user interfaces combine several layout containers. They may use an arrangement with more than one Grid or mix the Grid with other layout containers like the StackPanel.

The following markup presents a simple example of this principle. It creates a basic dialog box with OK and Cancel buttons in the bottom right-hand corner, and a large content region that's sized to fit its content (the text in a TextBlock). The entire package is centered in the middle of the page by setting the alignment properties on the Grid.

```
<Grid ShowGridLines="True" Background="SteelBlue"
 HorizontalAlignment="Center" VerticalAlignment="Center">
  <Grid.RowDefinitions>
    <RowDefinition Height="*"></RowDefinition>
    <RowDefinition Height="Auto"></RowDefinition>
  </Grid.RowDefinitions>

  <TextBlock Margin="10" Grid.Row="0" Foreground="White"
   Text="This is simply a test of nested containers."></TextBlock>
  <StackPanel Grid.Row="1" HorizontalAlignment="Right" Orientation="Horizontal">
    <Button Margin="10,10,2,10" Padding="3" Content="OK"></Button>
    <Button Margin="2,10,10,10" Padding="3" Content="Cancel"></Button>
  </StackPanel>
</Grid>
```

You'll notice that this Grid doesn't declare any columns. This is a shortcut you can take if your grid uses just one column and that column is proportionately sized (so it fills the entire width of the Grid). Figure 2-9 shows the rather pedestrian dialog box this markup creates.

Figure 2-9. A basic dialog box

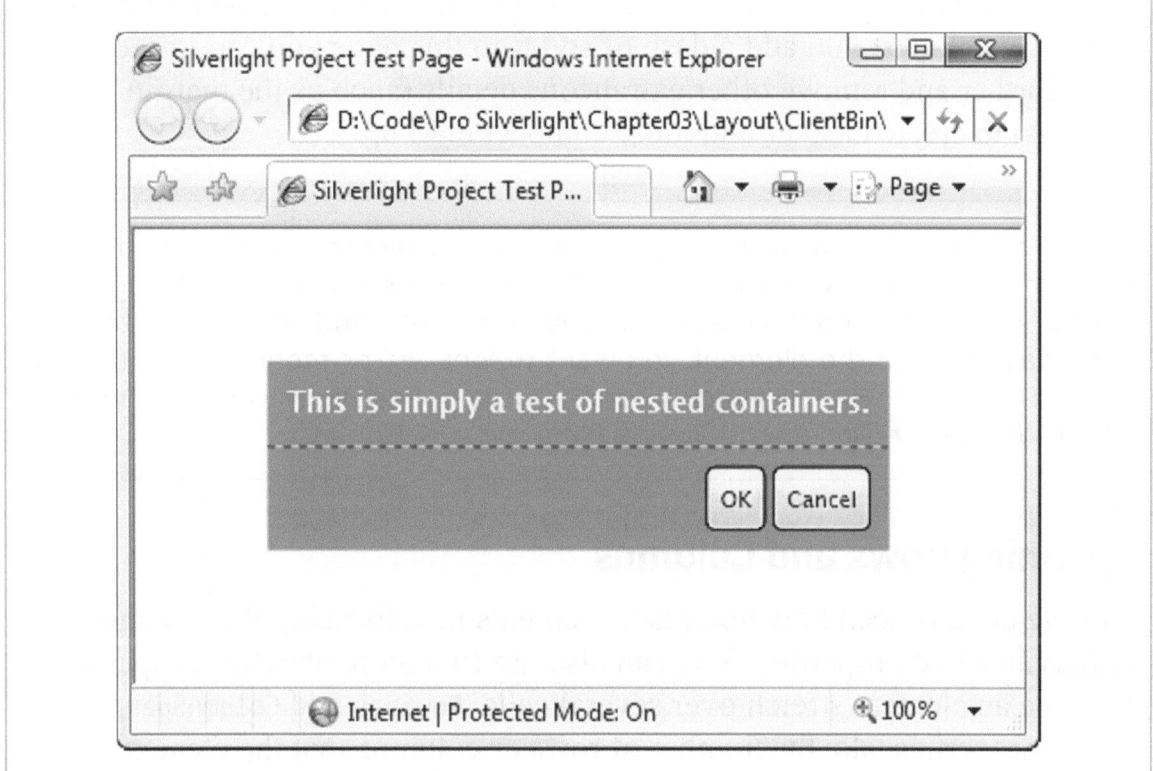

At first glance, nesting layout containers seems like a fair bit more work than placing controls in precise positions using coordinates. And in many cases, it is. However, the longer setup time is compensated by the ease with which you can change the user interface in the future. For example, if you decide you want the OK and Cancel buttons to be centered at the bottom of the page, you simply need to change the alignment of the StackPanel that contains them:

```
<StackPanel Grid.Row="1" HorizontalAlignment="Center" ... >
```

Similarly, if you need to change the amount of content in the first row, the entire `Grid` will be enlarged to fit, and the buttons will move obligingly out of the way. And if you add a dash of styles to this page you can improve it even further and remove other extraneous details (such as the margin settings) to create cleaner and more compact markup.

Tip If you have a densely nested tree of elements, it's easy to lose sight of the overall structure. Visual Studio provides a handy feature that shows you a tree representation of your elements and allows you to click your way down to the element you want to look at (or modify). This feature is the Document Outline window, and you can show it by choosing View ➤ Other Windows ➤ Document Outline from the menu.

Spanning Rows and Columns

You've already seen how you place elements in cells using the `Row` and `Column` attached properties. You can also use two more attached properties to make an element stretch over several cells: `RowSpan` and `ColumnSpan`. These properties take the number of rows or columns that the element should occupy.

Row and column spanning can achieve some interesting effects and is particularly handy when you need to fit elements in a tabular structure that's broken up by dividers or longer sections of content.

Using the GridSplitter

Every Windows user has seen *splitter bars*—draggable dividers that separate one section of a window from another. For example, when you use Windows Explorer, you're presented with a list of folders (on the left) and a list of files (on the right). You can drag the splitter bar in between to determine what proportion of the window is given to each pane.

A **Grid** usually contains no more than a single **GridSplitter**. However, you can nest one **Grid** inside another, and if you do, each **Grid** may have its own **GridSplitter**. This allows you to create a page that's split into two regions (for example, a left and right pane), and you can then further subdivide one of these regions (say, the pane on the right) into more sections (such as a resizable top and bottom portion).

Coordinate-Based Layout with the Canvas

The only layout container you haven't considered yet is the **Canvas**. It allows you to place elements using exact coordinates, which is a poor choice for designing rich data-driven forms and standard dialog boxes, but a valuable tool if you need to build something a little different (such as a drawing surface for a diagramming tool). The **Canvas** is also the most lightweight of the layout containers. That's because it doesn't include any complex layout logic to negotiate the sizing preferences of its children. Instead, it simply lays them all out at the position they specify, with the exact size they want.

To position an element on the **Canvas**, you set the attached **Canvas.Left** and **Canvas.Top** properties. **Canvas.Left** sets the number of pixels between the left edge of your element and the left edge of the **Canvas**. **Canvas.Top** sets the number of pixels between the top of your element and the top of the **Canvas**.

Optionally, you can size your element explicitly using its **Width** and **Height** properties. This is more common when using the **Canvas** than it is in other panels because the **Canvas** has no layout logic of its own. (And often, you'll use the **Canvas** when you need precise control over how a combination of elements is arranged.) If you don't set the **Width** and **Height** properties, your element will get its desired size—in other words, it will grow just large enough to fit its content. If you change the size of the Canvas, it has no effect on the Controls inside.

Here's a simple Canvas that includes four buttons:

```
<Canvas Background="White">
  <Button Canvas.Left="10" Canvas.Top="10" Content="(10,10)"></Button>
  <Button Canvas.Left="120" Canvas.Top="30" Content="(120,30)"></Button>
  <Button Canvas.Left="60" Canvas.Top="80" Width="50" Height="50"
  Content="(60,80)"></Button>
  <Button Canvas.Left="70" Canvas.Top="120" Width="100" Height="50"
  Content="(70,120)"></Button>
</Canvas>
```

Figure 2-10 shows the result.

Figure 2-10. Explicitly positioned buttons in a Canvas

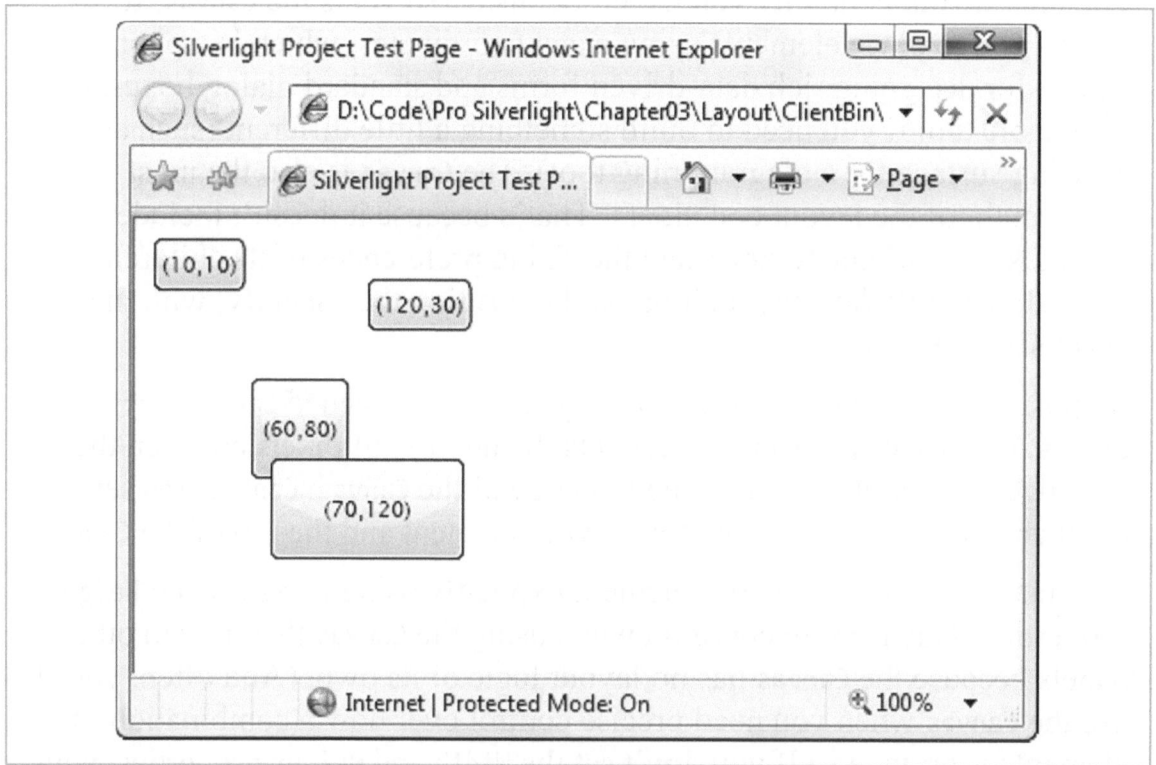

Like any other layout container, the Canvas can be nested inside a user interface. That means you can use the Canvas to draw some detailed content in a portion of your page, while using more standard Silverlight panels for the rest of your elements.

If you have more than one overlapping element, you can set the attached Canvas.ZIndex property to control how they are layered.

The ZIndex property is particularly useful if you need to change the position of an element programmatically. Just call Canvas.SetZIndex() and pass in the element you want to modify and the new ZIndex you want to apply. Unfortunately, there is no BringToFront() or SendToBack() method—it's up to you to keep track of the highest and lowest ZIndex values if you want to implement this behavior.

CHOOSING THE RIGHT LAYOUT CONTAINER

As a general rule of thumb, the Grid and StackPanel are best when dealing with business-style applications (for example, when displaying data entry forms or documents). They deal well with changing window sizes and dynamic content (for example, blocks of text that can grow or shrink depending on the information at hand). They also make it easier to modify, localize, and reskin the application, because adjacent elements will bump each other out of the way as they change size. The Grid and StackPanel are also closest to the way ordinary HTML pages work.

The Canvas is dramatically different. Because all of its children are arranged using fixed coordinates, you need to go to more work to position them (and even more work if you want to tweak the layout later on in response to new elements or new formatting). However, the Canvas makes sense in certain types of graphically rich applications, such as games. In these applications, you need fine-grained control, text and graphics often overlap, and you often change coordinates programmatically. Here, the emphasis isn't on flexibility, but on achieving a specific visual appearance, and the Canvas makes more sense.

And if none of the layout containers gives you the layout you really want, there's still another option—you can build your own. The developers of Silverlight have intentionally limited the available containers to include just the three most useful, which keeps the Silverlight framework (and its download size) small. However, there's no reason you can't re-create some of the more specialized layout containers that exist in the WPF world.

The Page

As you've already seen, the top-level container for each Silverlight page is a custom class that derives from `UserControl`. The `UserControl` class adds a single property, named `Content`, to Silverlight's basic element infrastructure. The `Content` property accepts a single element, which becomes the content of that user control.

User controls don't include any special functionality—they're simply a convenient way to group together a block of related elements. However, the way you size your user control can affect the appearance of your entire user interface, so it's worth taking a closer look.

You've already seen how you can use different layout containers and a variety of layout properties to control whether your elements size to fit their content, the available space, or hard-coded dimensions. Many of the same options are available when you're sizing a page. Your options include the following:

- **Fixed size**: Set the `Width` and `Height` properties of the user control to give your page an exact size. If you have controls inside the page that exceed these dimensions, they will be truncated. When using a fixed-size window, it's common to change the `HorizontalAlignment` and `VerticalAlignment` properties of the user control to `Center`, so it floats in the center of the browser window rather than being locked into the top-left corner.

- **Browser size**: Remove the `Width` and `Height` properties to let your page take the full space allocated to it in the Silverlight content region. By default,

Visual Studio creates an entry page that sizes the Silverlight content region to take 100% of the browser window. If you use this approach, it's still possible to create elements that stretch off the bounds of the display region, but the user can now observe the problem and resize the browser window to see the missing content. If you want to preserve some blank space between your page and the browser window when using this approach, you can set the user control's `Margin` property.

- **Constrained size**: Remove the `Width` and `Height` properties but use the `MaxWidth`, `MaxHeight`, `MinWidth`, and `MinHeight` properties instead. Now the user control will resize itself to fit the browser windows within a sensible range, and it will stop resizing when the window reaches very large or very small dimensions, ensuring it's never scrambled beyond recognition.

- **Unlimited size**: In some cases it makes sense to let your Silverlight content region take more than the full browser window. In this situation, the browser will add scrollbars, much as it does with a long HTML page. To get this effect, you need to remove the `Width` and `Height` properties and edit the entry page (`TestPage.html`). In the entry page, remove the `width="100%"` and `height="100%"` attributes in the `<object>` element. This way, the Silverlight content region will be allowed to grow to fit the size of your user control.

All of these approaches are reasonable choices. It simply depends on the type of user interface that you're building. When you use a non-fixed-size page, your application can take advantage of the extra space in the browser window by reflowing its layout to fit. The disadvantage is that extremely large or small windows may make your content more difficult to read or use. You can design for these issues, but it takes more work. On the other hand, the disadvantage of hard-coded sizes is that your application will be forever locked in a specific window size no matter what the browser window looks like. This can lead to oceans of empty space (if you've hard-coded a size that's smaller than the browser window) or make the application unusable (if you've hard-coded a size that's bigger than the browser window).

As a general rule of thumb, resizable pages are more flexible and preferred where possible. They're usually the best choice for business applications and applications with a more traditional user interface that isn't too heavy on the graphics. On the other hand, graphically rich applications and games often need more precise control over what's taking place in the page, and are more likely to use fixed page sizes.

Tip If you're testing out different approaches, it helps to make the bounds of the page more obvious. One easy way to do so is to apply a nonwhite background to the top-level content element (for example, setting the **Background** property of a **Grid** to **Yellow**). You can't set the **Background** property on the user control itself, because the **UserControl** class doesn't provide it. Another option is to use a **Border** element as your top-level element, which allows you to outline the page region.

There are also a few more specialized sizing options: scrollable interfaces, scalable interfaces, and full-screen interfaces.

Scrolling

None of the containers you've seen have provided support for *scrolling*, which is a key feature for fitting large amounts of content in a limited amount of space. In Silverlight, scrolling support is easy to get, but it requires another ingredient: the **ScrollViewer** content control.

In order to get scrolling support, you need to wrap the content you want to scroll inside a **ScrollViewer**. Although the **ScrollViewer** can hold anything, you'll typically use it to wrap a layout container.

Scaling

Earlier in this chapter, you saw how the `Grid` can use proportional sizing to make sure your elements take all the available space. Thus, the `Grid` is a great tool for building resizable interfaces that grow and shrink to fit the browser window.

Although this resizing behavior is usually what you want, it isn't always suitable. Changing the dimensions of controls changes the amount of content they can accommodate and can have subtle layout-shifting effects. In graphically rich applications, you might need more precise control to keep your elements perfectly aligned. However, that doesn't mean you need to use fixed-size pages. Instead, you can use another trick, called *scaling*.

Essentially, scaling resizes the entire visual appearance of the control, not just its outside bounds. No matter what the scale, a control can hold the same content—it just looks different. Conceptually, it's like changing the zoom level.

Full Screen

Silverlight applications also have the capability to enter a full-screen mode, which allows them to break out of the browser window altogether. In full-screen mode, the Silverlight plug-in fills the whole display area, and is shown on top of all other applications, including the browser.

Full-screen mode has some serious limitations:

- **You can only switch into full-screen mode when responding to a user input event**: In other words, you can switch into full-screen mode when the user clicks a button or hits a key. However, you can't switch into full-screen mode as soon as your application loads up. (If you attempt to do so, you're code will simply be ignored.) This limitation is designed to prevent a Silverlight application from fooling a user into thinking it's actually another local application or a system window.

- **While in full-screen mode, you can't respond to keyboard events**: For example, if you have a text box control, it's impossible for users to type into it. This limitation is designed to prevent users from being tricked into typing into your application when they're trying to access another one, but it seems unnecessarily restrictive. It prevents you from creating many types of full-screen games.

Note   Full-screen mode was primarily designed for showing video content in a large window.

Navigation

With the know-how you've picked up in this chapter, you're ready to create pages that use a variety of different layouts. However, there's still something missing—the ability to transition from one page to another. After all, traditional rich client applications are usually built around different windows that encapsulate distinct tasks.

The short answer is a bit disappointing. Surprisingly, Silverlight doesn't give you any built-in navigation capability. Although you can add multiple user controls to your project, there's no automated way to jump from one to another. Silverlight does include a `HyperlinkButton` control, but it's designed to navigate between HTML pages. In other words, when a user clicks a `HyperlinkButton` control, the current Silverlight application is abandoned and the browser requests a new URL. The new page may or may not have its own Silverlight application—but if it does, that application needs to be downloaded to the client and will start from scratch.

The lack of navigation in Silverlight is a clear drawback. However, there are several commonly used techniques to compensate for this limitation, as you'll see in the following sections.

Loading Child User Controls

One approach is to create a central page that acts as the main window for your application for its entire lifetime. However, this page can modify itself by loading new user controls into its hierarchy of elements.

Dynamically loading a user control is easy—you simply need to create an instance of the appropriate class and then add it to a suitable container, such as a `Border`, `ScrollViewer`, `StackPanel`, or `Grid`.

Hiding Elements

Creating a dynamic page that adds and removes subsections is a more commonly used approach than removing all the content of a page and loading a different one. If you decide to create a dynamic page, it's important to realize that you aren't limited to adding and removing content. You can also temporarily hide it. The trick is to set the `Visibility` property, which is defined in the base `UIElement` class and inherited by all elements.

```
panel.Visibility = Visibility.Hidden;
```

The `Visibility` property uses an enumeration that provides just two values, `Visible` and `Hidden`. WPF included a third value, `Collapsed`, which is not supported in Silverlight. Although you can set the `Visibility` property of individual elements, usually you'll show and hide entire containers (`Border`, `StackPanel`, or `Grid` objects) at once.

When an element is hidden, it takes no space in the page and doesn't receive any input events. The rest of your interface will resize itself to fill the available space (unless you've positioned your other elements with fixed coordinates using a layout container like the `Canvas`).

Tip   Many applications use panels that collapse or slide out of the way. To create this effect, you can combine this code with a dash of Silverlight animation. The animation will change the elements you want to hide—for example, shrinking, compressing, or moving it.

The Last Word

In this chapter, you saw how to organize Silverlight content in an attractive and flexible way using layout containers. You also saw how these containers can be modified and manipulated to fit your requirements and considered special case scenarios such as scrolling navigation and scaling.

Chapter 3: Dependency Properties and Routed Events

At this point, you're probably itching to dive into a realistic, practical example of Silverlight coding. But before you can get started, you need to understand a few more fundamentals. In this chapter, you'll get a whirlwind tour of two key Silverlight concepts: *dependency properties* and *routed events*.

Both of these concepts first appeared in Silverlight's big brother technology, WPF. They came as quite a surprise to most developers—after all, few expected a user interface technology to retool core parts of .NET's object abstraction. However, WPF's changes weren't designed to improve .NET but to support key WPF features. The new property model allowed WPF elements to plug into services such as data binding, animation, and styles. The new event model allowed WPF to adopt a layered content model without horribly complicating the task of responding to user actions like mouse clicks and key presses.

Silverlight borrows both concepts, albeit in a streamlined form.

Note   If you're an experienced WPF programmer, you're probably well versed in the intricacies of dependency properties and routed events. However, the Silverlight implementation of dependency properties and routed events is much simpler than that of WPF, because Silverlight is designed to be more compact, more streamlined, and more easily ported to different computing platforms. Dependency properties do not support the extensive metadata that WPF uses, and routed events are able to bubble but not tunnel—and even then, the bubbling only applies to a small set of built-in input events.

Dependency Properties

Essentially, a dependency property is a property that can be set directly (for example, by your code) or by one of Silverlight's services (such as data binding, styles, or animation). The key feature of this system is the way that these different property providers are *prioritized*. For example, an animation will take precedence over all other services while it's running. These overlapping factors make for a very flexible system. They also give dependency properties their name—in essence, a dependency property *depends* on multiple property providers, each with its own level of precedence.

Most of the properties that are exposed by WPF elements are dependency properties. For example, the Text property of the TextBlock, the Content property of the Button, and the Background property of the Grid—all of which you saw in the simple example in Chapter 1—are all dependency properties. This hints at an important principle of Silverlight dependency properties—they're designed to be consumed in the same way as normal properties. That's because the dependency properties in the Silverlight libraries are always wrapped by ordinary property definitions.

Although dependency features can be read and set in code like normal properties, they're implemented quite differently behind the scenes. The simple reason why is performance. If the designers of Silverlight simply added extra features on top of the .NET property system, they'd need to create a complex, bulky layer for your code to travel through. Ordinary properties could not support all the features of dependency properties without this extra overhead.

Tip   As a general rule, you don't need to know that a property is a dependency property in order to use it. However, some Silverlight features are limited to dependency properties. Furthermore, you'll need to know all about dependency properties to create them in your own classes.

Defining and Registering a Dependency Property

You'll spend much more time using dependency properties than creating them. However, there are still many reasons you'll need to create your own dependency properties. Obviously, they're a key ingredient if you're designing a custom Silverlight element. They're also required in some cases if you want to add data binding, animation, or another Silverlight feature to a portion of code that wouldn't otherwise support it.

Creating a dependency property isn't difficult, but the syntax takes a little getting used to. It's thoroughly different from creating an ordinary .NET property.

The first step is to define an object that *represents* your property. This is an instance of the DependencyProperty class (which is found in the System.Windows namespace). The information about your property needs to be available all the time. For that reason, your DependencyProperty object must be defined as a static field in the associated class.

For example, consider the FrameworkElement class from which all Silverlight elements inherit. FrameworkElement defines a Margin dependency property that all elements share. It's defined like this:

```
public class FrameworkElement: UIElement
{
    public static readonly DependencyProperty MarginProperty;

    ...
}
```

By convention, the field that defines a dependency property has the name of the ordinary property, plus the word "Property" at the end. That way, you can separate the dependency property definition from the name of the actual property. The field is defined with the readonly keyword, which means it can only be set in the static constructor for the FrameworkElement.

> **Note**   Silverlight does not support WPF's system of property sharing—in other words, defining a dependency property in one class and reusing it in another. However, dependency properties follow the normal rules of inheritance, which means that a dependency property like Margin that's defined in the `FrameworkElement` class applies to all Silverlight elements, because all Silverlight elements derive from `FrameworkElement`.

Defining the `DependencyProperty` object is just the first step. In order for it to become usable, you need to register your dependency property with Silverlight. This step needs to be completed before any code uses the property, so it must be performed in a static constructor for the associated class.

Silverlight ensures that `DependencyProperty` objects can't be instantiated directly, because the `DependencyObject` class has no public constructor. Instead, a `DependencyObject` instance can be created only using the static `DependencyProperty.Register()` method. Silverlight also ensures that `DependencyProperty` objects can't be changed after they're created, because all `DependencyProperty` members are read-only. Instead, their values must be supplied as arguments to the `Register()` method.

The following code shows an example of how a `DependencyProperty` must be created. Here, the `FrameworkElement` class uses a static constructor to initialize the `MarginProperty`:

```
static FrameworkElement()
{
    MarginProperty = DependencyProperty.Register("Margin",
      typeof(Thickness), typeof(FrameworkElement), null);
    ...
}
```

The DependencyProperty.Register() method accepts the following arguments:

- The property name (**Margin** in this example).

- The data type used by the property (the **Thickness** structure in this example).

- The type that owns this property (the **FrameworkElement** class in this example).

- A callback that will be triggered when the property is changed. For example, the **TextBox** reacts when the **Text** property is changed, and then fires the **TextChanged** event to notify the application. If you don't need to use the property-changed callback, supply null (as in this example).

With these details in place, you're able to register a new dependency property so that it's available for use.

Note   The Silverlight model for dependency properties makes three simplifications from the richer WPF model. It doesn't use a metadata object to indicate additional information, it doesn't support validation (automatically rejecting incorrect values), and it doesn't support coercion (automatically changing incorrect values to acceptable ones).

The Property Wrapper

The final step is to wrap your Silverlight property in a traditional .NET property. However, whereas typical property procedures retrieve or set the value of a private field, the property procedures for a Silverlight property use the **GetValue()** and **SetValue()** methods that are defined in the base **DependencyObject** class. Here's an example:

```
public Thickness Margin
{
    get { return (Thickness)GetValue(MarginProperty); }
    set { SetValue(MarginProperty, value); }
}
```

When you create the property wrapper, you should include nothing more than a call to `SetValue()` and a call to `GetValue()`, as in the previous example. You should *not* add any extra code to validate values, raise events, and so on. That's because other features in Silverlight may bypass the property wrapper and call `SetValue()` and `GetValue()` directly. (One example is when the Silverlight parser reads your XAML markup and uses it to initialize your user interface.)

You now have a fully functioning dependency property, which you can set just like any other .NET property using the property wrapper:

```
myElement.Margin = new Thickness(5);
```

Dynamic Value Resolution

As you've already learned, dependency properties depend on multiple different services, called property providers. To determine the current value of a property, Silverlight has to decide which one takes precedence. This process is called *dynamic value resolution*.

When evaluating a property, Silverlight follows this order of precedence:

1. **Animations**: If an animation is currently running, and that animation is changing the property value, Silverlight uses the animated value.

2. **Local value**: If you've explicitly set a value in XAML or in code, Silverlight uses the local value. Remember, you can set a value using the `SetValue()` method or the property wrapper. If you set a property using a data binding or a resource, it's considered to be a locally set value.

3. **The template parent**: If an element is part of a data template or a control template, it can inherit certain details from its parent element. If so, they come into effect now.

4. **Styles**: Silverlight styles allow you to configure multiple controls with one rule. If you've set a style that applies to this control, it comes into play now.

Attached Properties

An attached property is a full-fledged dependency property and, like all dependency properties, it's managed by the Silverlight property system. The difference is that an attached property applies to a class other than the one where it's defined.

The most common example of attached properties is found in layout containers. For example, the Grid class defines the attached properties Row and Column, which you set on the contained elements to indicate where they should be positioned. Similarly, the Canvas defines the attached properties Left and Top that let you place elements using absolute coordinates.

When creating an attached property, you don't define the .NET property wrapper. That's because attached properties can be set on *any* dependency object. For example, the Grid.Row property may be set on a Grid object (if you have one Grid nested inside another) or on some other element. In fact, the Grid.Row property can be set on an element even if that element isn't in a Grid—and even if there isn't a single Grid object in your element tree.

Instead of using a .NET property wrapper, attached properties require a pair of static methods that can be called to set and get the property value. These methods use the familiar SetValue() and GetValue() methods (inherited from the DependencyObject class). The static methods should be named SetPropertyName() and GetPropertyName().

Here are the static methods that implement the Grid.Row attached property:

```
public static int GetRow(UIElement element)
{
    return (int)element.GetValue(Grid.RowProperty);
}

public static void SetRow(UIElement element, int value)
{
    element.SetValue(Grid.RowProperty, value);
}
```

And here's an example that positions an element in the first row of a `Grid` using code:

```
Grid.SetRow(txtElement, 0);
```

This sets the `Grid.Row` property to 0 on the `txtElement` object, which is a `TextBox`. Because `Grid.Row` is an attached property, Silverlight allows you to apply it to any other element.

Routed Events

Every .NET developer is familiar with the idea of *events*—messages that are sent by an object (such as a Silverlight element) to notify your code when something significant occurs. WPF enhanced the .NET event model with a new concept of *event routing*, which allows an event to originate in one element but be raised by another one. For example, event routing allows a click that begins in a button to rise up to that button's container and then to the containing page before it's handled by your code.

Silverlight borrows some of WPF's routed event model, but in a dramatically simplified form. While WPF supports several types of routed events, Silverlight only allows one: *bubbled events* that rise up the containment hierarchy from deeply nested elements to their containers. Furthermore, Silverlight's event bubbling is linked to a few keyboard and mouse input events (like `MouseMove` and `KeyDown`). As you'll see, Silverlight doesn't use event bubbling for higher-level control events (like `Click`) and you can't use event routing with the events in your own custom controls.

The Core Element Events

Elements inherit their basic set of events from two core classes: `UIElement` and `FrameworkElement`.

The `UIElement` class defines the most important events for handling user input and the only events that use event bubbling. Table 3-1 provides a list of all the `UIElement` events.

Table 3-1. The UIElement Events

EVENT	BUBBLES	DESCRIPTION
KeyDown	Yes	Occurs when a key is pressed.
KeyUp	Yes	Occurs when a key is released.
GotFocus	Yes	Occurs when the focus changes to this element (when the user clicks it or tabs to it). The element that has focus is the control that will receive keyboard events first.
LostFocus	Yes	Occurs when the focus leaves this element.
MouseLeftButtonDown	Yes	Occurs when the left mouse button is pressed while the mouse pointer is positioned over the element. Silverlight does not provide events for other mouse events, like mouse wheeling scrolling or right-button clicking. (When the right mouse button is clicked over the Silverlight window, a Silverlight system menu pops up with one option: Silverlight Configuration.)
MouseLeftButtonUp	Yes	Occurs when a mouse button is released.

Table 3-1. continued

EVENT	BUBBLES	DESCRIPTION
MouseEnter	No	Occurs when the mouse pointer first moves onto an element. This event doesn't bubble, but if you have several nested elements, they'll all fire MouseEnter events as you move to the most deeply nested element, passing over the bounding line that delineates the others.
MouseLeave	No	Occurs when the mouse pointer moves off of an element.
MouseMove	No	Occurs when the mouse moves while over an element. The MouseMove event is fired frequently—for example, if the user slowly moves the mouse pointer across the face of a button, you'll quickly receive hundreds of MouseMove events. For that reason, you shouldn't perform time-consuming tasks when reacting to this event.

In some cases, higher-level events may effectively replace some of the UIElement events. For example, the Button class provides a Click event that's triggered when the user presses and releases the mouse button, or when the button has focus and the user hits the spacebar. Thus, when handling button clicks, you should always respond to the Click event, not MouseLeftButtonDown or MouseLeftButtonUp. Similarly, the TextBox provides a `TextChanged` event that fires when the text is changed by any mechanism in addition to the basic `KeyDown` and `KeyUp` events.

The `FrameworkElement` class adds just a few more events to this model, as detailed in Table 3-2. None of these events use event bubbling.

Table 3-2. The FrameworkElement Events

EVENT	DESCRIPTION
Loaded	Occurs after an element has been created, configured, and arranged in the window for the first time. After this point, you may want to perform additional customization to the element in code.
SizeChanged	Occurs after the size of an element changes. As you saw in Chapter 3, you can react to this event to implement scaling.
LayoutUpdated	Occurs after the layout inside an element changes. For example, if you create a page that uses no fixed size (and so fits the browser window), and you resize the browser window, the controls will be rearrange to fit the new dimensions, and the LayoutUpdated event will fire for your top-level layout container.

Event Bubbling

Bubbling events are events that travel *up* the containment hierarchy. For example, `MouseLeftButtonDown` is a bubbling event. It's raised first by the element that is clicked. Next, it's raised by that element's parent, and then by *that* element's parent, and so on, until Silverlight reaches the top of the element tree.

Bubbling events allow you to do two useful things:

- **Centralize event handling logic**: For example, you may have a layout panel full of Image elements. When an image is clicked, you want to display some information about it in another part of your user interface. Rather than connect each Image element to the same event handler that does the work, you could attach the event handler once, at the container level.

- **Deal with content controls**: Certain controls have the ability to hold virtually other elements. One example is the Button class, which can hold a piece of text or a layout panel that might contain a combination of text, shapes, and images. In order to react to button clicks, the button needs to be able to intercept mouse actions that happen to any of its contained elements.

Mouse Movements

Along with the obvious mouse clicking events (MouseLeftButtonDown and MouseLeftButtonUp), Silverlight also provides mouse events that fire when the mouse pointer is moved. These events include MouseEnter (which fires when the mouse pointer moves over the element), MouseLeave (which fires when the mouse pointer moves away), and MouseMove (which fires at every point in between).

All of these events provide your code with the same information: a MouseEventArgs object. The MouseEventArgs object includes one important ingredient: a GetPosition() method that tells you the coordinates of the mouse in relation to an element of your choosing. Here's an example that displays the position of the mouse pointer:

```
private void MouseMoved(object sender, MouseEventArgs e)
{
    Point pt = e.GetPosition(this);
    lblInfo.Text =
      String.Format("You are at ({0},{1}) in page coordinates",
      pt.X, pt.Y);
}
```

In this case, the coordinates are measured from the top-left corner of the page area (just below the title bar of the browser).

Tip   In order to receive mouse events in a layout container, the `Background` property must be set to a nonnull value—for example, a solid white fill.

Capturing the Mouse

Ordinarily, every time an element receives a mouse button down event, it will receive a corresponding mouse button up event shortly thereafter. However, this isn't always the case. For example, if you click an element, hold down the mouse, and then move the mouse pointer off the element, the element won't receive the mouse up event.

In some situations, you may want to have a notification of mouse up events, even if they occur after the mouse has moved off your element. To do so, you need to *capture* the mouse by calling the `MouseCapture()` method of the appropriate element. (`MouseCapture()` is defined by the base `UIElement` class, so it's supported by all Silverlight elements.) From that point on, you'll receive mouse down and mouse up events until you call `Mouse.Capture()` again and pass in a null reference. Other elements won't receive mouse events while the mouse is captured. That means the user won't be able to click buttons elsewhere in the page, click inside text boxes, and so on. Mouse capturing is sometimes used to implement draggable and resizable elements.

While the mouse has been captured by an element, the user won't be able to interact with other elements. (For example, the user won't be able to click another element in your page.) However, clicking another application or a part of the browser window outside of the Silverlight content region will cause your application to lose its mouse capture. Mouse capturing is generally used for short-term operations such as drag and drop.

Mouse Cursors

A common task in any application is to adjust the mouse cursor to show when the application is busy or to indicate how different controls work. You can set the mouse pointer for any element using the `Cursor` property, which is inherited from the `FrameworkElement` class.

Every cursor is represented by a `System.Windows.Input.Cursor` object. The easiest way to get a `Cursor` object is to use the static properties of the `Cursors` class (from the `System.Windows.Input` namespace). They include all the standard Windows cursors, such as the hourglass, the hand, resizing arrows, and so on. Here's an example that sets the hourglass for the current page:

```
this.Cursor = Cursors.Wait;
```

Now when you move the mouse over the current page, the mouse pointer changes to the familiar hourglass icon (in Windows XP) or the swirl (in Windows Vista).

Note   The properties of the `Cursors` class draw on the cursors that are defined on the computer. If the user has customized the set of standard cursors, the application you create will use those customized cursors.

If you set the cursor in XAML, you don't need to use the `Cursors` class directly. That's because the type converter for the `Cursor` property is able to recognize the property names and retrieve the corresponding `Cursor` object from the `Cursors` class. That means you can write markup like this to show the "help" cursor (a combination of an arrow and a question mark) when the mouse is positioned over a button:

```
<Button Cursor="Help" Content="Help Me"></Button>
```

It's possible to have overlapping cursor settings. In this case, the most specific cursor wins. For example, you could set a different cursor on a button and on the page that contains the button. The button's cursor will be shown when you move the mouse over the button, and the page's cursor will be used for every other region in the page.

Tip   Unlike WPF, Silverlight does not support custom mouse cursors. However, you can hide the mouse cursor (set it to `Cursors.None`) and then make a small image follow the mouse pointer using code like that shown in the previous section.

Key Presses

As you saw in Table 3-1, Silverlight elements use `KeyDown` and `KeyUp` events to notify you when a key is pressed. These events use bubbling, so they travel up from the element that currently has focus to the containing elements.

When you react to a key press event, you receive a `KeyEventArgs` object that provides two additional pieces of information: `Key` and `PlatformKeyCode`. `Key` indicates the key that was pressed is a value from the `System.Windows.Input.Key` enumeration (for example, `Key.S` is the S key). `PlatformKeyCode` is an integer value that must be interpreted based on the hardware and operating system that's being used on the client computer. For example, a nonstandard key that Silverlight can't recognize will return a `Key.Unknown` value for the `Key` property, but will provide a `PlatformKeyCode` that's up to you to interpret. An example of a platform-specific key is Scroll Lock on Microsoft Windows computers.

Note   In general, it's best to avoid any platform-specific coding. But if you really do need to evaluate a nonstandard key, you can use the `BrowserInformation` class from the `System.Windows.Browser` namespace to get more information about the client computer where your application is running.

Key Modifiers

When a key press occurs, you often need to know more than just what key was pressed. It's also important to find out what other keys were held down at the same time. That means you might want to investigate the state of other keys, particularly modifiers such as Shift and Ctrl, both of which are supported on all platforms. Although you can handle the events for these keys separately and keep track of them in that way, it's much easier to use the static `Modifiers` property of the `Keyboard` class.

To test for a `Keyboard.Modifier`, you use bitwise logic. For example, the following code checks whether the Ctrl key is currently pressed.

```
if ((Keyboard.Modifiers & ModifierKeys.Control) == ModifierKeys.Control)
{
    message += "You are holding the Control key.";
}
```

Note   The browser is free to intercept keystrokes. For example, in Internet Explorer, you won't see the `KeyDown` event for the Alt key, because the browser intercepts it. The Alt key opens the Internet Explorer menu (when used alone) or triggers a shortcut (when used with another key).

Focus

In the Windows world, a user works with one control at a time. The control that is currently receiving the user's key presses is the control that has *focus*. Sometimes this control is drawn slightly differently. For example, the Silverlight button uses blue shading to show that it has the focus.

To move the focus from one element to another, the user can click the mouse or use the Tab and arrow keys. In previous development frameworks, programmers have been forced to take great care to make sure that the Tab key moves focus in a logical manner (generally from left to right and then down the window) and that the right control has focus when the window first appears. In Silverlight, this extra work is seldom necessary because Silverlight uses the hierarchical layout of your elements to implement a tabbing sequence. Essentially, when you press the Tab key, you'll move to the first child in the current element or, if the current element has no children, to the next child at the same level. For example, if you tab through a window with two `StackPanel` containers, you'll move through all the controls in the first `StackPanel` and then through all the controls in the second container.

If you want to take control of tab sequence, you can set the `TabIndex` property for each control to place it in numerical order. The control with a `TabIndex` of 0 gets the focus first, followed by the next highest `TabIndex` value (for example, 1, then 2, then 3, and so on). If more than one element has the same `TabIndex` value, Silverlight uses the automatic tab sequence, which means it jumps to the nearest subsequent element.

Tip   By default, the `TabIndex` property for all controls is set to 1. That means you can designate a specific control as the starting point for a window by setting its `TabIndex` to 0 but rely on automatic navigation to guide the user through the rest of the window from that starting point, according to the order that your elements are defined.

The TabIndex property is defined in the Control class, along with an IsTabStop property. You can set IsTabStop to false to prevent a control from being included in the tab sequence. A control that has IsTabStop set to false can still get the focus in another way—either programmatically (when your code calls its Focus() method) or by a mouse click.

Controls that are invisible or disabled ("grayed out") are skipped in the tab order and are not activated regardless of the TabIndex and IsTabStop settings. To hide or disable a control, you set the Visibility and IsEnabled properties, respectively.

The Last Word

In this chapter, you took a look at Silverlight dependency properties and routed events. First, you saw how dependency properties are defined and registered. Next, you explored event bubbling. Finally, you considered the basic set of mouse and keyboard events that all elements provide.

Tip   One of the best ways to learn more about the internals of Silverlight is to browse the code for basic Silverlight elements, such as Button, UIElement, and FrameworkElement. One of the best tools to perform this browsing is Lutz Roeder's Reflector, which is available at http://www.aisto.com/roeder/dotnet. Using Reflector, you can see the definitions for dependency properties and routed events, browse through the static constructor code that initializes them, and even explore how the properties and events are used in the class code.

Chapter 4: Elements

Now that you've learned the fundamentals of layout and mouse and keyboard handling, you're ready to take a closer look at the elements Silverlight includes. In this chapter, you'll take a quick tour of Silverlight's elements and explore many that you haven't already encountered. You'll learn how to display wrapped, formatted text with the `TextBlock`. You'll learn about content controls, including Silverlight's many different flavors of button and the `ToolTip` control. Finally, you'll take a quick look at Silverlight's list, range, and date controls.

The Silverlight Elements

You've already met quite a few of Silverlight's core elements, including the layout containers. Some of the more specialized elements, such as the ones used for drawing 2D graphics, displaying "deep zoom" images and video, won't be covered in this book. But this chapter deals with all the basics—fundamental widgets like buttons, text boxes, lists, and check boxes—which every client developer has used in some form. Table 4-1 provides an at-a-glance look at all the elements that Silverlight includes.

Table 4-1. Silverlight Elements

CLASS	DESCRIPTION
Border	A rectangular or rounded border, which you can draw around another element.
Button	The familiar button, complete with a shaded gray background, which the user clicks to launch a task.
Calendar	A one-month-at-a-time calendar view that allows the user to select a single date.

Table 4-1. continued

CLASS	DESCRIPTION
Canvas	A layout container that allows you to lay out elements with precise coordinates.
CheckBox	A box that can be checked or unchecked, with optional content displayed next to it.
ContentControl	The base from which all content controls (controls that can contain another element as their content) derive.
DataGrid	A multicolumn, multirow list filled with a collection of data objects.
DatePicker	A text box for date entry, with a drop-down calendar for easy selection.
Ellipse	A shape drawing element that represents an ellipse.
Grid	A layout container that places children in an invisible grid of cells.
GridSplitter	A resizing bar that allows users to change the height or adjacent rows or width of adjacent columns in a Grid.
HyperlinkButton	A link that directs the user to another web page.
Image	An element that displays a supported image file.
Line	A shape drawing element that represents a line.
ListBox	A list of items, out of which a single one can be selected.

CLASS	DESCRIPTION
MediaElement	A media file, such as a video window.
MultiScaleImage	An image that supports Silverlight's deep zoom feature and allows the user to zoom in.
RadioButton	A small circle that represents one choice out of a group of options, with optional content displayed next to it.
Rectangle	A shape-drawing element that represents a rectangle.
RepeatButton	A button that fires click events continuously when pressed (like the buttons on either side of a scrollbar).
ScrollBar	A track with an arrow button an either side, which allows the user to move through a large content region that can't be shown all at once. Used in the ScrollViewer.
ScrollViewer	A container that holds any large content and makes it scrollable.
Slider	An input control that lets the user set a numeric value by dragging a thumb along a track.
StackPanel	A layout container that stacks items from top to bottom or left to right.
TextBlock	An all-purpose text display control that includes the ability to give different formatting to multiple pieces of inline text.
TextBox	The familiar text-entry control.
ToggleButton	A button that has two states, on or off, and can be switched from one to another by clicking (like the check box).

Table 4-1. continued

CLASS	DESCRIPTION
ToolTip	A pop-up box that shows content when the user moves the mouse pointer over an element.
WatermarkedTextBox	A text box that adds the ability to show a prompt when it's blank and doesn't have focus.

In the following sections, you'll explore many of these elements.

Static Text

Silverlight doesn't include a Label control. The lynchpin for text display is the TextBlock element, which you've seen at work in several examples over the past three chapters.

The TextBlock element is refreshingly straightforward. It provides a Text property, which accepts a string with the text you want to display.

```
<TextBlock Text="This is the content."></TextBlock>
```

Alternatively, you can supply the text as nested content:

```
<TextBlock>This is the content.</TextBlock>
```

The chief advantage of this approach is that you can add line breaks and tabs to make large sections of text more readable in your code. Silverlight follows the standard rules of XML, which means it *collapses* whitespace. Thus a series of spaces, tabs, and hard returns is rendered using a single space character. If you really do want to split text over lines at an explicit position, you need to use separate TextBlock elements or use a LineBreak inside the TextBlock element, as shown here:

```
<TextBlock>
    This is line 1.<LineBreak/>
    This is line 2.
</TextBlock>
```

> **Note**   When using inline text, you can't use the < and > characters, because these have a specific XML meaning. Instead, you need to replace the angled brackets with the character entities < (for the less than symbol) and > (for the greater than symbol), which will be rendered as < and >.

Unsurprisingly, text is colored black by default. You can change the color of your text using the **Foreground** property. You can set it using a color name in XAML:

```
<TextBlock x:Name="txt" Text="Hello World" Foreground="Red"></TextBlock>
```

or in code:

```
txt.Foreground = new SolidColorBrush(Colors.Red);
```

Instead of using a color name, you can use RGB values. You can also use partially transparent colors that allow the background to show through. Both topics are covered in Chapter 2 when discussing how to paint the background of a panel.

> **Tip**   Ordinarily, you'll use a solid color brush to fill in text. (The default is obviously a black brush.) However, you can create more exotic effects by filling in your text with gradients and tiled patterns using the fancy brushes discussed in Chapter 7.

The **TextBlock** also provides a **TextAlignment** property (which allows you to center or right-justify text), a **Padding** property (which sets the space between the text and the outer edges of the **TextBlock**), and a few more properties for controlling fonts, inline formatting, and text wrapping.

Font Properties

The TextBlock class defines font properties that determine how text appears in a control. These properties are outlined in Table 4-2.

Table 4-2. Font-Related Properties of the Control Class

NAME	DESCRIPTION
FontFamily	The name of the font you want to use. Because Silverlight is a client-side technology, it's limited to just nine built-in fonts (Arial, Arial Black, Comic Sans MS, Courier New, Georgia, Lucida, Times New Roman, Trebuchet MS, and Verdana). However, you can also distribute custom fonts by doing a bit more work and packing them up with your project assembly.
FontSize	The size of the font in pixels. Ordinary Windows applications measure fonts using *points*, which are assumed to be 1/72 of an inch on a standard PC monitor, while pixels are assumed to be 1/96 of an inch. Thus, if you want to turn a Silverlight font size into a more familiar point size, you can use a handy trick—just multiply by 3/4. For example, a 20-pixel FontSize is equivalent to a traditional 15-point font size.
FontStyle	The angling of the text, as represented as a FontStyle object. You get the FontStyle preset you need from the static properties of the FontStyles class, which includes Normal and Italic lettering. If you apply italic lettering to a font that doesn't provide an italic variant, Silverlight will simply slant the letters. However, this behavior only gives a crude approximation of a true italic typeface.

NAME	DESCRIPTION
FontWeight	The heaviness of text, as represented as a FontWeight object. You get the FontWeight preset you need from the static properties of the FontWeights class. Normal and Bold are the most obvious of these, but some typefaces provide other variations such as Heavy, Light, ExtraBold, and so on. If you use Bold on a font that doesn't provide a bold variant, Silverlight will paint a thicker border around the letters, thereby simulating a bold font.
FontStretch	The amount that text is stretched or compressed, as represented by a FontStretch object. You get the FontStretch preset you need from the static properties of the FontStretches class. For example, UltraCondensed reduces fonts to 50% of their normal width, while UltraExpanded expands them to 200%. Font stretching is an OpenType feature that is not supported by many typefaces. The built-in Silverlight fonts don't support any of these variants.

Obviously, the most important of these properties is FontFamily. A *font family* is a collection of related typefaces—for example, Arial Regular, Arial Bold, Arial Italic, and Arial Bold Italic are all part of the Arial font family. Although the typographic rules and characters for each variation are defined separately, the operating system realizes they're related. As a result, you can configure an element to use Arial Regular, set the FontWeight property to Bold, and be confident that Silverlight will switch over to the Arial Bold typeface.

When choosing a font, you must supply the full family name, as shown here:

```
<TextBlock x:Name="txt" FontFamily="Times New Roman" FontSize="18">
 Some Bold Text</Button>
```

It's much the same in code:

```
txt.FontFamily = "Times New Roman";
txt.FontSize = "18";
```

When identifying a `FontFamily`, a shortened string is not enough. That means you can't substitute Times or Times New instead of the full name Times New Roman.

Optionally, you can use the full name of a typeface to get italic or bold, as shown here:

```
<TextBlock FontFamily="Times New Roman Bold">A Button</TextBlock >
```

However, it's clearer and more flexible to use just the family name and set other properties (such as `FontStyle` and `FontWeight`) to get the variant you want. For example, the following markup sets the `FontFamily` to Times New Roman and sets the `FontWeight` to `FontWeights.Bold`:

```
<TextBlock FontFamily="Times New Roman" FontWeight="Bold">A Button</TextBlock >
```

Standard Fonts

Silverlight supports nine core fonts, which are guaranteed to render correctly on any browser and operating system that supports Silverlight. They're shown in Figure 4-1.

Figure 4-1. Silverlight's built-in fonts

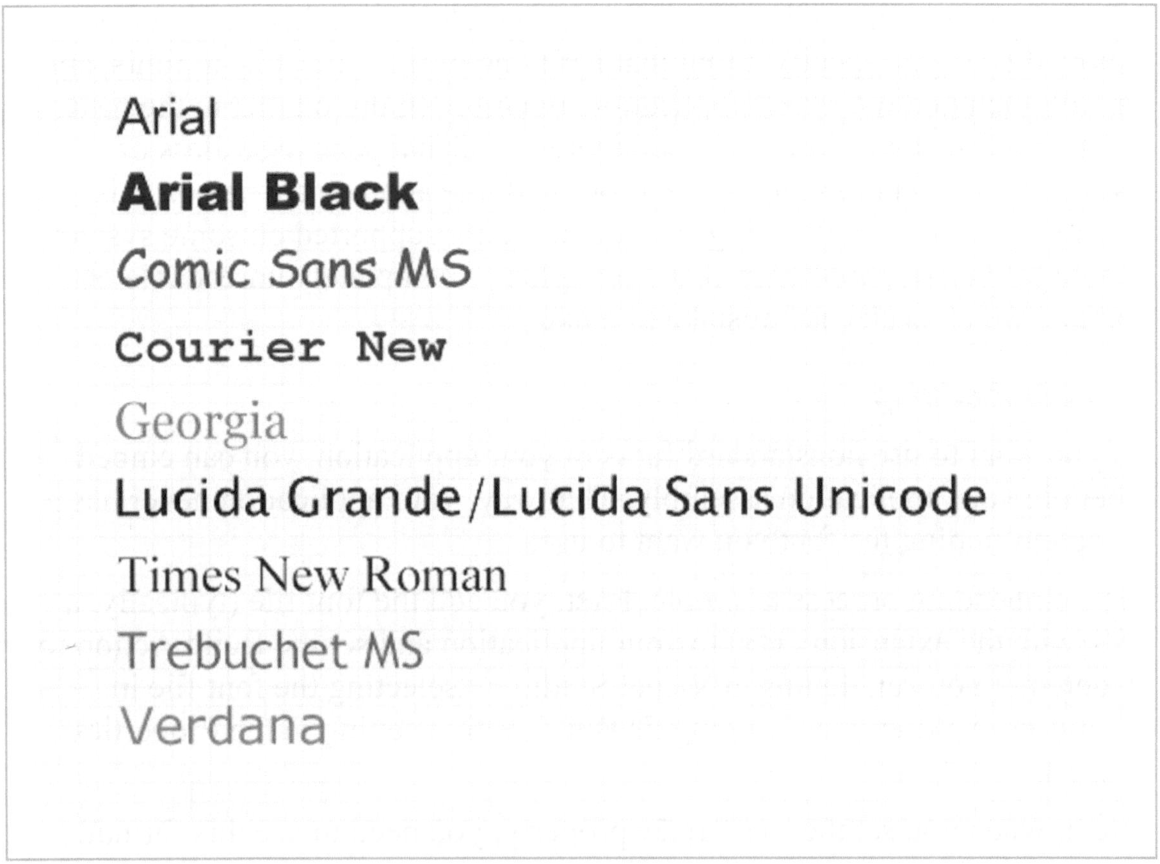

Arial

Arial Black

Comic Sans MS

Courier New

Georgia

Lucida Grande/Lucida Sans Unicode

Times New Roman

Trebuchet MS

Verdana

In the case of Lucida, there are two variants with slightly different names: Lucida Sans Unicode is included with Windows, while Lucida Grande is an almost identical font that's included with Mac OS X. To allow this system to work, the `FontFamily` property supports font fallback—in other words, you can supply a comma-separated list of font names, and Silverlight will used the first supported font. The default `TextBlock` font is equivalent to setting the `FontFamily` property to the string "Lucida Sans Unicode, Lucida Grande."

You might think that you can use more specialized fonts, which may or may not be present on the client's computer. However, Silverlight doesn't allow this. If you specify a font that isn't one of the nine built-in fonts, and it isn't included with your application assembly (more on that in the next section), your font setting will be ignored. This happens regardless of whether the client has an installed font with the appropriate name. This makes sense—after all, using a font that's only supported on some systems could lead to an application that's mangled or completely unreadable on others, which is an easy mistake to make.

Font Embedding

If you want to use nonstandard fonts in your application, you can embed them in your application assembly. That way, your application never has a problem finding the font you want to use.

The embedding process is simple. First, you add the font file (typically, a file with the extension .ttf) to your application and set the Build Action to Content. (You can do this in Visual Studio by selecting the font file in Solution Explorer and changing its Build Action setting in the Properties page.)

Next, when you set the FontFamily property, you need to use this format:

`FileName#FontName`

The file is the XAP file that's created with your compiled project files when you run your application in Visual Studio. For example, if you have a project named Elements that includes a font file with a font named Bayern, you would use markup like this:

```
<TextBlock FontFamily="Elements.xap#Bayern">This is an embedded font</TextBlock>
```

Note that the font name is the name that's defined for the font, *not* the name of the font file (which is irrelevant).

Although this process is easy enough, font embedding raises obvious licensing concerns. Unfortunately, most font vendors allow their fonts to be embedded in documents (such as PDF files) but not applications (such as Silverlight assemblies). The problem is obvious—users can download the XAP file by hand, unzip it, and install the font file on their local computers. Silverlight doesn't make any attempt to enforce font licensing, but you should make sure you're on solid legal ground before you redistribute a font.

You can check a font's embedding permissions using Microsoft's free font properties extension utility, which is available at `http://www.microsoft.com/typography/TrueTypeProperty21.mspx`. Once you install this utility, right-click any font file, and choose Properties to see more detailed information about it. In particular, check the Embedding tab for information about the allowed embedding for this font. Fonts marked with Installed Embedding Allowed are suitable for Silverlight applications, while fonts with Editable Embedding Allowed may not be. Consult with the font vendor for licensing information about a specific font.

Note   If all else fails, you can get around licensing issues by changing your fonts to graphics. This works for small pieces of graphical text (for example, headings), but isn't appropriate for large blocks of text. You can save graphical text as a bitmap in your favorite drawing program, or you can convert text to a series of shapes using Silverlight's **Path** element. You can convert graphical text to a path using Expression Designer or Expression Blend (simply select the **TextBlock** and choose Object → Path → Convert to Path).

Underlining

You can add underlining to any font by setting the `TextDecorations` property to `Underline`:

```
<TextBlock TextDecorations="Underline">Underlined text</TextBlock>
```

In WPF, there are several types of text decorations, including overlines and strikethrough. However, at present Silverlight only includes underlining.

If you want to underline an individual word in a block of text, you'll need to use inline elements, as described in the next section.

Runs

In many situations, you'll want to format individual bits of text, but keep them together in a single paragraph in a TextBlock. To accomplish this, you need to use a Run object inside the TextBlock element. Here's an example that formats several words differently (the result of which is shown in Figure 4-2):

```
<TextBlock FontFamily="Georgia" FontSize="20" >
  This <Run FontStyle="Italic" Foreground="YellowGreen">is</Run> a
  <Run FontFamily="Comic Sans MS" Foreground="Red" FontSize="40">test.</Run>
</TextBlock>
```

Figure 4-2. Formatting text with runs

A run supports the same key formatting properties as the TextBlock, including Foreground, TextDecorations, and the five font properties (FontFamily, FontSize, FontStyle, FontWeight, and FontStretch).

Technically, a Run object is not a true element. Instead, it's an *inline*. Silverlight provides two just types of inlines—the LineBreak class that you saw earlier and the Run class. You can interact with the runs in your TextBlock through the TextBlock.Inlines collection. In fact, the TextBlock actually has two overlapping content models. You can set text through the simple Text property, or you can supply it through the Inlines collection. However, the changes you make in one affect the other, so if you set the Text property, you'll wipe out the current collection of inlines.

Note   The inline classes are the only part of WPF's document model that survives in Silverlight.

Wrapping Text

To wrap text over several lines, you use the TextWrapping property. Ordinarily, TextWrapping is set to TextWrapping.NoWrap, and content is truncated if it extends past the right edge of the containing element. If you use TextWrapping.Wrap, your content will be wrapped over multiple lines when the width of the TextBlock element is constrained in some way. (For example, you place it into a proportionately sized or fixed-width Grid cell.) When wrapping, the TextBlock splits lines at the nearest space. If you have a word that is longer than the available line width, the TextBlock will split that word wherever it can to make it fit.

When wrapping text, the LineHeight and LineStackingStrategy properties become important. The LineHeight property can set a fixed height (in pixels) that will be used for every line. However, the LineHeight can only be used to increase the line height—if you specify a height that's smaller than what's required to show the text, your setting will be ignored. The `LineStackingStrategy` determines what the `TextBlock` will do when dealing with multiline content that uses different fonts. You can choose to use the standard behavior, `MaxHeight`, which makes each line as high as it needs to be to fit the tallest piece of text it contains, or you can use `BlockLineHeight`, which sets the lines to one fixed height according to the font size of the `TextBlock` itself. Shorter text will then have extra space, and taller text will overlap with other lines. Figure 4-3 compares the different options.

Figure 4-3. Two different ways to calculate line height

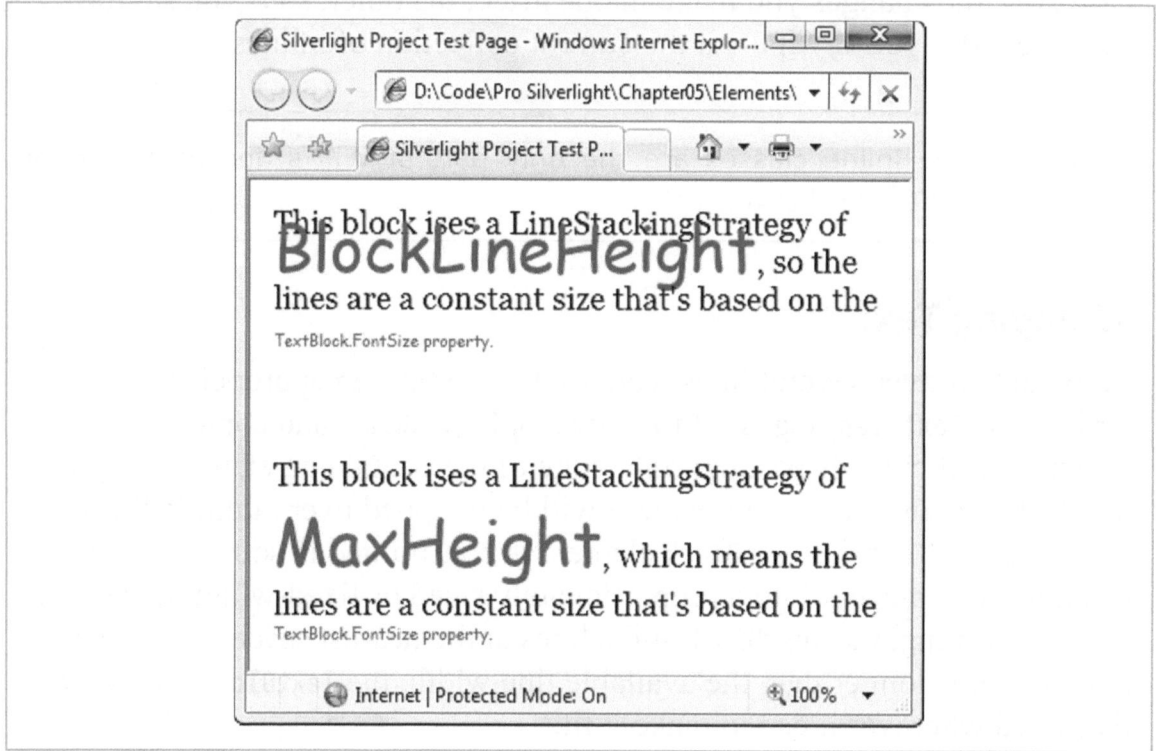

Content Controls

Content controls are a specialized type of control designed to hold (and display) a piece of content. Technically, a content control is a control that can contain a *single* nested element. The one-child limit is what differentiates content controls from layout containers, which can hold as many nested elements as you want.

All Silverlight layout containers derive from the Panel class, which gives the support for holding multiple elements. Similarly, all content controls derive from the ContentControl class. Figure 4-4 shows the class hierarchy.

As Figure 4-4 shows, several common controls are actually content controls, including the Tooltip, Button, RadioButton, and the CheckBox. There are also a few more specialized content controls, such as ScrollViewer, and some controls that are designed for being used with another specific control. (For example, the ListBox control holds ListBoxItem content controls, the Calendar requires the DayButton and MonthButton, and the DataGrid uses the DataGridCell, DataGridRowHeader, and DataColumnHeader).

Figure 4-4. The hierarchy of content controls

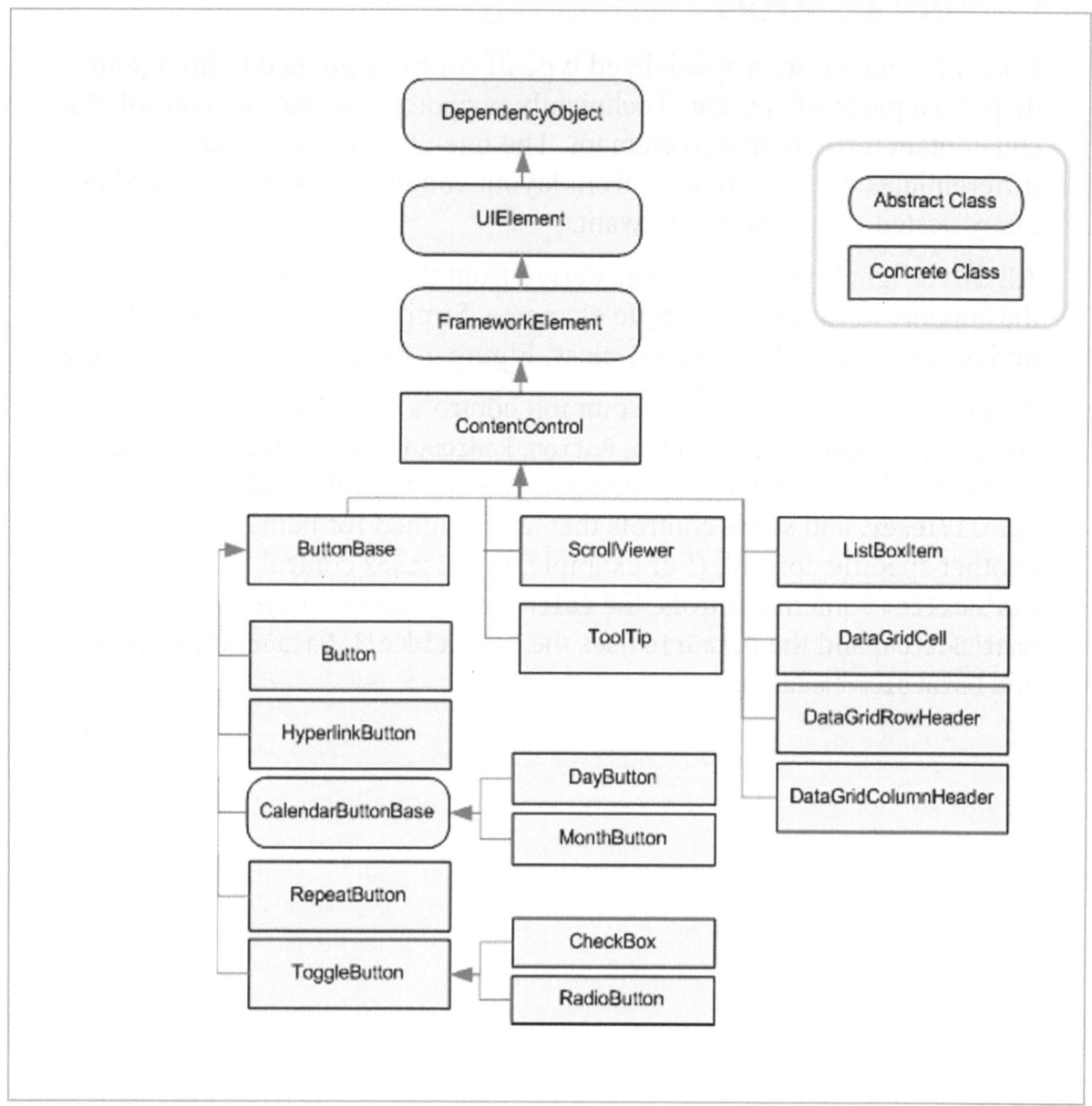

The Content Property

Whereas the `Panel` class adds the `Children` collection to hold nested elements, the `ContentControl` class adds a `Content` property, which accepts a single object. The `Content` property supports any type of object. It gives you three ways to show content:

- **Elements**: If you use an object that derives from `UIElement` for the content of a content control, that element will be rendered.

- **Other objects**: If you place a nonelement object into a content control, the control will simply call `ToString()` to get the text representation for that control. For some types of objects, `ToString()` produces a reasonable text representation. For others, it simply returns the fully qualified class name of the object, which is the default implementation.

- **Other objects, with a data template**: If you place a nonelement object into a content control, and you set the `ContentTemplate` property with a data template, the content control will render the data template and use the expressions it contains to pull information out of the properties of your object. This approach is particularly useful when dealing with collections of data objects.

To understand how this works, consider the humble button. An ordinary button may just use a simple string object to generate its content:

```
<Button Margin="3" Content="Text content"></Button>
```

This string is set as the button content and displayed on the button surface.

Tip   When filling a button with unformatted text, you may want to use the font-related properties that the **Button** class inherits from `ContentControl`, which duplicate the `TextBlock` properties listed in Table 3-1.

However, you can get more ambitious by placing other elements inside the button. For example, you can place an image inside using the Image class:

```
<Button Margin="3">
  <Image Source="happyface.jpg"></Image>
</Button>
```

Or you could combine text and images by wrapping them all in a layout container like the StackPanel:

```
<Button Margin="3">
  <StackPanel>
    <TextBlock Margin="3" Text="Image and text button"></TextBlock>
    <Image Source="happyface.jpg" />
    <TextBlock Margin="3" Text="Courtesy of the StackPanel"></TextBlock>
  </StackPanel>
</Button>
```

If you want to create a truly exotic button, you could even place other content controls such as text boxes and buttons inside (and nest still elements inside these). It's doubtful that such an interface would make much sense, but it is possible.

At this point, you might be wondering whether the Silverlight content model is really worth all the trouble. After all, you might choose to place an image inside a button, but you're unlikely to embed other controls and entire layout panels. However, there are a few important advantages to the content model.

For example, the previous markup placed a bitmap into a button. However, this approach isn't as flexible as creating a vector drawing out of Silverlight shapes. Using a vector drawing, you can create a button image that's rescalable and can be changed programmatically (for example, with different colors, a transform, or an animation). Using a vector-based button opens you up to the possibility of creating a dynamic interface that responds to state changes and user actions.

The key fact you should understand now is that the vector drawing model integrates seamlessly with content controls because they have the ability to hold any element. For example, this markup creates a simple graphical button that uses two diamond shapes (as shown in Figure 4-5):

```
<Button Margin="3" Height="70" Width="214">
  <Grid Margin="4">
    <Polygon Points="100,24 124,0 200,24 124,40"
     Fill="LightSteelBlue" />
    <Polygon Points="100,24 74,0 0,24 74,40"
     Fill="White"/>
  </Grid>
</Button>
```

Figure 4-5. A button with shape content

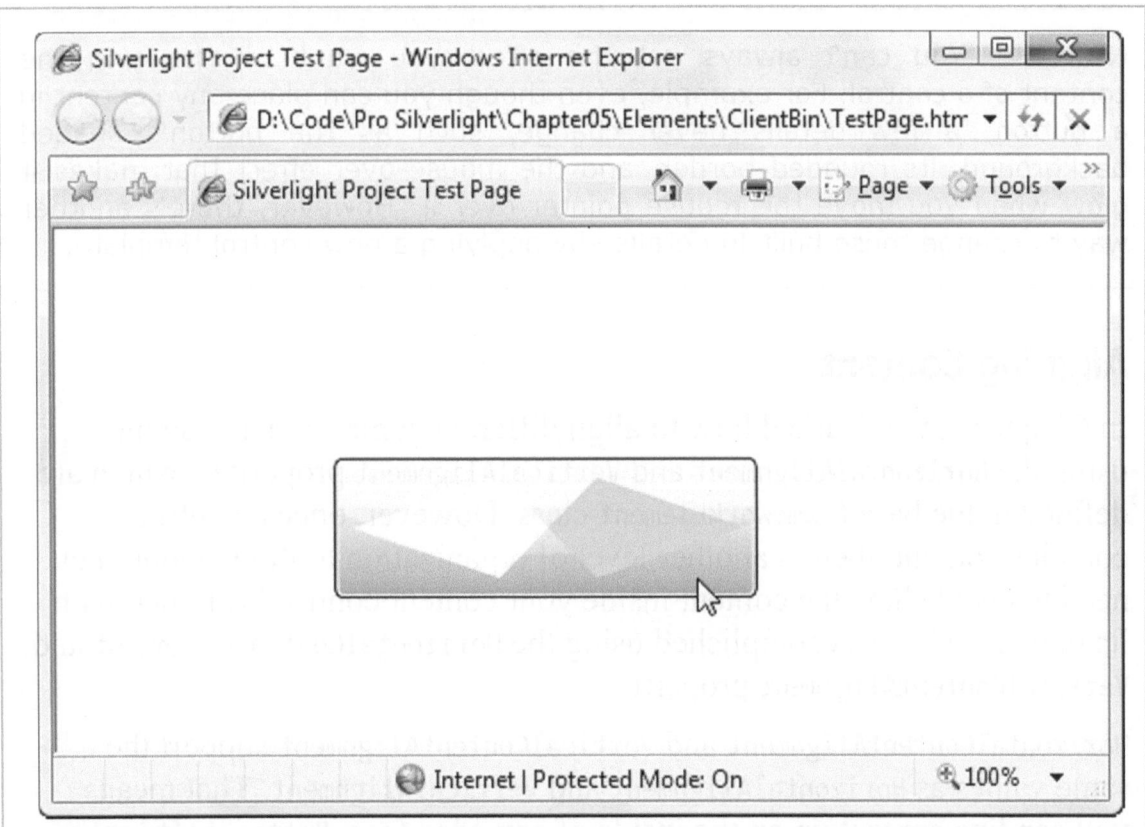

Clearly, in this case the nested content model is simpler than adding extra properties to the Button class to support the different types of content. Not only is the nested content model more flexible, but it also allows the Button class to expose a simpler interface. And because all content controls support content nesting in the same way, there's no need to add different content properties to multiple classes.

In essence, the nested content model is a trade. It simplifies the class model for elements because there's no need to use additional layers of inheritance to add properties for different types of content. However, you need to use a slightly more complex *object* model—elements that can be built out of other nested elements.

Note   You can't always get the effect you want by changing the content of a control. For example, even though you can place any content in a button, a few details never change, such as the button's shaded background, its rounded border, and the mouse-over effect that makes it glow when you move the mouse pointer over it. However, there's another way to change these built-in details—by applying a new control template.

Aligning Content

In Chapter 2, you learned how to align different controls in a container using the HorizontalAlignment and VerticalAlignment properties, which are defined in the base FrameworkElement class. However, once a control contains content, there's another level of organization to think about. You need to decide how the content inside your content control is aligned with its borders. This is accomplished using the HorizontalContentAlignment and VerticalContentAlignment properties.

HorizontalContentAlignment and VerticalContentAlignment support the same values as HorizontalAlignment and VerticalAlignment. That means you can line content up on the inside of any edge (Top, Bottom, Left, or

Right), you can center it (Center), or you can stretch it to fill the available space (Stretch). These settings are applied directly to the nested content element, but you can use multiple levels of nesting to create a sophisticated layout. For example, if you nest a StackPanel in a Button element, the Button.HorizontalContentAlignment determines where the StackPanel is placed, but the alignment and sizing options of the StackPanel and its children will determine the rest of the layout.

The Margin property allows you to add whitespace between adjacent elements. Content controls use a complementary property named Padding, which inserts space between the edges of the control and the edges of the content. To see the difference, compare the following two buttons:

```
<Button Content="Absolutely No Padding"></Button>
<Button Padding="3" Content="Well Padded"></Button>
```

The button that has no padding (the default) has its text crowded up against the button edge. The button that has a padding of 3 pixels on each side gets a more respectable amount of breathing space.

Note   The HorizontalContentAlignment, VerticalContentAlignment, and Padding properties are all defined as part of the Control class, not the more specific ContentControl class. That's because there may be controls that aren't content controls but still have some sort of content. One example is the TextBox—its contained text (stored in the Text property) is adjusted using the alignment and padding settings you've applied.

Buttons

Silverlight recognizes three types of button controls: the familiar Button, the CheckBox, and the RadioButton. All of these controls are content controls that derive from ButtonBase.

The `ButtonBase` class includes only a few members. It defines the `Click` event and adds support for commands, which allow you to wire buttons to higher-level application tasks. Finally, the `ButtonBase` class adds a `ClickMode` property, which determines when a button fires its `Click` event in response to mouse actions. The default value is `ClickMode.Release`, which means the `Click` event fires when the mouse is clicked and released. However, you can also choose to fire the `Click` event mouse when the mouse button is first pressed (`ClickMode.Press`) or, oddly enough, whenever the mouse moves over the button and pauses there (`ClickMode.Hover`).

Note   All button controls support access keys, which work similarly to mnemonics in the `Label` control. You add the underscore character to identify the access key. If the user presses Alt and the access key, a button click is triggered.

The HyperlinkButton

The ordinary `Button` control is simple enough—you click it and it fires a `Click` event that you handle in code. But what about the other variants that Silverlight offers?

One of the simplest is the `HyperlinkButton`. When clicked, it directs the browser to another web page, effectively ending the current Silverlight application. The `HyperlinkButton` class adds two properties: `NavigateUri` (a relative or absolute path that points to a web page) and `TargetName` (which, optionally, identifies a bookmark in that page).

```
<HyperlinkButton Content="Buy Now" NavigateUri="shopping.aspx"></HyperlinkButton>
```

The `HyperlinkButton` doesn't draw the standard button background. Instead, it simply renders the content that you supply. If you use text in the `HyperlinkButton`, it appears blue by default, but it's not underlined. (Use the `TextDecorations` property if you want that effect.)

When you move the mouse over a HyperlinkButton, the mouse cursor changes to the pointing hand. You can override this effect by setting the Cursor property.

The ToggleButton and RepeatButton

Alongside Button and HyperlinkButton, three more classes derive from ButtonBase:

- CalendarButtonBase, which is used to build the clickable month and day buttons in the Calendar control.

- RepeatButton, which fires Click events continuously, as long as the button is held down. Ordinary buttons fire one Click event per user click.

- ToggleButton, which represents a button that has two states (pushed or unpushed). When you click a ToggleButton, it stays in its pushed state until you click it again to release it. This is sometimes described as "sticky click" behavior.

Both RepeatButton and ToggleButton are defined in the System.Windows.Controls.Primitives namespace, which indicates they aren't often used on their own. Instead, they're used to build more complex controls by composition or extended with features through inheritance. For example, the RepeatButton is used to build the higher-level ScrollBar control (which, ultimately, is a part of the even higher-level ScrollViewer). The RepeatButton gives the arrow buttons at the ends of the scrollbar their trademark behavior—scrolling continues as long as you hold it down. Similarly, the ToggleButton is used to derive the more useful CheckBox and RadioButton classes described next. However, neither the RepeatButton nor the ToggleButton is an abstract class, so you can use both of them directly in your user interfaces or to build custom controls if the need arises.

The CheckBox

Both the CheckBox and the RadioButton are buttons of a different sort. They derive from ToggleButton, which means they can be switched on or off by the user, hence their "toggle" behavior. In the case of the CheckBox, switching the control "on" means placing a check mark in it.

The CheckBox class doesn't add any members, so the basic CheckBox interface is defined in the ToggleButton class. Most important, ToggleButton adds an IsChecked property. IsChecked is a nullable Boolean, which means it can be set to true, false, or null. Obviously, true represents a checked box, while false represents an empty one. The null value is a little trickier—it represents an indeterminate state, which is displayed as a shaded box. The indeterminate state is commonly used to represent values that haven't been set or areas where some discrepancy exists. For example, if you have a check box that allows you to apply bold formatting in a text application, and the current selection includes both bold and regular text, you might set the check box to null to show an indeterminate state.

To assign a null value in Silverlight markup, you need to use the null markup extension, as shown here:

```
<CheckBox IsChecked="{x:Null}" Content="A check box in indeterminate state">
</CheckBox>
```

Along with the IsChecked property, the ToggleButton class adds a property named IsThreeState, which determines whether the user is able to place the check box into an indeterminate state. If IsThreeState is false (the default), clicking the check box alternates its state between checked and unchecked, and the only way to place it in an indeterminate state is through code. If IsThreeState is true, clicking the check box cycles through all three possible states.

The ToggleButton class also defines three events that fire when the check box enters specific states: Checked, Unchecked, and Indeterminate. In most cases, it's easier to consolidate this logic into one event handler by handling the Click event that's inherited from ButtonBase. The Click event fires whenever the button changes state.

The RadioButton

The RadioButton also derives from ToggleButton and uses the same IsChecked property and the same Checked, Unchecked, and Indeterminate events. Along with these, the RadioButton adds a single property named GroupName, which allows you to control how radio buttons are placed into groups.

Ordinarily, radio buttons are grouped by their container. That means if you place three RadioButton controls in a single StackPanel, they form a group from which you can select just one of the three. On the other hand, if you place a combination of radio buttons in two separate StackPanel controls, you have two independent groups on your hands.

The GroupName property allows you to override this behavior. You can use it to create more than one group in the same container or to create a single group that spans multiple containers. Either way, the trick is simple—just give all the radio buttons that belong together the same group name.

Consider this example:

```
<StackPanel>
  <Border Margin="4" Padding="4" BorderBrush="Yellow" BorderThickness="1"
   CornerRadius="4">
    <StackPanel>
      <RadioButton Content="Group 1"></RadioButton>
      <RadioButton Content="Group 1"></RadioButton>
      <RadioButton Content="Group 1"></RadioButton>
      <RadioButton GroupName="Group2" Content="Group 2"></RadioButton>
    </StackPanel>
  </Border>
  <Border Margin="4" Padding="4" BorderBrush="Yellow" BorderThickness="1"
   CornerRadius="4">
    <StackPanel>
      <RadioButton Content="Group 3"></RadioButton>
      <RadioButton Content="Group 3"></RadioButton>
      <RadioButton Content="Group 3"></RadioButton>
      <RadioButton GroupName="Group2" Content="Group 2"></RadioButton>
    </StackPanel>
```

```
    </Border>
</StackPanel>
```

Here, there are two containers holding radio buttons, but three groups. The final radio button at the bottom of each group box is part of a third group (see Figure 4-6). In this example, it makes for a confusing design, but there may be some scenarios where you want to separate a specific radio button from the pack in a subtle way without causing it to lose its group membership.

Figure 4-6. Grouping radio buttons

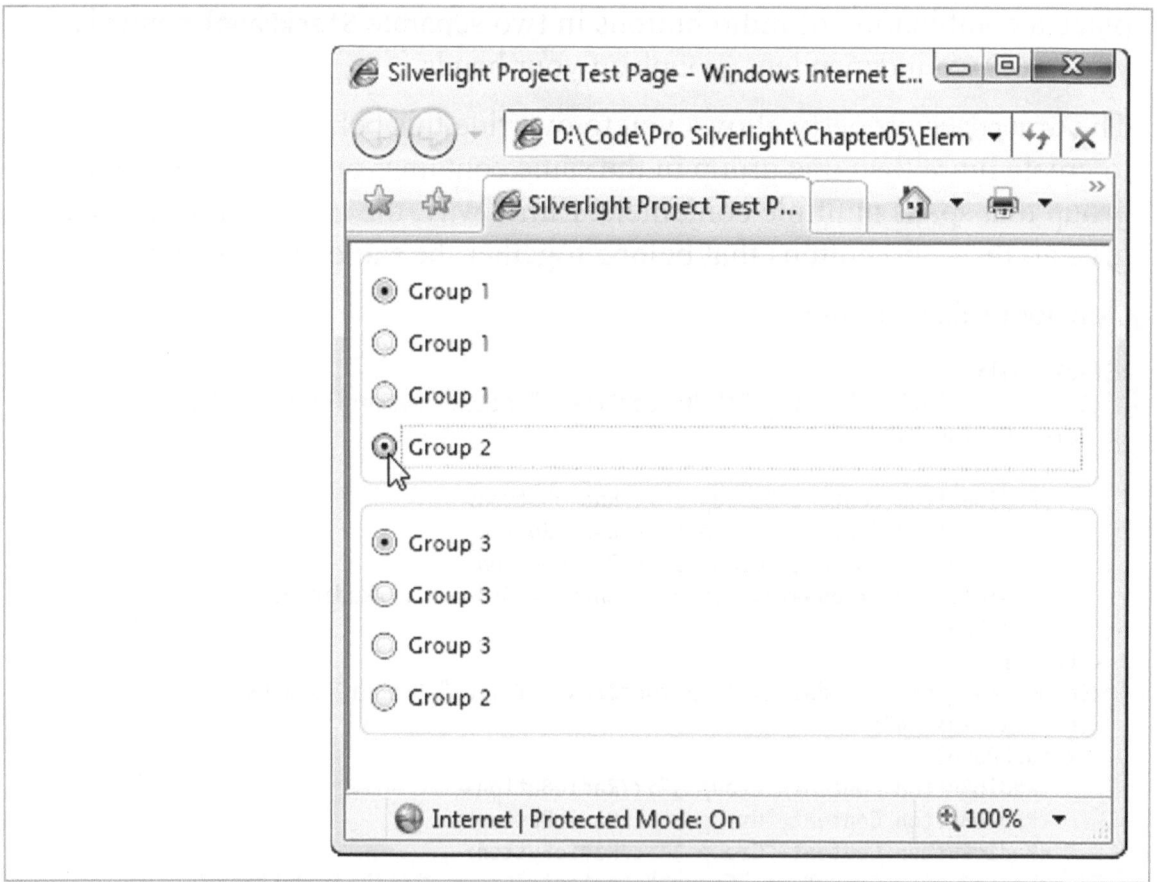

Tooltips

Silverlight has a flexible model for *tooltips* (those infamous yellow boxes that pop up when you hover over something interesting). Because tooltips in Silverlight are content controls, you can place virtually anything inside a tooltip. You can also tweak various timing settings to control how quickly tooltips appear and disappear.

The easiest way to show a tooltip doesn't involve using the `ToolTip` class directly. Many elements, including all content controls, include a `ToolTip` that you can set directly. For example, here's a button that has a basic tooltip:

```
<Button ToolTip="This is my tooltip" Content="I have a tooltip"></Button>
```

When you hover over this button, the text "This is my tooltip" appears in a gray pop-up box.

If you want to supply more ambitious tooltip content, such as a combination of nested elements, you need to break the `ToolTip` property out into a separate element. Here's an example that sets the `ToolTip` property of a button using more complex nested content:

```
<Button Content="I have a fancy tooltip">
  <Button.ToolTip>
    <StackPanel>
      <TextBlock Margin="3" Text="Image and text"></TextBlock>
      <Image Source="happyface.jpg"></Image>
      <TextBlock Margin="3" Text="Image and text"></TextBlock>
    </StackPanel>
  </Button.ToolTip>
</Button>
```

As in the previous example, Silverlight implicitly creates a `ToolTip` object. The difference is that in this case the `ToolTip` object contains a `StackPanel` rather than a simple string.

Note   Don't put user-interactive controls in a tooltip because the ToolTip page can't accept focus. For example, if you place a button in a ToolTip, the button will appear, but it isn't clickable. (If you attempt to click it, your mouse click will just pass through to the page underneath.) If you want a tooltip-like page that can hold other controls, consider using the Popup instead, which is discussed shortly in the section "The Popup."

The ToolTip Control

The previous example shows how you can customize the content of a tooltip, but what if you want to configure other ToolTip-related settings ? You actually have two options. The first technique you can use is to explicitly define the ToolTip element in your markup. That gives you the chance to directly set a variety of ToolTip properties.

The ToolTip is a content control, so you can adjust size and alignment properties (like Width, Height, MaxWidth, HoriztontalContentAlignment, Padding, and so on), font (FontFamily, FontSize, FontStyle, and so on), and color (Background and Foreground). You can also use the HorizontalOffset and VerticalOffset properties to nudge the tooltip away from the mouse pointer and into the position you want, with negative or positive values.

Using the ToolTip properties, the following markup creates a tooltip that has no drop shadow but uses a transparent red background that lets the underlying page (and controls) show through:

```
<Button Content="I have a fancy tooltip">
  <Button.ToolTip>
    <ToolTip Background="#60AA4030" Foreground="White">
      <StackPanel>
        <TextBlock Margin="3" Text="Image and text"></TextBlock>
        <Image Source="happyface.jpg"></Image>
        <TextBlock Margin="3" Text="Image and text"></TextBlock>
      </StackPanel>
    </ToolTip>
  </Button.ToolTip>
```

```
    </Button.ToolTip>
</Button>
```

If you assign a name to your tooltip, you can also interact with it programmatically. For example, you can use the `IsEnabled` property to temporarily disable a `ToolTip` and `IsOpen` to programmatically show or hide a tooltip (or just check whether the tooltip is open). You can also handle its `Opened` and `Closed` events, which is useful if you want to generate the content for a tooltip dynamically, just as it opens.

The ToolTipService

Some tooltip properties can't be configured using the properties of the `ToolTip` class. In this case, you need to use a different class, which is named `ToolTipService`. `ToolTipService` allows you to configure the time delays associated with the display of a tooltip. All the properties of the `ToolTipService` class are attached properties, so you can set them directly in your control tag, as shown here:

```
<Button ToolTipService.InitialShowDelay="1">
  ...
</Button>
```

The `ToolTipService` class defines the properties listed in Table 4-3.

Table 4-3. ToolTipService Properties

NAME	DESCRIPTION
InitialShowDelay	Sets the delay (in milliseconds) before this tooltip is shown when the mouse hovers over the element.
ShowDuration	Sets the amount of time (in milliseconds) that this tooltip is shown before it disappears, if the user does not move the mouse.

Table 4-3. continued

NAME	DESCRIPTION
BetweenShowDelay	Sets a time page (in milliseconds) during which the user can move between tooltips without experiencing the InitialShowDelay. For example, if BetweenShowDelay is 4000, the user has five seconds to move to another control that has a tooltip. If the user moves to another control within that time period, the new tooltip is shown immediately. If the user takes longer, the BetweenShowDelay page expires, and the InitialShowDelay kicks into action. In this case, the second tooltip isn't shown until after the InitialShowDelay period.
ToolTip	Sets the content for the tooltip. Setting ToolTipService.ToolTip is equivalent to setting the ToolTip property of an element.

The Popup

The Popup control has a great deal in common with the ToolTip control, although neither one derives from the other.

Like the ToolTip, the Popup can hold a single piece of content, which can include any Silverlight element. (This content is stored in the Popup.Child property, rather than the ToolTip.Content property.) Also, like the ToolTip, the content in the Popup can extend beyond the bounds of the page. Lastly, the Popup can be placed using the same placement properties and shown or hidden using the same IsOpen property.

The differences between the Popup and ToolTip are more important. They include the following:

- **The Popup is never shown automatically**: You must set the IsOpen property for it to appear. The Popup does not disappear until you explicitly set its IsOpen property to false.

- **The Popup can accept focus**: Thus, you can place user-interactive controls in it, such as a Button. This functionality is one of the key reasons to use the Popup instead of the ToolTip.

- **The Popup is placed at the top-left of the page**: You can move it down and to the left using the HorizontalOffset and VerticalOffset properties.

Because the Popup must be shown manually, you may choose to create it entirely in code. However, you can define it just as easily in XAML markup—just make sure to include the Name property so you can manipulate it in code. The placement of the Popup in your markup isn't important, because its top-left will always be aligned with the top-left corner of the Silverlight content region.

```
<StackPanel Margin="20">
  <TextBlock TextWrapping="Wrap" MouseLeftButtonDown="txt_MouseLeftButtonDown"
   Text="Click here to open the PopUp."></TextBlock>

  <Popup x:Name="popUp" MaxWidth="200" HorizontalOffset="20" VerticalOffset="20">
    <TextBox Margin="10" MouseLeftButtonDown="popUp_MouseLeftButtonDown"
     Text="This is the PopUp."></TextBox>
  </Popup>
</StackPanel>
```

The only remaining detail is the relatively trivial code that shows the Popup when the user clicks it, and the code that hides the Popup when it's clicked:

```
private void txt_MouseLeftButtonDown(object sender, MouseButtonEventArgs e)
{
    popUp.IsOpen = true;
}

private void popUp_MouseLeftButtonDown(object sender, MouseButtonEventArgs e)
{
    popUp.IsOpen = false;
}
```

Figure 4-7 shows the Popup in action.

Figure 4-7. A tooltip-like effect with the Popup

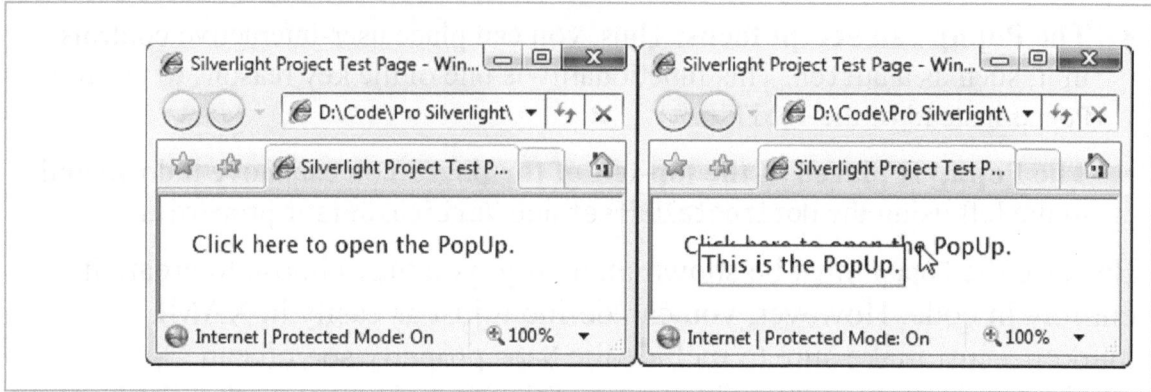

List Controls

Controls that wrap collections of items generally derive from the ItemsControl class. Silverlight provides a single example: the ListBox. Oddly enough, it has no ComboBox for drop-down list display, although one will certainly be developed in the future.

The ItemsControl class fills in the basic plumbing that's used by all list-based controls. Notably, it gives you two ways to fill the list of items. The most straightforward approach is to add them directly to the Items collection, using code or XAML. However, in Silverlight it's more common to use data binding. In this case, you set the ItemsSource property to the object that has the collection of data items you want to display.

To add items to the ListBox, you can nest ListBoxItem elements inside the ListBox element. For example, here's a ListBox that contains a list of colors:

```
<ListBox>
  <ListBoxItem Content="Green"></ListBoxItem>
  <ListBoxItem Content="Blue"></ListBoxItem>
  <ListBoxItem Content="Yellow"></ListBoxItem>
```

```
  <ListBoxItem Content="Red"></ListBoxItem>
</ListBox>
```

Different controls treat their nested content in different ways. The ListBox stores each nested object in its Items collection.

Note   Unlike WPF (and HTML forms), the Silverlight ListBox does not support multiple selection. It provides a SelectionMode property for future use, but currently the only possible value is Single.

The ListBox is a remarkably flexible control. Not only can it hold ListBoxItem objects, but it can also host any arbitrary element. This works because the ListBoxItem class derives from ContentControl, which gives it the ability to hold a single piece of nested content. If that piece of content is a UIElement-derived class, it will be rendered in the ListBox. If it's some other type of object, the ListBoxItem will call ToString() and display the resulting text.

For example, if you decided you want to create a list with images, you could create markup like this:

```
<ListBox>
  <ListBoxItem>
    <Image Source="happyface.jpg"></Image>
  </ListBoxItem>
  <ListBoxItem>
    <Image Source="happyface.jpg"></Image>
  </ListBoxItem>
</ListBox>
```

The ListBox is actually intelligent enough to create the ListBoxItem objects it needs implicitly. That means you can place your objects directly inside the ListBox element. Here's a more ambitious example that uses nested StackPanel objects to combine text and image content:

```
<ListBox>
  <StackPanel Orientation="Horizontal">
    <Image Source="happyface.jpg"  Width="30" Height="30"></Image>
    <TextBlock VerticalAlignment="Center" Text="A happy face"></TextBlock>
  </StackPanel>
  <StackPanel Orientation="Horizontal">
    <Image Source="redx.jpg" Width="30" Height="30"></Image>
    <TextBlock VerticalAlignment="Center" Text="A warning sign"></TextBlock>
  </StackPanel>
  <StackPanel Orientation="Horizontal">
    <Image Source="happyface.jpg"  Width="30" Height="30"></Image>
    <TextBlock VerticalAlignment="Center" Text="A happy face"></TextBlock>
  </StackPanel>
</ListBox>
```

In this example, the StackPanel becomes the item that's wrapped by the ListBoxItem. This markup creates the list shown in Figure 4-8.

Figure 4-8. A list of images

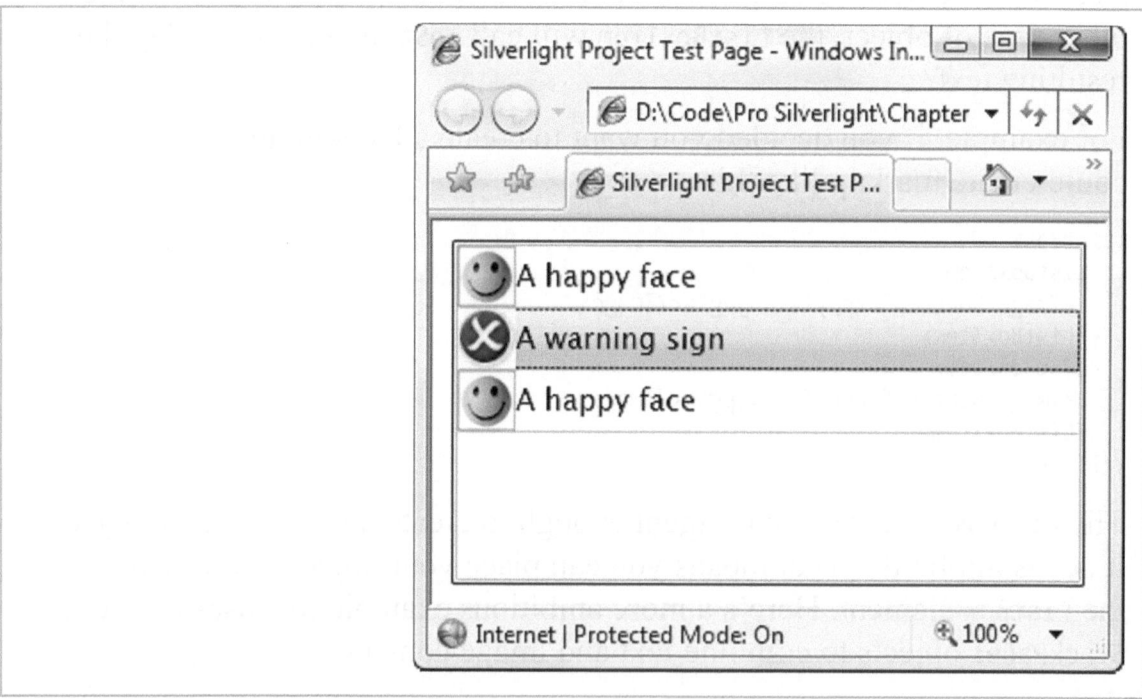

This ability to nest arbitrary elements inside list box items allows you to create a variety of list-based controls without needing to use specialized classes. For example, you can display a check box next to every item by nesting the CheckBox element inside the ListBox.

There's one caveat to be aware of when you use a list with different elements inside. When you read the SelectedItem value (and the SelectedItems and Items collections), you won't see ListBoxItem objects—instead, you'll see whatever objects you placed in the list. In the previous example, that means SelectedItem provides a StackPanel object.

When manually placing items in a list, it's up to you whether you want to place the items in directly or explicitly wrap each one in a ListBoxItem object. The second approach is often cleaner, albeit more tedious. The most important consideration is to be consistent. For example, if you place StackPanel objects in your list, the ListBox.SelectedItem object will be a StackPanel. If you place StackPanel objects wrapped by ListBoxItem objects, the ListBox.SelectedItem object will be a ListBoxItem, so code accordingly. And there's a third option—you can place data objects inside your ListBox and use a data template to display the properties you want.

The ListBoxItem offers a little bit of extra functionality from what you get with directly nested objects. Namely, it defines an IsSelected property that you can read (or set) and a Selected and Unselected event that tells you when that item is highlighted. However, you can get similar functionality using the members of the ListBox class, such as the SelectedItem (or SelectedItems) property and the SelectionChanged event.

Text Controls

Silverlight includes two text-entry controls: the standard `TextBox` and the slightly more enhanced `WatermarkedTextBox`.

Unlike the content controls you've seen, the text boxes are limited in the type of content they can contain. A text box always stores a string (provided by the `Text` property). You can change the alignment of that text using the `TextAlignment` property, and you can use all the properties listed earlier in the chapter in Table 4-2 to control the font of the text inside the text box.

Ordinarily, the `TextBox` control stores a single line of text. (You can limit the allowed number of characters by setting the `MaxLength` property.) Unfortunately, it does not support automatic text wrapping. However, you can allow multiline content by setting the `AcceptsReturn` property to true. Now, when the user presses the Enter key, a line break wil be inserted.

Sometimes, you'll create a text box purely for the purpose of displaying text. In this case, set the `IsReadOnly` property to true to prevent editing. This is preferable to disabling the text box by setting `IsEnabled` to false because a disabled text box shows grayed-out text (which is more difficult to read) and does not support selection (or copying to the clipboard).

Text Selection

As you already know, you can select text in any text box by clicking and dragging with the mouse or holding down Shift while you move through the text with the arrow keys. The `TextBox` class also gives you the ability to determine or change the currently selected text programmatically, using the `SelectionStart`, `SelectionLength`, and `SelectedText` properties.

`SelectionStart` identifies the zero-based position where the selection begins. For example, if you set this property to 10, the first selected character is the 11th character in the text box. The `SelectionLength` indicates the total number of selected characters. (A value of 0 indicates no selected characters.) Finally, the `SelectedText` property allows you to quickly examine or change the selected text in the text box.

You can react to the selection being changed by handling the `SelectionChanged` event. Here's an example that reacts to this event and displays the current selection information:

```
private void txt_SelectionChanged(object sender, RoutedEventArgs e)
{
    if (txtSelection == null) return;

    txtSelection.Text = String.Format(
      "Selection from {0} to {1} is \"{2}\"",
      txt.SelectionStart, txt.SelectionLength, txt.SelectedText);
}
```

Figure 4-9 shows the result.

Figure 4-9. Selecting text

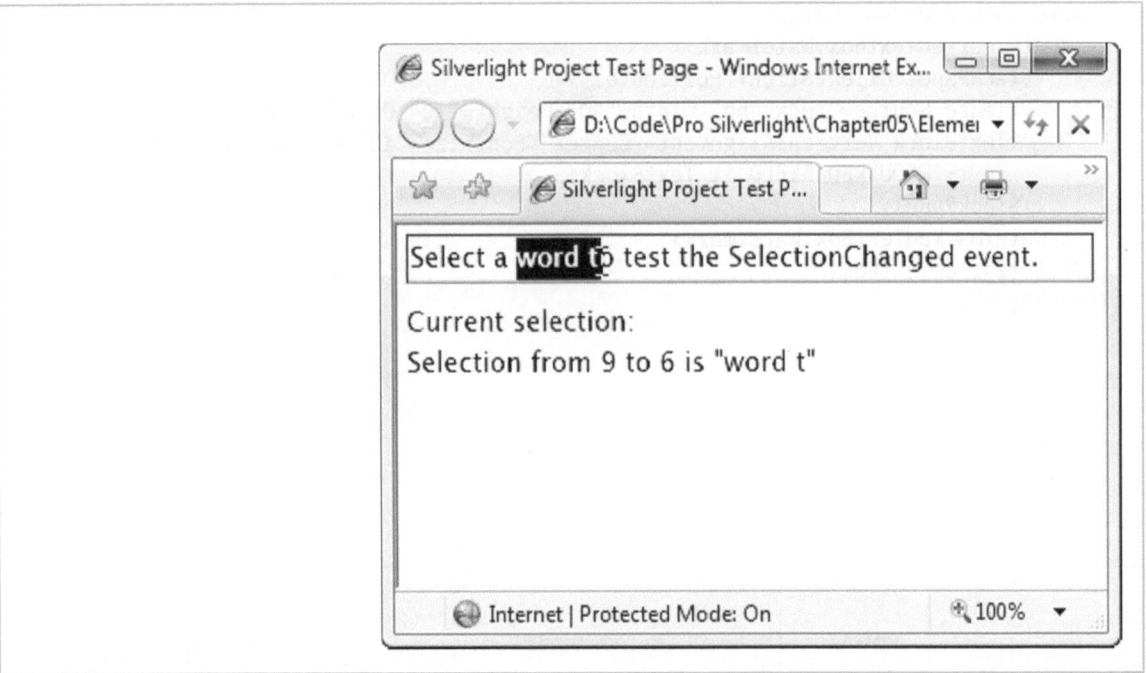

The WatermarkedTextBox

The WatermarkedTextBox derives from TextBox and adds a single feature: the ability to display some content in the button when it's empty and doesn't have focus. Usually, this content is a prompt that tells the user what to type of information to enter (or simply indicates the information is still needed).

By default, a WatermarkedTextBox gets the watermark "<enter text here>" displayed in light gray lettering. To supply a custom watermark, you set the Watermark property. You can use ordinary text, in which case the watermark will be displayed in light gray, or you can supply any element (with any formatting you like). Here's an example that defines the different watermarks shown in Figure 4-10:

```
<StackPanel Margin="10">
  <WatermarkedTextBox Margin="3"></WatermarkedTextBox>
  <WatermarkedTextBox Margin="3"></WatermarkedTextBox>
  <WatermarkedTextBox Margin="3" Watermark="- Optional -"></WatermarkedTextBox>

  <WatermarkedTextBox Margin="3">
    <WatermarkedTextBox.Watermark>
      <StackPanel Orientation="Horizontal">
        <Image Source="redx.jpg" Width="30" Height="30" Opacity="0.4"></Image>
        <TextBlock VerticalAlignment="Center" FontSize="10" Foreground="LightBlue"
        Text="REQUIRED FIELD"></TextBlock>
      </StackPanel>
    </WatermarkedTextBox.Watermark>
  </WatermarkedTextBox>
</StackPanel>
```

Figure 4-10. Simple and custom watermarks

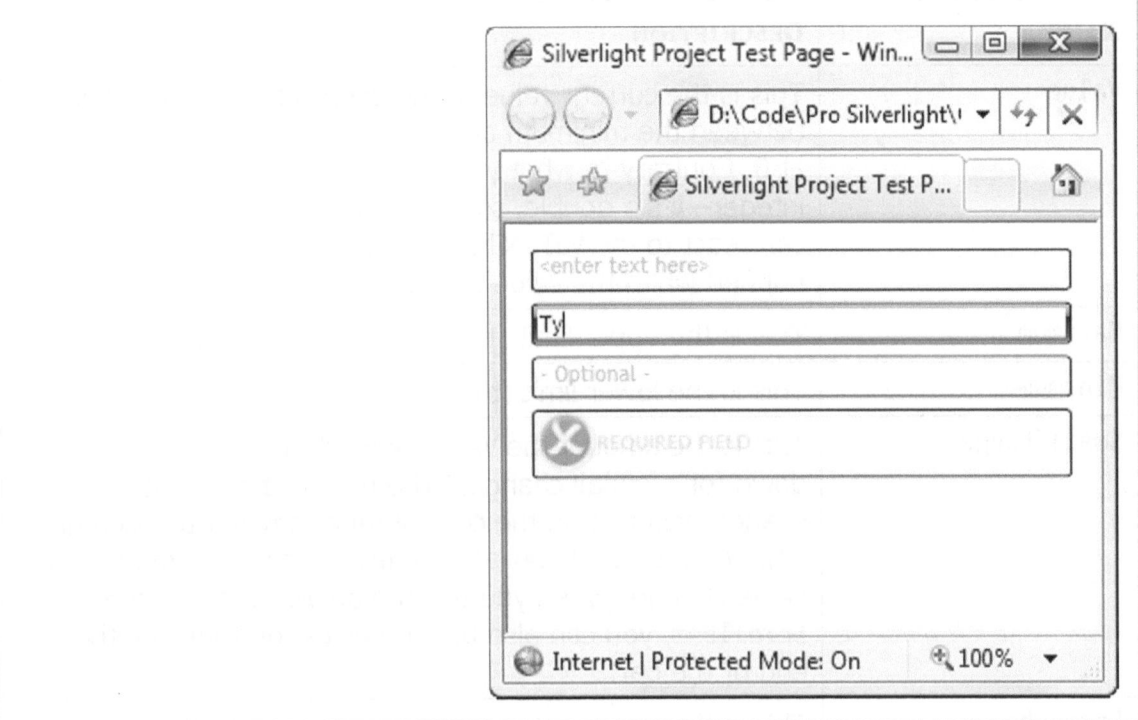

Range-Based Controls

Silverlight includes two controls that use the concept of a *range*. These controls take a numeric value that falls in between a specific minimum and maximum value. These controls—ScrollBar and Slider—derive from the RangeBase class (which itself derives from the Control class). The RangeBase class adds a ValueChanged event, a Tooltip property, and the range properties shown in Table 4-4.

Table 4-4. Properties of the RangeBase Class

NAME	DESCRIPTION
Value	This is the current value of the control (which must fall between the minimum and maximum). By default, it starts at 0. Contrary to what you might expect, Value isn't an integer—it's a double, so it accepts fractional values. You can react to the ValueChanged event if you want to be notified when the value is changed.
Maximum	This is the upper limit (the largest allowed value).
Minimum	This is the lower limit (the smallest allowed value).
SmallChange	This is the amount the Value property is adjusted up or down for a "small change." The meaning of a small change depends on the control (and may not be used at all). For the ScrollBar and Slider, this is the amount the value changes when you use the arrow keys. For the ScrollBar, you can also use the arrow buttons at either end of the bar.
LargeChange	This is the amount the Value property is adjusted up or down for a "large change." The meaning of a large change depends on the control (and may not be used at all). For the ScrollBar and Slider, this is the amount the value changes when you use the Page Up and Page Down keys or when you click the bar on either side of the thumb (which indicates the current position).

Ordinarily, there's no need to use the ScrollBar control directly. The higher-level ScrollViewer control, which wraps two ScrollBar controls, is typically much more useful. (The ScrollViewer was mentioned in Chapter 2.) However, the Slider is a specialized control that's occasionally useful. You might use it to set numeric values in situations where the number itself isn't particularly significant. For example, it makes sense to set the volume in a media player by dragging the thumb in a slider bar from side to side.

The general position of the thumb indicates the relative loudness (normal, quiet, loud), but the underlying number has no meaning to the user.

Here's an example that creates the horizontal slider shown in Figure 4-11:

```
<Slider Orientation="Horizontal" Minimum="0" Maximum="10" Width="100" />
```

Figure 4-11. A basic slider

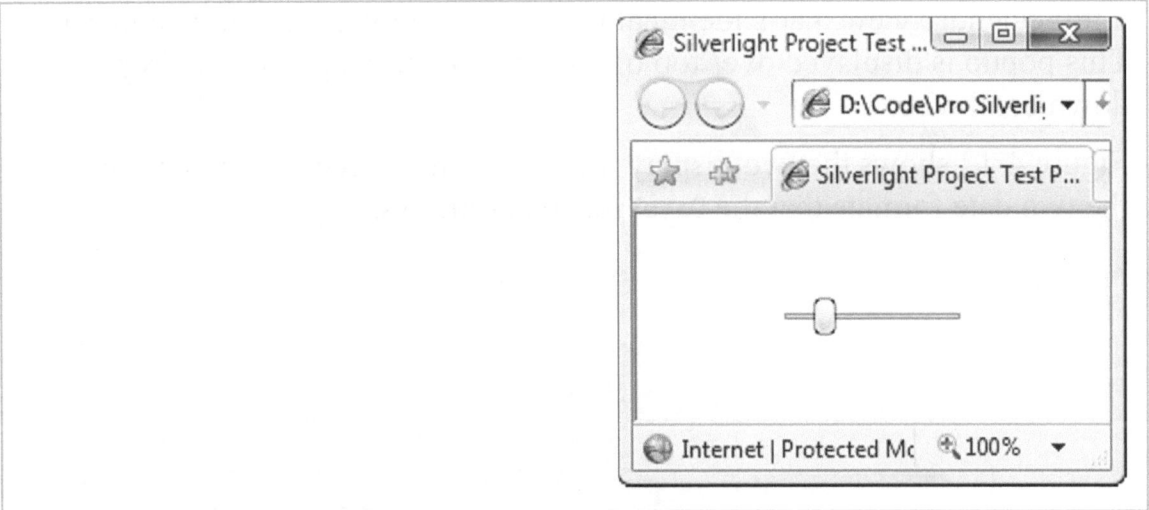

Unlike WPF, the Silverlight slider doesn't provide any properties for adding tick marks. However, as with any control, you can change its appearance while leaving its functionality intact using the control templating feature.

Date Controls

Silverlight adds two date controls, `Calendar` and `DateTimePicker` (also known as `DatePicker`), neither of which exists in the WPF control library. Both are designed to allow the user to choose a single date.

The `Calendar` control displays a calendar that's similar to what you see in the Windows operating system (for example, when you configure the system date). It shows a single month at a time and allows you to step through from month to month (by clicking the arrow buttons) or jump to a specific month (by clicking the month header to view an entire year, and then clicking the month).

The DateTimePicker requires less space. It's modeled after a simple text box, which holds a date string in long or short date format. However, the DateTimePicker provides a drop-down arrow that, when clicked, pops open a full calendar view that's identical to that shown by the Calendar control. This popup is displayed over top of any other content, just like a drop-down combo box.

Figure 4-12 shows the two display modes that the Calendar supports and the two date formats that the DateTimePicker allows.

Figure 4-12. The Calendar and DatePicker

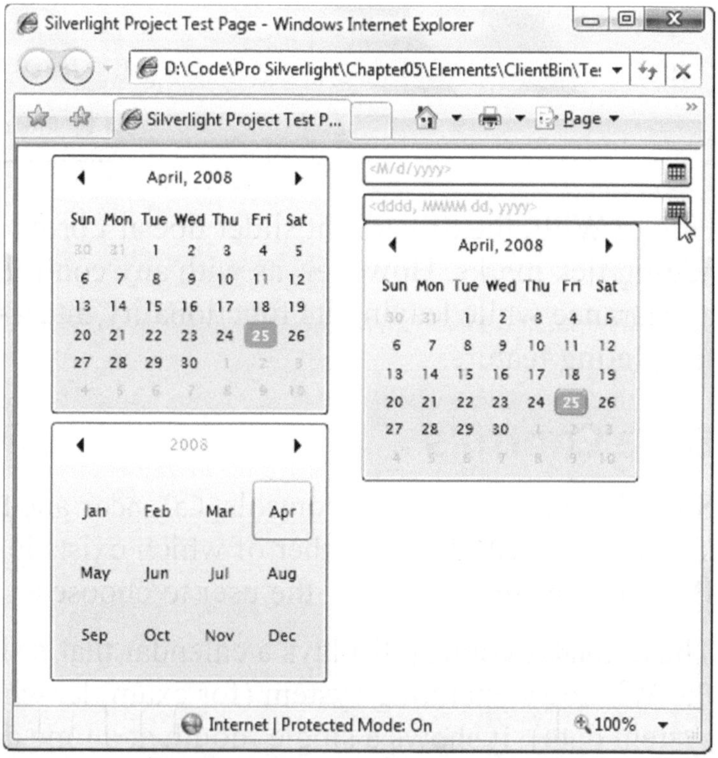

The `Calendar` and `DateTimePicker` include properties that allow you to determine which dates are shown and which dates are selectable (provided they fall in a contiguous range). Table 4-5 lists the properties you can use.

Table 4-5. Properties of the Calendar and DateTimePicker Classes

PROPERTY	DESCRIPTION
`AreDatesInPastSelectable`	Controls whether the user can pick dates that are later than the current date (true) or not (false). The default is true. This property is only used when the `SelectableDateStart` and `SelectableDateEnd` properties are null.
`DisplayDateStart` and `DisplayDateEnd`	Set the range of dates that are displayed in the view from the first, earliest date to the last, oldest date (`DisplayDateEnd`). The user won't be able to navigate to months that don't have any displayable dates. To show all dates, set `DisplayDateStart` to `DateTime.MinValue` and `DisplayDateEnd` to `DateTime.MaxValue`.
`SelectableDateStart` and `SelectableDateEnd`	Set the range of dates that the user can select. This range must be the same as or fall inside of the displayed date range. Dates that are displayable but not selectable are displayed as dimmed and disabled.
`SelectedDate`	Provides the selected date as a `DateTime` object (or a null value if not date is selected). It can be set programmatically, by the user clicking the date in the calendar or by the user typing in a date string (in the `DatePicker`).
`DisplayDate`	Determines what month is shown in the calendar view. If null, the month of the `SelectedDate` is shown. If `DisplayDate` and `SelectedDate` are both null, the current month is used.

Table 4-5. continued

PROPERTY	DESCRIPTION
FirstDayOfWeek	Determines the day of the week that will be displayed at the start of each calendar row, in the leftmost position.
IsTodayHighlighted	Determines whether the calendar view uses highlighting to point out the current date.
DisplayMode (Calendar only)	Determines the initial display month of the calendar. If set to Month, the Calendar shows the standard single-month view. If set to Year, the Calendar shows the months in the current year (similar to when the user clicks the month header). Once the user clicks a month, the Calendar shows the full calendar view for that month.
IsDropDownOpen (DatePicker only)	Determines whether the calendar view drop-down is open in the DatePicker. You can set this property programmatically to show or hide the calendar.
SelectedDateFormat (DatePicker only)	Determines how the selected date will be displayed in the text part of the DatePicker. You can choose Short or Long. The actual display format is based on the client computer's regional settings. For example, if you use Short, the date might be rendered in the yyyy/mm/dd format or dd/mm/yyyy. The long format generally includes the month and day names.

> **Note** Don't rely on the `AreDatesInPastSelectable`, `SelectableDateStart`, and `SelectableDateEnd` properties to prevent all invalid input. They use the clock on the client computer, which could be inaccurate.

The date controls also provide a few different events. Most useful is `DateSelected`, which both date controls support. You can react to `DateSelected` to reject specific date selections, such as dates that fall on a weekend:

```
private void Calendar_DateSelected(object sender, CalendarDateChangedEventArgs e)
{
    if (e.AddedDate != null)
    {
        if (e.AddedDate.Value.DayOfWeek == DayOfWeek.Saturday ||
            e.AddedDate.Value.DayOfWeek == DayOfWeek.Sunday)
        {
            lblError.Text = "Weekends are not allowed";

            // Revert to previous date selection.
            ((Calendar)sender).SelectedDate = e.RemovedDate;
        }
    }
}
```

The `Calendar` also adds a `DisplayDateChanged` event (when the user browses to a new month). The `DateTimePicker` adds a `CalendarOpened` and `CalendarClosed` event (which fire when the calendar drop-down is displayed and closed) and a `TextParseError` event (which fires when the user types a value in the text entry portion that can't be interpreted as a valid date). Ordinarily, invalid values are discarded when the user opens the calendar view, but here's an option that fills in some text to alert the user of the problem:

```
private void DatePicker_TextParseError(object sender,
  DatePickerTextParseErrorEventArgs e)
 {
     lblError.Text = "'" + e.Text +
       "' is not a valid value because " + e.Exception.Message;
}
```

The Last Word

In this chapter, you saw all the fundamental Silverlight elements. You considered several categories:

- The TextBlock, which allows you to display richly formatted text using built-in and custom fonts

- Content controls that can contain nested elements, including various types of buttons and the ToolTip

- List controls that contain a collection of items, such as the ListBox and the ComboBox

- Text controls for text editing (the TextBox) and, optionally, watermark display (the WatermarkedTextBox)

- Range-based controls that take a numeric value from a range, such as the Slider

Although you haven't had an exhaustive look at every detail of XAML markup, you've learned enough to reap all its benefits.

Chapter 5: The Application Model

Over the past five chapters, you've taken a detailed look at the different types of visual elements you can put inside Silverlight pages. You've learned how to use layout containers and common controls, and how to respond to mouse and keyboard events. Now it's time to take a second look at the Silverlight application model, which shapes how your application is deployed and hosted.

In this chapter, you'll consider the application events that allow you to respond when your application is created, unloaded, or runs into trouble with an unhandled exception. Along the way, you'll see how to use initialization parameters, how to navigate from one page to another, and how to show a custom splash screen. Next, you'll take a detailed look at the many options Silverlight provides for retrieving resources, including large files (like images and video) and dependent assemblies. You'll learn how to include essential resources in your application package for easy deployment or download them on demand to streamline performance.

Application Events

In Chapter 1, you took your first look at the life cycle of a Silverlight application. Here's a quick review:

1. The user requests the HTML entry page in the browser.

2. The Silverlight plug-in is loaded. It downloads the XAP file with your application.

3. The Silverlight plug-in reads the `AppManifest.xml` file from the XAP to find out what assemblies your application uses. It creates the Silverlight runtime environment and then loads your application assembly (and any dependencies) into it.

4. The Silverlight plug-in creates an instance of your custom application class (which is defined in the `App.xaml` and `App.xaml.cs` files).

5. The default constructor of the application class raises the **Startup** event.

6. Your application handles the **Startup** event and creates the startup page.

From this point on, your page code takes over, until it encounters an unhandled error (`UnhandledException`) or finally ends (`Exit`). These events—Startup, UnhandledException, and Exit—are the only events that the `Application` class provides.

If you look at the code in the `App.cs` file, you'll see pregenerated code in the application constructor. This code attaches event handlers to the three application events:

```
public App()
{
    this.Startup += this.Application_Startup;
    this.Exit += this.Application_Exit;
    this.UnhandledException += this.Application_UnhandledException;

    InitializeComponent();
}
```

As with the page and element events you've considered in earlier chapters, there are actually two ways to attach application event handlers. Instead of using code, you could add event attributes to the XAML markup, as shown here:

```
<Application ... x:Class="SilverlightApplication1.App"
 Startup="Application_Startup" >
```

In the following sections, you'll see how you can write code that plugs into the application events.

Application Startup

By default, the `Application_Startup` method simply creates the first page and assign it to the `Application.RootVisual` property, ensuring that it becomes the main application element.

```
private void Application_Startup(object sender, StartupEventArgs e)
{
    this.RootVisual = new Page();
}
```

Although you can change the root visual by adding or removing elements, you can't reassign the RootVisual property. After the application starts, it's essentially read-only. However, you'll learn how to manipulate the root visual to simulate the effect of changing pages in the "Changing the Page" section later in this chapter.

Application Shutdown

At some point, your Silverlight application ends. Most commonly, this occurs when the user surfs to another page in the web browser or closes the browser window. It also occurs if the user refreshes the page (effectively abandoning the current instance of the application and launching a new one), if the page runs JavaScript code that removes the Silverlight content region or changes its source, or if an unhandled exception derails your code.

Just before the application is released from memory, Silverlight gives you the chance to run some code by responding to the Application.Exit event. This event is commonly used to store user-specific information locally in isolated storage, so it's available the next time the user runs your application.

The Exit event doesn't provide any additional information in its event arguments.

Unhandled Exceptions

Although you should use disciplined exception handling code in situations where errors are possible (for example, when reading a file, downloading web content, or accessing a web service), it's not always possible to anticipate all possible sources of error. If your application encounters an error that isn't handled, it will end, and the Silverlight content region will revert to a blank space. If you've included JavaScript code that reacts to potential errors from the Silverlight plug-in (as described in Chapter 1), that code will run. Otherwise, you won't receive any indication about the error that's just occurred.

The `Application.UnhandledException` event gives you a last-ditch chance to respond to an exception before it reaches the Silverlight plug-in and terminates your application. This code is notably different from the JavaScript error-handling code that you may add to the page, because it has the ability to mark an exception as handled. Doing so effectively neutralizes the exception, preventing it from rising to the plug-in and ending your application.

Here's an example that checks the exception type and decides whether to allow the application to continue:

```
public void App_UnhandledException(object sender,
    ApplicationUnhandledExceptionEventArgs e)
{
    if (e.ExceptionObject is FileNotFoundException)
    {
        // Suppress the exception and allow the application to continue.
        e.Handled = true;
    }
}
```

Ideally, an exception like this will be handled closer to where it occurs—for example, in your page code. Application-level error handling is awkward because it's difficult to notify the user of the problem. Although the application has access to the `RootVisual` property, it doesn't know what this object is.

If your application has a single page, the application could cast the root visual to the appropriate type and call a custom method, like the `ReportError()` method shown in this example:

```
((Page1)this.RootVisual).ReportError(e.ExceptionObject)
```

You could then use this method to update the user interface with an error message.

Another option is to make the **RootVisual** a simple layout container (like a **Grid**) that includes two rows—a proportionately sized row that shows the current page and an auto-sized row that shows any error message. You'll see how to use this pattern later in this chapter, in the "Changing the Page" section.

XAML Resources

Although the most important part of your application is the logic in the code-behind file (**App.xaml.cs**), there is one ingredient you want to add to the application markup file (**App.xaml**)—*application resources*.

XAML allows you to define objects in a resources collection and then use them in your markup. Resources allow you to centralize changing details (like vector drawings and formatting preferences), and they make it easier to reuse them throughout your markup.

Resources use a hierarchical lookup system. In other words, when you use a resource in an element, Silverlight checks the resources in that element, then those in that element's container, and so on, eventually ending up at the resources collection of the top-level user control that represents your page. However, resource lookup doesn't stop there. It continues for one more level, to the application resources collection, which is defined in the **App.xaml** collection. For instance, here's an example that defines a brush in the application resources collection:

```
<Application xmlns="http://schemas.microsoft.com/client/2007"
 xmlns:x="http://schemas.microsoft.com/winfx/2006/xaml"
 x:Class="SilverlightApplication1.App">
  <Application.Resources>
    <LinearGradientBrush x:Key="PageBackgroundBrush">
      <LinearGradientBrush.GradientStops>
        <GradientStop Offset="0.00" Color="Yellow" />
        <GradientStop Offset="0.50" Color="White" />
```

```
        <GradientStop Offset="1.00" Color="Purple" />
      </LinearGradientBrush.GradientStops>
    </LinearGradientBrush>
  </Application.Resources>
</Application>
```

The advantage of placing resources in the application collection is that they're completely removed from the markup in your page, and they can be reused in all the pages in your application:

```
<Grid Name="grid1" Background="{StaticResource PageBackgroundBrush}">
```

Furthermore, pages can selectively override a resource by defining a replacement with the same name in their resource collections.

Unfortunately, Silverlight doesn't currently allow you to merge resource dictionaries, which means there's no way to split your application resources into separate files and then merge them into your application (which is possible in WPF).

Note   XAML resources shouldn't be confused with the binary resources you'll explore later in this chapter. XAML resources are objects that are declared in your markup. Binary resources are nonexecutable files that are inserted into your assembly or XAP file when your project is compiled.

Application Tasks

Now that you understand the lifecycle of a Silverlight application and the content of the `App.xaml` and `App.xaml.cs` files, you're ready to take a look at a few common scenarios. In the following sections, you'll consider how you can process initialization parameters, support page navigation, and show a splash screen while your application is loading.

Accessing the Current Application

You can retrieve a reference to the application object at any time, at any point in your code, using the static `Application.Current` property. However, the application object is typed as a `System.Windows.Application` object. To use any custom properties or methods that you've added to your derived application class, you must cast the reference to the `App` type:

```
((App)Application.Current).DoSomething()
```

Along with the `Current` property, the `Application` class also provides three more important members:

- **Host**: The `Host` property allows you to interact with the browser, and through it the rest of the HTML content on the web page.

- **GetResourceStream()**: This method is used to retrieve resources in code.

- **LoadComponent()**: This method accepts a XAML file and instantiates the corresponding elements (much as Silverlight does automatically when you create a page class and the constructor calls the `InitializeComponent()` method). You'll see an example that uses this method.

Initialization Parameters

The `Startup` event passes in a `StartupEventArgs` object that includes one additional detail—initialization parameters. This mechanism allows the page that hosts the Silverlight control to pass in custom information. This is particularly useful if you host the same Silverlight application on different pages or you want the Silverlight application to vary based on user-specific or session-specific information. For example, you might customize the application's view depending on whether users are entering from the customers page or the employees page. Or, you might choose to load up different information based on the product that the user is currently viewing. Just remember that the initialization parameters come from the tags of the HTML entry page, and a malicious user can alter them.

For example, imagine you want to pass a `ViewMode` parameter that has two possible values, Customer or Employee, as represented by this enumeration:

```
public enum ViewMode
{
    Customer, Employee
}
```

You'll need to change a variety of details based on this information, so it makes sense to store it somewhere that's accessible throughout your application. The logical choice is to add a property to your custom application class, as shown here:

```
private ViewMode viewMode = ViewMode.Customer;
public ViewMode ViewMode
{
    get { return viewMode; }
}
```

This property defaults to customer view, so it only needs to be changed if the web page specifically requests the employee view.

To pass the parameter into your Silverlight application, you need to add a `<param>` element to the markup in the Silverlight content region. This parameter must have the name `initParams`. Its value is a comma-separated list of name-value pairs that set your custom parameters. For example, to add a parameter named `viewMode`, you would add the following line (shown in bold) to your markup:

```
<div id="silverlightControlHost">
  <object data="data:application/x-silverlight,"
   type="application/x-silverlight-2-b1" width="100%" height="100%">
    <param name="source" value="TransparentSilverlight.xap"/>
    <param name="onerror" value="onSilverlightError" />
    <param name="background" value="white" />
    <param name="initParams" value=" viewMode=Customer" />
    ...
  </object>
```

```
<iframe style='visibility:hidden;height:0;width:0;border:0px'></iframe>
</div>
```

Then, you can retrieve this from the **StartupEventArgs.InitParams** collection. However, you must check first that it exists:

```
private void Application_Startup(object sender, StartupEventArgs e)
{
    // Take the view mode setting and store in an application property.
    if (e.InitParams.ContainsKey("viewMode"))
    {
        string view = e.InitParams["viewMode"];
        if (view == "Employee") this.view = ViewMode.Employee;
    }

    // Create the root page.
    this.RootVisual = new Page();
}
```

If you have many possible values, you can use the following leaner code to convert the string to the corresponding enumeration value, assuming the text matches exactly:

```
string view = e.InitParams["viewMode"];
try
{
    this.viewMode = (ViewMode)Enum.Parse(typeof(ViewMode), view, true);
}
catch { }
```

Now, different pages are free to pass in a different parameter and launch your application with different view settings (see Figure 5-1). Because the view information is stored as a property in the custom application class (named **App**), you can retrieve it anywhere in your application:

```
lblViewMode.Text = "Current view mode: " +
  ((App)Application.Current).ViewMode.ToString();
```

Figure 5-1. Displaying an initialization parameter

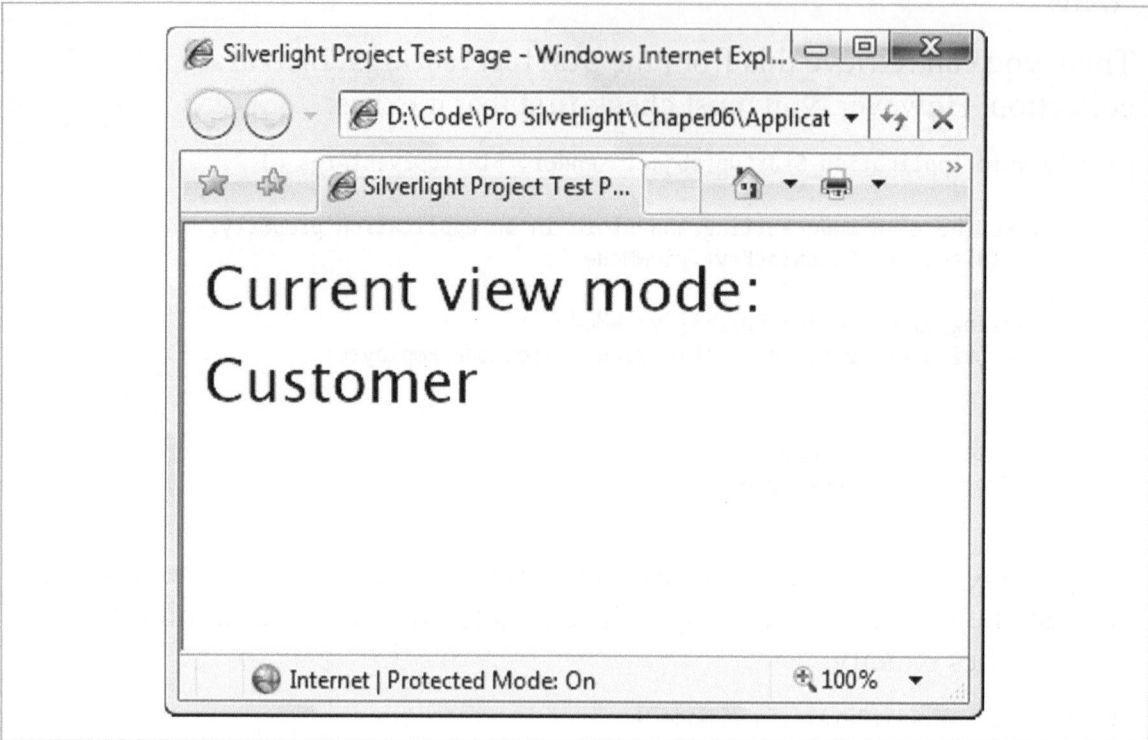

If you have more than one initialization parameter, simply pass them all in one comma-delimited string. Initialization values should be made up of alphanumeric characters. There's currently no support for escaping special characters like commas in parameter values.

```
<param name="initParams" value="startPage=Page1,viewMode=Customer" />
```

Now the event handler for the `Startup` event can retrieve the `StartPage` value and use it to choose the application's root page. You can load the correct page using a block of conditional logic that distinguishes between the available choices, or you can write a more general solution that uses reflection to attempt to create the class with the requested name, as shown here:

```
UserControl startPage = null;
if (e.InitParams.ContainsKey("startPage"))
{
    try
    {
        // Create an instance of the page.
        Type type = this.GetType();
        Assembly assembly = type.Assembly;
        startPage = (UserControl)assembly.CreateInstance(
            type.Namespace + "." + startPageName);
    }
    catch
    {
        startPage = null;
    }
}
// If no parameter was supplied or the class couldn't be created, use a default.
if (startPage == null) startPage = new MenuPage;

this.RootVisual = startPage;
```

Changing the Page

Once you've set the RootVisual property and your application has finished
loading up, you can't change it. That means there's no way to unload a
page and replace it with a new one. However, you can achieve much the
same effect by changing what you use for your root visual. Instead of
setting it with a custom user control, you can use something a bit more
flexible—a simple container like the Border or layout panel like the Grid.
Here's an example of the latter approach:

```
// This Grid will host your pages.
private Grid rootVisual = new Grid();

private void Application_Startup(object sender, StartupEventArgs e)
{
    // Load the first page.
    this.RootVisual = rootVisual;
    rootVisual.Children.Add(new Page());
}
```

Now, you can switch to another page by removing the first page from the Grid and adding a different one. To make this process relatively straightforward, you can add a static method like this to the App class:

```
public static void Navigate(UserControl newPage)
{
    // Get the current application object and cast it to
    // an instance of the custom (derived) App class.
    App currentApp = (App)Application.Current;

    // Change the currently displayed page.
    currentApp.rootVisual.Children.Clear();
    currentApp.rootVisual.Children.Add(newPage);
}
```

Now you can navigate at any point using code like this:

```
App.Navigate(new Page2());
```

Retaining Page State

If you plan to allow the user to navigate frequently between complex pages, it makes more sense to create them once and keep the page instance in memory until later. (This also has the sometimes-important side effect of maintaining that page's current state, including all the values in any input controls.) To implement this pattern, you first need a system to identify pages. You could fall back on string names, but an enumeration gives you better error prevention:

```
public enum Pages
{
    MainWindow, ReviewPage, AboutPage
}
```

You can then store the pages of your application in private fields in your custom application class. Here's a simple dictionary that does the trick:

```
private static Dictionary<Pages, UserControl> pageCache =
  new Dictionary<Pages,UserControl>();
```

In your **Navigate()** method, create the page only if it needs to be created—in other words, the corresponding private field is null.

```
public static void Navigate(Pages newPage)
{
    // Get the current application object and cast it to
    // an instance of the custom (derived) App class.
    App currentApp = (App)Application.Current;

    // Check if the page has been created before.
    if (!pageCache.ContainsKey(newPage))
    {
        // Create the first instance of the page,
        // and cache it for future use.
        Type type = currentApp.GetType();
        Assembly assembly = type.Assembly;
        pageCache[newPage] = (UserControl)assembly.CreateInstance(
            type.Namespace + "." + newPage.ToString());
    }

    // Change the currently displayed page.
    currentApp.rootVisual.Children.Clear();
    currentApp.rootVisual.Children.Add(pageCache[newPage]);
}
```

Now you can navigate by indicating the page you want with the **Pages** enumeration:

```
App.Navigate(Pages.MainWindow);
```

Because there's only one version of the page ever created, and it's kept in memory over the lifetime of the application, all the page's state remains intact when you navigate away and back again (see Figure 5-2).

Figure 5-2. Moving from one page to another

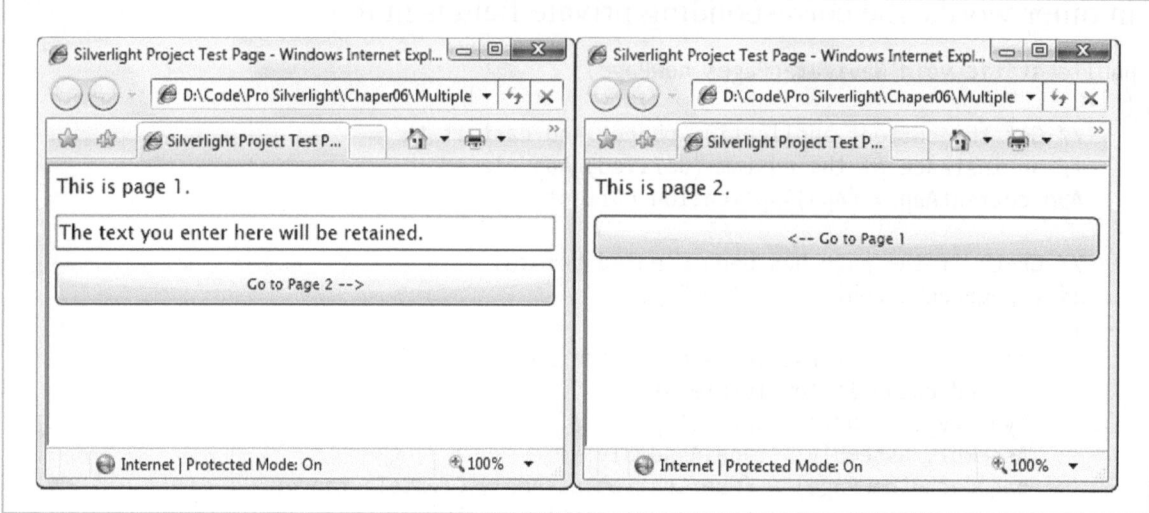

Browser History

The only limitation with the navigation methods described in this section is the fact that the browser has no idea you've changed from one page to another. If you want to allow the user to go back, it's up to you to add the controls that do it. The browser's Back button will only send you to the previous HTML page (thereby exiting your Silverlight application). If you want to create an application that integrates more effectively with the browser and supports the Back button, it is possible—but you'll need the HTML interaction techniques.

Tip   You can add a dash of Silverlight animation and graphics to create a more pleasing transition between pages, such as a gentle fade or wipe.

Splash Screens

If a Silverlight application is small, it will be downloaded quickly and appear in the browser. If a Silverlight application is large, it may take a few seconds to download. As long as your application takes longer than 500 milliseconds to download, Silverlight will show an animated splash screen.

The built-in splash screen isn't too exciting—it's little more than a percentage that tells you how much of the application has downloaded so far. However, you can easily create your own custom splash screen. Essentially, a splash screen is a XAML file with the graphical content you want to display and a dash of JavaScript code that updates the splash screen as the application is downloaded. You can't use C# code at this point, because the management Silverlight programming environment hasn't been initialized yet.

Furthermore, the XAML file for your splash screen can't be a part of your Silverlight XAP file, because the XAP file is still in the process of being downloaded. Instead, the splash screen XAML must be in a separate file that's placed alongside your XAP file at the same web location.

Note   Testing a custom splash screen requires a bit of work. Ordinarily, you won't see the splash screen while testing because the application is sent to the browser too quickly. To slow down your application enough to see the splash screen, you need to first ensure that you're using an ASP.NET test site, which ensures that your Silverlight application is hosted by Visual Studio test web server (as described in Chapter 1). Then, you need to add multiple large resource files to your Silverlight project—say, a handful of MP3 files—and set the build action of each one to Resource so it's added to the XAP file.

Resources

As you learned in Chapter 1, a Silverlight application is actually a package of files that's archived using ZIP compression and stored as a single file with the extension **.xap**. In a simple application, the **.xap** file has little more than a manifest (which list the files your project uses) and your application assembly. However, there's something else you can place in the XAP file—resources.

A XAP resource is a distinct file that you want to make available to your compiled application. Common examples include graphical *assets*—images, sounds, and video files that you want to display in your user interface.

However, using resources can be unnecessarily complicated because of the wealth of different options Silverlight provides for storing them. Here's a quick roundup of your options:

- **In the application assembly**: The resource file is embedded in the compiled DLL file for your project, such as `SilverlightApplication1.dll`. This is the default approach.

- **In the application package**: The resource file is placed in the XAP file alongside your application assembly. It's still just as easy to deploy, but now it's a bit easier to manage, because you replace or modify your assets by editing the XAP file without compiling your application.

- **On the site of origin**: The resource file is placed on the web site alongside your XAP file. Now you have more deployment headaches, because you need to make sure you deploy both the XAP file and the resource file. However, you gain the ability to use your resource in other ways—for example, you can use an image in ordinary HTML web pages or make videos available for easy downloading. You can reduce the size of the initial XAP download, which is important if the resources are large.

These aren't all your options. You can also place resources in other assemblies that your application uses. (This approach gives you more advanced options for controlling the way you share content between different Silverlight applications.)

Class Library Assemblies

So far, all the examples you've seen in this book have placed all their code into a single assembly. For a small or modest-sized Silverlight application, this straightforward design makes good sense. However, it's not hard to imagine that you might want to factor out certain functionality and place it in a separate class library assembly. Usually, you'll take this step because you want to reuse that functionality with more than one Silverlight application. Alternatively, you might just want to separate it so it can be coded, compiled, debugged, and revised separately, which is particularly important if that code is being created by a different development team.

Creating a Silverlight class library is easy. In fact, it's essentially the same process you follow to create and use class library assemblies in ordinary .NET applications. First, create a new project in Visual Studio using the Silverlight Class Library project template. Then, add a reference in your Silverlight application that points to that project or assembly. The dependent assembly will be copied into the XAP package when you build your application.

Using Resources in an Assembly

Class libraries give you another way to share resources. You can embed a resource in a class library and then retrieve it in your application. In fact, this technique is easy—the only trick is constructing the right URIs. Here's the format to use:

```
/ClassLibraryFileName;component/ResourceFileName
```

The leading slash represents the root of the XAP file. This URI points to the dependent assembly in that file, and then indicates a resource in that assembly.

For example, consider the ResourceClassLibrary assembly in Figure 5-3. It includes a resource named happyface.jpg, and that file has a build action of Resource.

Figure 5-3. A resource in a XAP file

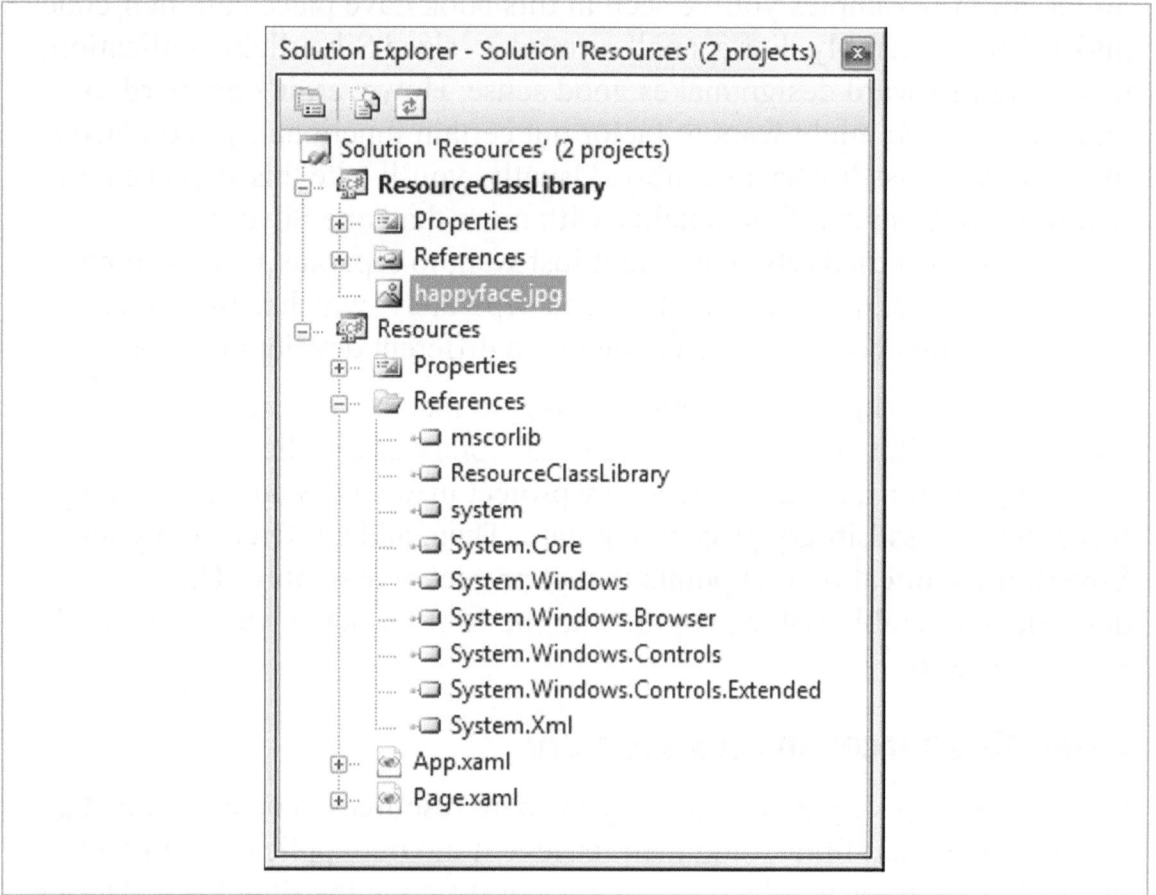

Here's an image file that uses the resource from the class library:

```
<Image Source="/ResourceClassLibrary;component/happyface.jpg"></Image>
```

Downloading Assemblies on Demand

In some situations, the code in a class library is used infrequently, or perhaps not at all for certain users. However, if the class library contains a significant amount of code or (more likely) has large embedded resources like graphics, including it with your application will increase the size of your XAP file and lengthen download times needlessly. In this case, you might want to create a separate component assembly—one that isn't downloaded until you need it. This scenario is similar to on-demand resource downloading. You place the separate resource in a separate file outside of the XAP file, but on the same web site.

Before you use assembly downloading, you need to make sure that the dependent assembly won't be placed in the XAP file. To do so, select the project reference that points to the assembly. In the Properties window, set Copy Local to false.

To implement on-demand downloading of assemblies, you need to use the `WebClient` in conjunction with the `AssemblyPart` class. The `WebClient` retrieves the assembly, and the assembly makes it available for downloading.

```
string uri = Application.Current.Host.Source.AbsoluteUri;
int index = url.IndexOf("/ClientBin");
// In this example, the URI includes the /ClientBin portion, because we've
// decided to place the DLL in the ClientBin folder.
uri = uri.Substring(0, index + 10) + "/ResourceClassLibrary.dll";

// Begin the download.
WebClient webClient = new WebClient();
webClient.OpenReadCompleted += webClient_OpenReadCompleted;
webClient.OpenReadAsync(new Uri(url));
```

When the assembly is downloaded, you use the `AssemblyPart.Load()` method to load it into the current application domain:

```
private void webClient_OpenReadCompleted(object sender,
  OpenReadCompletedEventArgs e)
{
    if (e.Error != null)
    {
        // (Add code to display error or downgrade gracefully.)
    }
    else
    {
        AssemblyPart assemblypart = new AssemblyPart();
        assemblypart.Load(e.Result);
        // (Now you can use code as though the assembly was always there.)
    }
}
```

Once you've performed this step, you can retrieve resources from your assembly and instantiate types from it. It's as though your assembly had been a part of the XAP file from the start.

Once again, it's important to keep track of whether you've downloaded an assembly, so you don't attempt to download it more than once. Some applications "daisy chain" assemblies, so one application downloads other dependent assemblies on demand, and these assemblies download additional assemblies when *they* need them.

The Last Word

In this chapter, you explored the Silverlight application model. You reexamined the application object, and considered how you can react to application events and store application resources. Next, you considered practical techniques that depend on the application class, such as passing initialization parameters from different web pages and moving from one page to another in your Silverlight application. Finally, you explored the resource system that Silverlight uses, and considered the many options for deploying resources and class libraries, from placing them alongside your assembly to downloading them only when needed.

Chapter 6: Shapes and Geometries

Silverlight's 2D drawing support is the basic foundation for many of its more sophisticated features, such as custom-drawn controls, interactive graphics, and animation. Even if you don't plan to create customized art for your application, you need to have a solid understanding of Silverlight's drawing fundamentals. You'll use it to add professional yet straightforward touches, like reflection. You'll also need it to add interactivity to your graphics—for example, to make shapes move or change in response to user actions.

Silverlight supports a surprisingly large subset of the drawing features from WPF, its more capable sibling. In this chapter, you'll explore the shape model, which allows you to construct graphics out of rectangles, ellipses, lines, and curves. You'll also see how you can convert existing vector art to the XAML format you need, which allows you to reuse existing graphics rather than build them from scratch.

Basic Shapes

The simplest way to draw 2D graphical content in a Silverlight user interface is to use *shapes*: dedicated classes that represent simple lines, ellipses, rectangles, and polygons. Technically, shapes are known as drawing *primitives*. You can combine these basic ingredients to create more complex graphics.

The most important detail about shapes in Silverlight is the fact that they all derive from `FrameworkElement`. As a result, shapes *are* elements. This has a number of important consequences:

- **Shapes draw themselves**: You don't need to manage the invalidation and painting process. For example, you don't need to manually repaint a shape when content moves, the page is resized, or the shape's properties change.

- **Shapes are organized in the same way as other elements**: In other words, you can place a shape in any of the layout containers you learned about in Chapter 2 (although the Canvas is obviously the most useful container because it allows you to place shapes at specific coordinates, which is important when you're building a complex drawing out of multiple pieces).

- **Shapes support the same events as other elements**: That means you don't need to go to any extra work to deal with key presses, mouse movements, and mouse clicks. You can use the same set of events you'd use with any element.

Silverlight uses a number of optimizations to make 2D drawing as fast as possible. For example, because shapes often overlap in complex drawings, Silverlight uses sophisticated algorithms to determine when part of a shape won't be visible, and thereby avoid the overhead of rendering and then overwriting it with another shape.

The Shape Classes

Every shape derives from the abstract System.Windows.Shapes.Shape class. Figure 6-1 shows the inheritance hierarchy for shapes.

As you can see, there's a relatively small set of classes that derive from the Shape class. Line, Ellipse, and Rectangle are all straightforward, while Polyline is a connected series of straight lines, and Polygon is a closed shape made up of a connected series of straight lines. Finally, the Path class is an all-in-one superpower that can combine basic shapes in a single element.

Figure 6-1. The Silverlight shape classes

Figure 6-1. The Silverlight shape classes

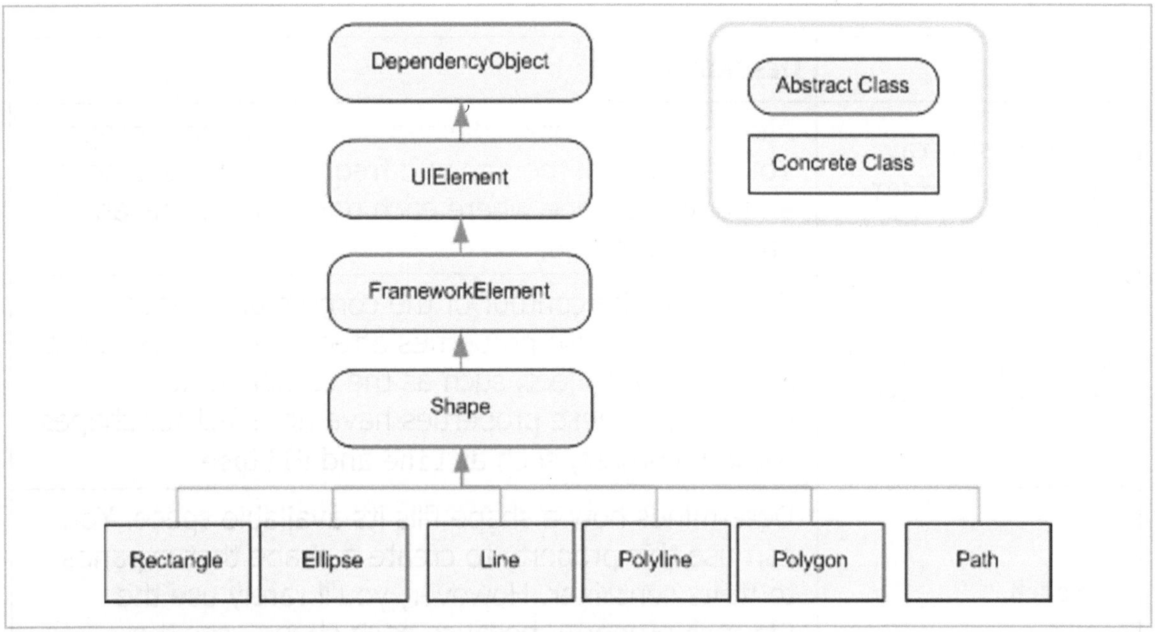

Although the Shape class can't do anything on its own, it defines a small set of important properties, which are listed in Table 6-1.

Table 6-1. Shape Properties

NAME	DESCRIPTION
Fill	Sets the brush object that paints the surface of the shape (everything inside its borders).
Stroke	Sets the brush object that paints the edge of the shape (its border).
StrokeThickness	Sets the thickness of the border, in pixels.
StrokeStartLineCap and StrokeEndLineCap	Determine the contour of the edge of the beginning and end of the line. These properties only have an effect for the Line, the Polyline, and (sometimes) the Path shapes. All other shapes are closed, and so have no starting and ending point.

Table 6-1. continued

NAME	DESCRIPTION
StrokeDashArray, StrokeDashOffset, and StrokeDashCap	Allow you to create a dashed border around a shape. You can control the size and frequency of the dashes and how the edge where each dash line begins and ends is contoured.
StrokeLineJoin and StrokeMiterLimit	Determine the contour of the corners of a shape. Technically, these properties affect the *vertices* where different lines meet, such as the corners of a Rectangle. These properties have no effect for shapes without corners, such as Line and Ellipse.
Stretch	Determines how a shape fills its available space. You can use this property to create a shape that expands to fit its container. However, you'll rarely use the Stretch property, because each shape uses the default value that makes most sense for it.
GeometryTransform	Allows you to apply a transform object that changes the coordinate system that's used to draw a shape. This allows you to skew, rotate, or displace a shape. Transforms are particularly useful when animating graphics. You'll learn about transforms in Chapter 7.

Rectangle and Ellipse

The Rectangle and Ellipse are the two simplest shapes. To create either one, set the familiar Height and Width properties (inherited from FrameworkElement) to define the size of your shape, and then set the Fill or Stroke property (or both) to make the shape visible. You're also free to use properties such as MinHeight, MinWidth, HorizontalAlignment, VerticalAlignment, and Margin.

Here's a simple example that stacks an ellipse on a rectangle (see Figure 6-2) using a **StackPanel**:

```
<StackPanel>
  <Ellipse Fill="Yellow" Stroke="Blue"
   Height="50" Width="100" Margin="5" HorizontalAlignment="Left"></Ellipse>
  <Rectangle Fill="Yellow" Stroke="Blue"
   Height="50" Width="100" Margin="5" HorizontalAlignment="Left"></Rectangle>
</StackPanel>
```

Figure 6-2. Two simple shapes

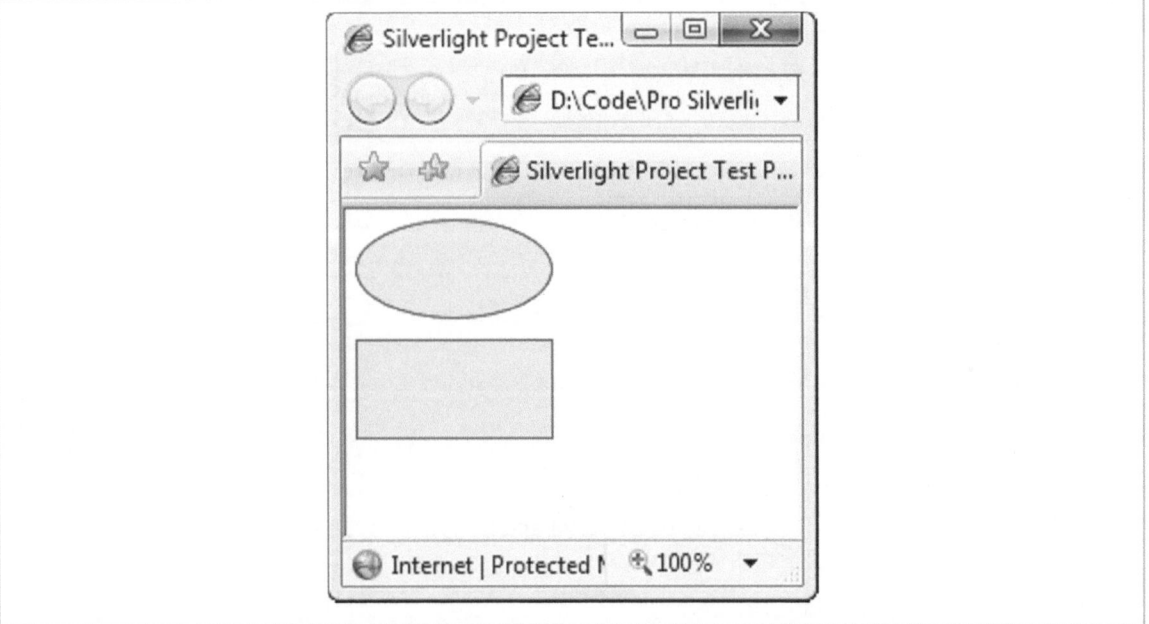

The **Ellipse** class doesn't add any properties. The **Rectangle** class adds just two: **RadiusX** and **RadiusY**. When set to nonzero values, these properties allow you to create nicely rounded corners.

You can think of RadiusX and RadiusY as describing an ellipse that's used just to fill in the corners of the rectangle. For example, if you set both properties to 10, Silverlight draws your corners using the edge of a circle that's 10 pixels wide. As you make your radius larger, more of your rectangle will be rounded off. If you increase RadiusY more than RadiusX, your corners will round off more gradually along the left and right sides and more sharply along the top and bottom edge. If you increase the RadiusX property to match your rectangle's width, and increase RadiusY to match its height, you'll end up converting your rectangle into an ordinary ellipse.

Figure 6-3 shows a few rectangles with rounded corners.

Figure 6-3. Rounded corners

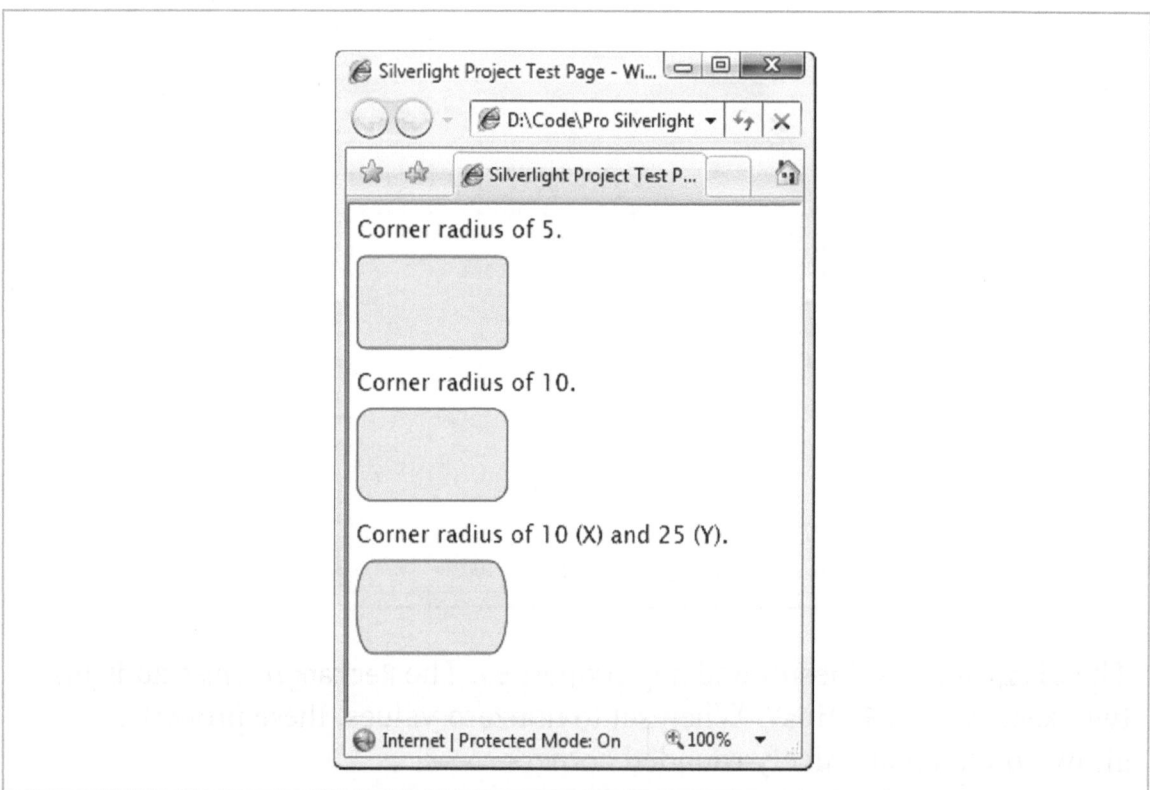

Sizing and Placing Shapes

As you already know, hard-coded sizes are usually not the ideal approach to creating user interfaces. They limit your ability to handle dynamic content, and they make it more difficult to localize your application into other languages.

When drawing shapes, these concerns don't always apply. Often, you'll need tighter control over shape placement. However, in many cases you can make your design a little more flexible. Both the Ellipse and the Rectangle have the ability to size themselves to fill the available space.

If you don't supply the Height and Width properties, the shape is sized based on its container. For example, if you use the proportional row-sizing behavior of the Grid, you can create an ellipse that fills a page with this stripped-down markup:

```
<Grid>
  <Ellipse Fill="Yellow" Stroke="Blue"></Ellipse>
</Grid>
```

Here, the Grid fills the entire page. The Grid contains a single proportionately sized row, which fills the entire Grid. Finally, the ellipse fills the entire row.

This sizing behavior depends on the value of the Stretch property (which is defined in the Shape class). By default, it's set to Fill, which stretches a shape to fill its container if an explicit size isn't indicated. Table 6-2 lists all your possibilities.

Table 6-2. Values for the Stretch Enumeration

NAME	DESCRIPTION
Fill	Your shape is stretched in width and height to fit its container exactly. (If you set an explicit height and width, this setting has no effect.)
None	The shape is not stretched. Unless you set a nonzero width and height (using the Height and Width or MinHeight and MinWidth properties), your shape won't appear.
Uniform	The width and height are sized up proportionately until the shape reaches the edge of the container. If you use this with an ellipse, you'll end up with the biggest circle that fits in the container. If you use it with a rectangle, you'll get the biggest possible square. (If you set an explicit height and width, your shape is sized within those bounds. For example, if you set a Width of 10 and a Height of 100 for a rectangle, you'll only get a 10×10 square.)
UniformToFill	The width and height are sized proportionately until the shape fills all the available height and width. For example, if you place a rectangle with this size setting into a page that's 100×200 pixels, you'll get a 200×200 rectangle, and part of it will be clipped off. (If you set an explicit height and width, your shape is sized within those bounds. For example, if you set a Width of 10 and a Height of 100 for a rectangle, you'll get a 100×100 rectangle that's clipped to fit an invisible 10×100 box.)

Figure 6-4 shows the difference between Fill, Uniform, and UniformToFill.

Figure 6-4. Filling three cells in a Grid

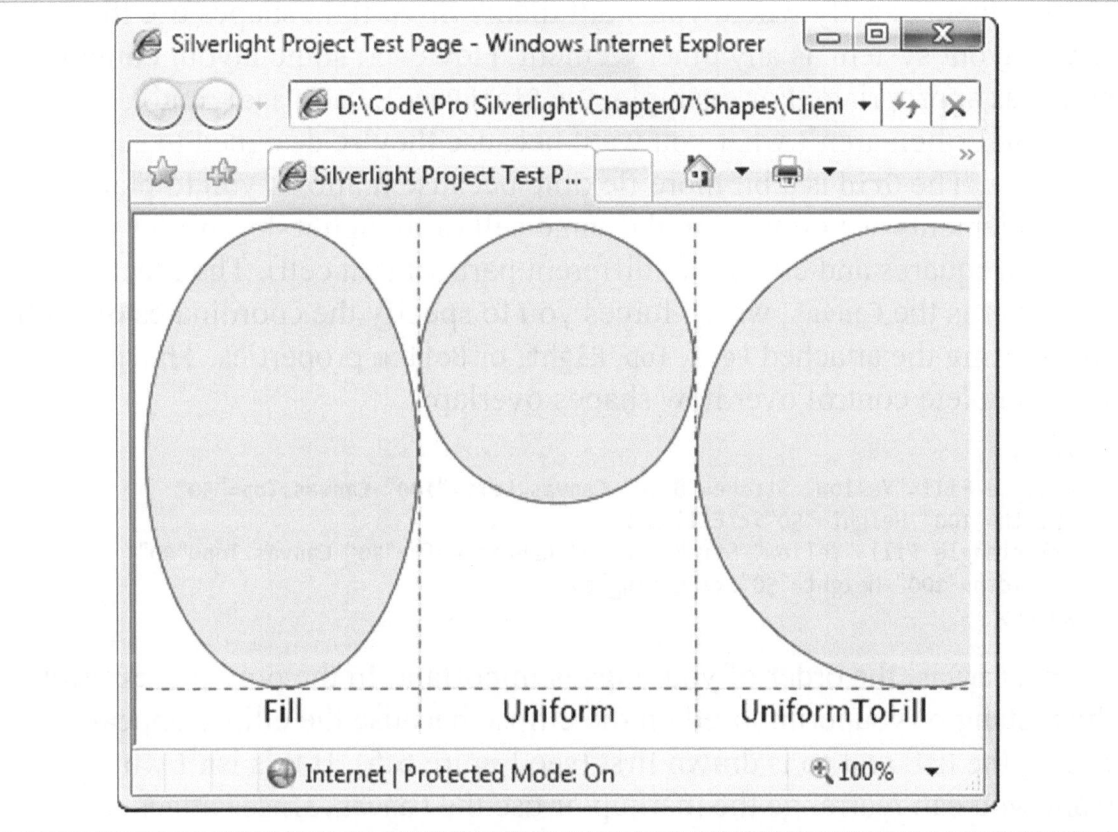

Usually, a `Stretch` value of `Fill` is the same as setting both `HorizontalAlignment` and `VerticalAlignment` to `Stretch`. The difference occurs if you choose to set a fixed `Width` or `Height` on your shape. In this case, the `HorizontalAlignment` and `VerticalAlignment` values are simply ignored. However, the `Stretch` setting still has an effect—it determines how your shape content is sized within the bounds you've given it.

Tip   In most cases, you'll size a shape explicitly or allow it to stretch to fit. You won't combine both approaches.

So far, you've seen how to size a `Rectangle` and an `Ellipse`, but what about placing them exactly where you want them? Silverlight shapes use the same layout system as any other element. However, some layout containers aren't as appropriate. For example, the `StackPanel`, `DockPanel`, and `WrapPanel` often aren't what you want because they're designed to separate elements. The `Grid` is a bit more flexible because it allows you to place as many elements as you want in the same cell (although it doesn't let you position squares and ellipses in different parts of that cell). The ideal container is the `Canvas`, which forces you to specify the coordinates of each shape using the attached `Left`, `Top`, `Right`, or `Bottom` properties. This gives you complete control over how shapes overlap:

```
<Canvas>
  <Ellipse Fill="Yellow" Stroke="Blue" Canvas.Left="100" Canvas.Top="50"
    Width="100" Height="50"></Ellipse>
    <Rectangle Fill="Yellow" Stroke="Blue" Canvas.Left="30" Canvas.Top="40"
      Width="100" Height="50"></Rectangle>
</Canvas>
```

With a `Canvas`, the order of your tags is important. In the previous example, the rectangle is superimposed on the ellipse because the ellipse appears first in the list, and so is drawn first (see Figure 6-5). If this isn't what you want, you can rearrange the markup or use the `Canvas.ZIndex` attached property to move an element to a specific layer.

Remember, a `Canvas` doesn't need to occupy an entire page. For example, there's no reason that you can't create a `Grid` that uses a `Canvas` in one of its cells. This gives you the perfect way to lock down fixed bits of drawing logic in a dynamic, free-flowing user interface.

Figure 6-5. Overlapping shapes in a Canvas

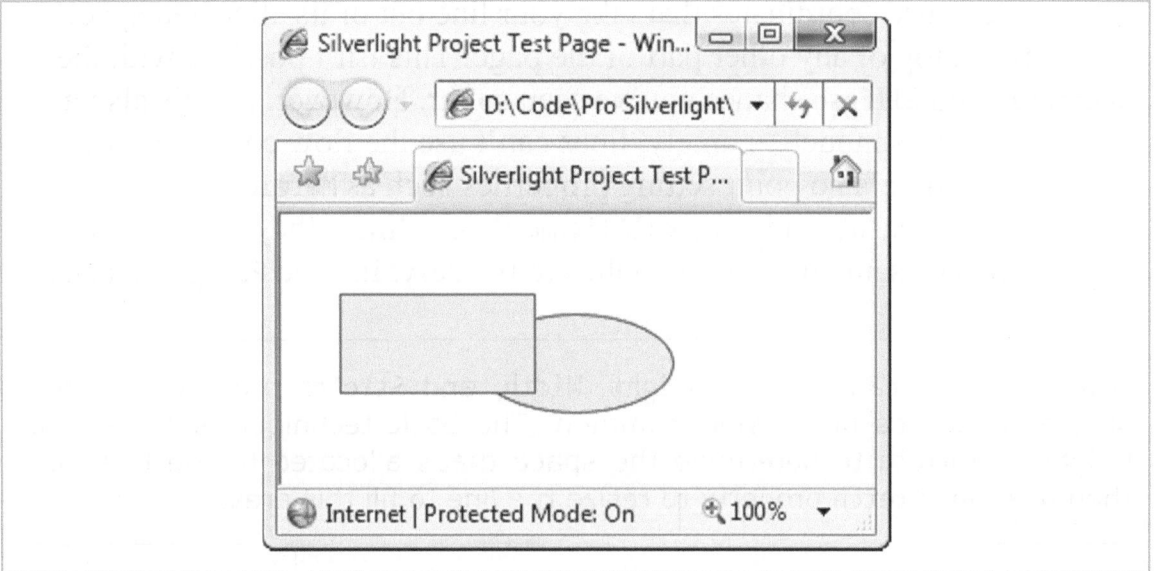

Line

The Line shape represents a straight line that connects one point to another. The starting and ending points are set by four properties: X1 and Y1 (for the first point) and X2 and Y2 (for the second). For example, here's a line that stretches from (0, 0) to (10, 100):

```
<Line Stroke="Blue" X1="0" Y1="0" X2="10" Y2="100"></Line>
```

The Fill property has no effect for a line. You must set the Stroke property.

The coordinates you use in a line are relative to the top-left corner where the line is placed. For example, if you place the previous line in a StackPanel, the coordinate (0, 0) points to wherever that item in the StackPanel is placed. It might be the top-left corner of the page, but it probably isn't. If the StackPanel uses a nonzero Margin, or if the line is preceded by other elements, the line will begin at a point (0, 0) some distance down from the top of the page.

However, it's perfectly reasonable to use negative coordinates for a line. In fact, you can use coordinates that take your line out of its allocated space and draw on top of any other part of the page. This isn't possible with the Rectangle and Ellipse shapes you've seen so far. However, there's also a drawback to this model—namely, lines can't use the flow content model. That means there's no point setting properties such as Margin, HorizontalAlignment, and VerticalAlignment on a line—they won't have any effect. The same limitation applies to the Polyline and Polygon shapes.

Note   You can use the Height, Width, and Stretch properties with a line, although it's not terribly common. The basic technique is to use the Height and Width to determine the space that's allocated to the line, and then use the Stretch property to resize the line to fill this area.

If you place a Line in a Canvas, the attached position properties (such as Top and Left) still apply. They determine the starting position of the line. In other words, the two line coordinates are offset by that amount. Consider this line:

```
<Line Stroke="Blue" X1="0" Y1="0" X2="10" Y2="100"
 Canvas.Left="5" Canvas.Top="100"></Line>
```

It stretches from (0, 0) to (10, 100), using a coordinate system that treats the point (5, 100) on the Canvas as (0, 0). That makes it equivalent to this line, which doesn't use the Top and Left properties:

```
<Line Stroke="Blue" X1="5" Y1="100" X2="15" Y2="200"></Line>
```

It's up to you whether you use the position properties when you place a Line on a Canvas. Often you can simplify your line drawing by picking a good starting point. You also make it easier to move parts of your drawing. For example, if you draw several lines and other shapes at a specific position in a Canvas, it's a good idea to draw them relative to a nearby point (by using the same Top and Left coordinates). That way, you can shift that entire part of your drawing to a new position as needed.

Note   There's no way to create a curved line with Line or Polyline shapes. Instead, you need the more advanced Path class described later in this chapter.

Polyline

The Polyline class allows you to draw a sequence of connected straight lines. You simply supply a list of x and y coordinates using the Points property. Technically, the Points property requires a PointCollection object, but you fill this collection in XAML using a lean string-based syntax. You simply need to supply a list of points and add a space or a comma between each coordinate.

A Polyline can have as few as two points. For example, here's a Polyline that duplicates the first line you saw in this section, which stretches from (5, 100) to (15, 200):

```
<Polyline Stroke="Blue" Points="5 100 15 200"></Polyline>
```

For better readability, use commas in between each x and y coordinate:

```
<Polyline Stroke="Blue" Points="5,100 15,200"></Polyline>
```

And here's a more complex Polyline that begins at (10, 150). The points move steadily to the right, oscillating between higher y values such as (50, 160) and lower ones such as (70, 130):

```
<Canvas>
  <Polyline Stroke="Blue" StrokeThickness="5" Points="10,150 30,140 50,160 70,130
90,170 110,120 130,180 150,110 170,190 190,100 210,240" >
  </Polyline>
</Canvas>
```

Figure 6-6 shows the final line.

Figure 6-6. A line with several segments

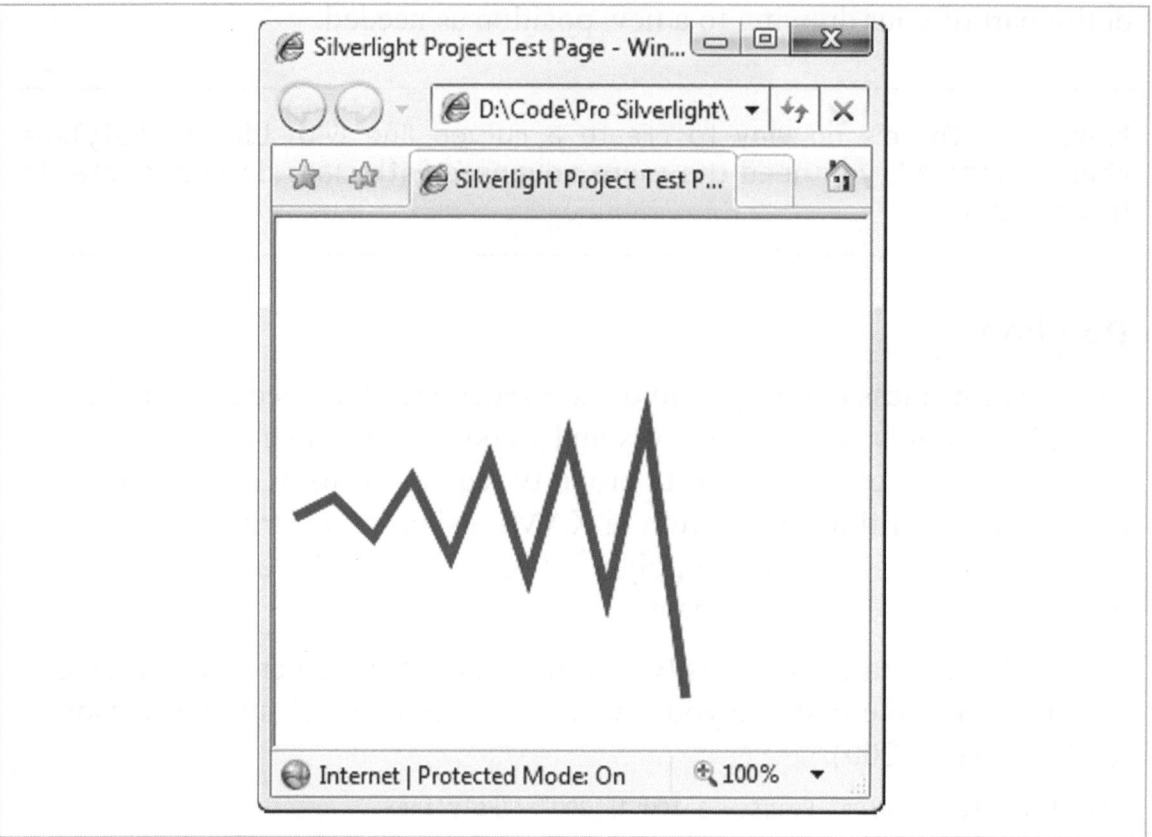

At this point, it might occur to you that it would be easier to fill the `Points` collection programmatically, using some sort of loop that automatically increments x and y values accordingly. This is true if you need to create highly dynamic graphics—for example, a chart that varies its appearance based on a set of data you extract from a database. But if you simply want to build a fixed piece of graphical content, you won't want to worry about the specific coordinates of your shapes at all. Instead, you (or a designer) will use another tool, such as Expression Design, to draw the appropriate graphics, and then export them to XAML.

Polygon

The Polygon is virtually the same as the Polyline. Like the Polyline class, the Polygon class has a Points collection that takes a list of coordinates. The only difference is that the Polygon adds a final line segment that connects the final point to the starting point. (If your final point is already the same as the first point, the Polygon class has no difference.) You can fill the interior of this shape using the Fill brush. Figure 6-7 shows the previous Polyline as a Polygon with a yellow fill.

Figure 6-7. A filled polygon

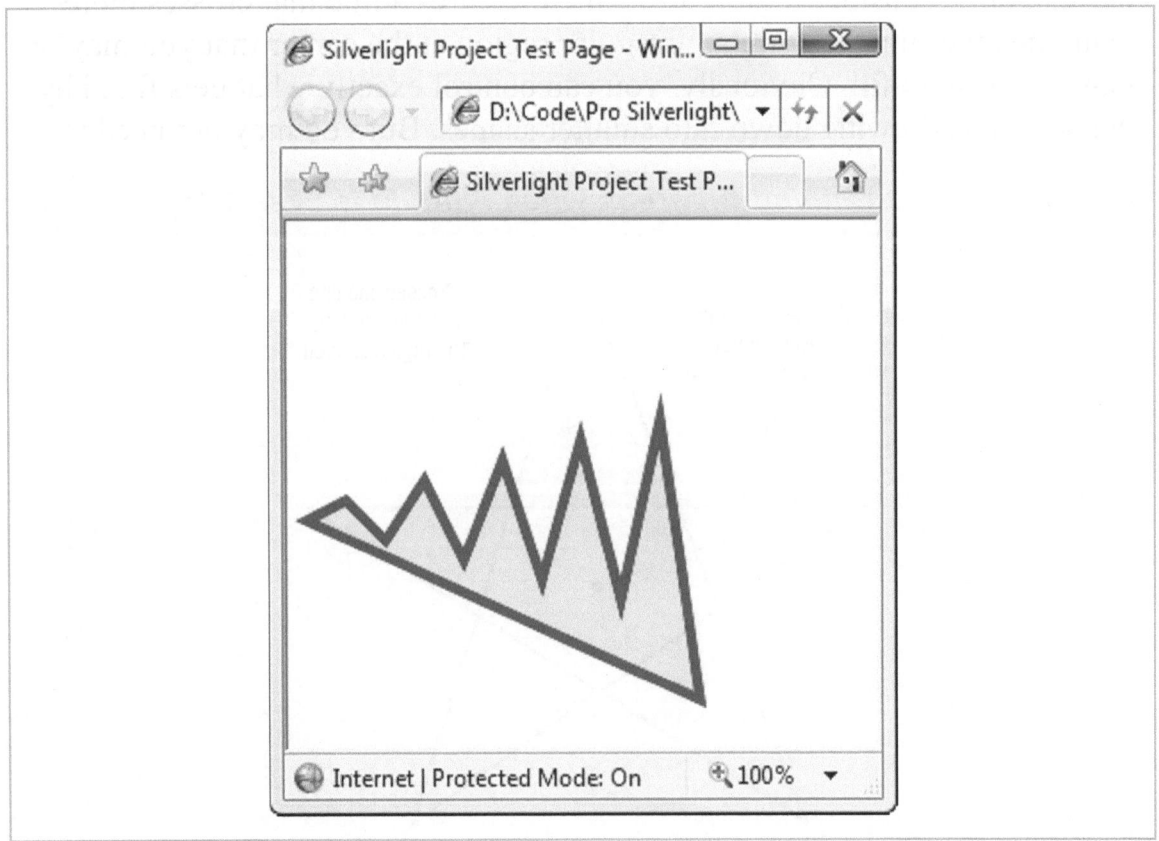

In a simple shape where the lines never cross, it's easy to fill the interior. However, sometimes you'll have a more complex `Polygon` where it's not necessarily obvious what portions are "inside" the shape (and should be filled) and what portions are outside.

For example, consider Figure 6-8, which features a line that crosses more than one other line, leaving an irregular region at the center that you may or may not want to fill. Obviously, you can control exactly what gets filled by breaking this drawing down into smaller shapes. But you may not need to.

Figure 6-8. Determining fill areas when FillRule is EvenOdd

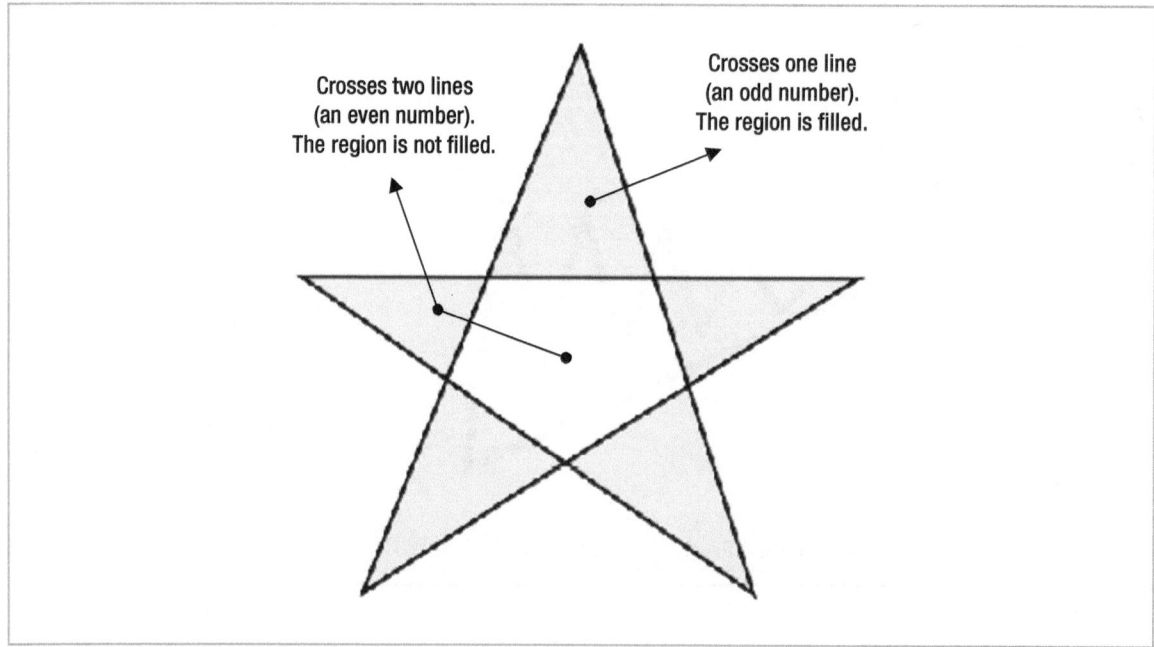

Every Polygon and Polyline includes a FillRule property that lets you choose between two different approaches for filling in regions. By default, FillRule is set to EvenOdd. In order to decide whether to fill a region, Silverlight counts the number of lines that must be crossed to reach the outside of the shape. If this number is odd, the region is filled in; if it's even, the region isn't filled. In the center area of Figure 6-9, you must cross two lines to get out of the shape, so it's not filled.

Silverlight also supports the Nonzero fill rule, which is a little trickier. Essentially, with Nonzero, Silverlight follows the same line-counting process as EvenOdd, but it takes into account the direction that each line flows. If the number of lines going in one direction (say, left to right) is equal to the number going in the opposite direction (right to left), the region is not filled. If the difference between these two counts is not zero, the region is filled. In the shape from the previous example, the interior region is filled if you set the FillRule to Nonzero. Figure 6-9 shows why. (In this example, the points are numbered in the order they are drawn, and arrows show the direction in which each line is drawn.)

Figure 6-9. Determining fill areas when FillRule is Nonzero

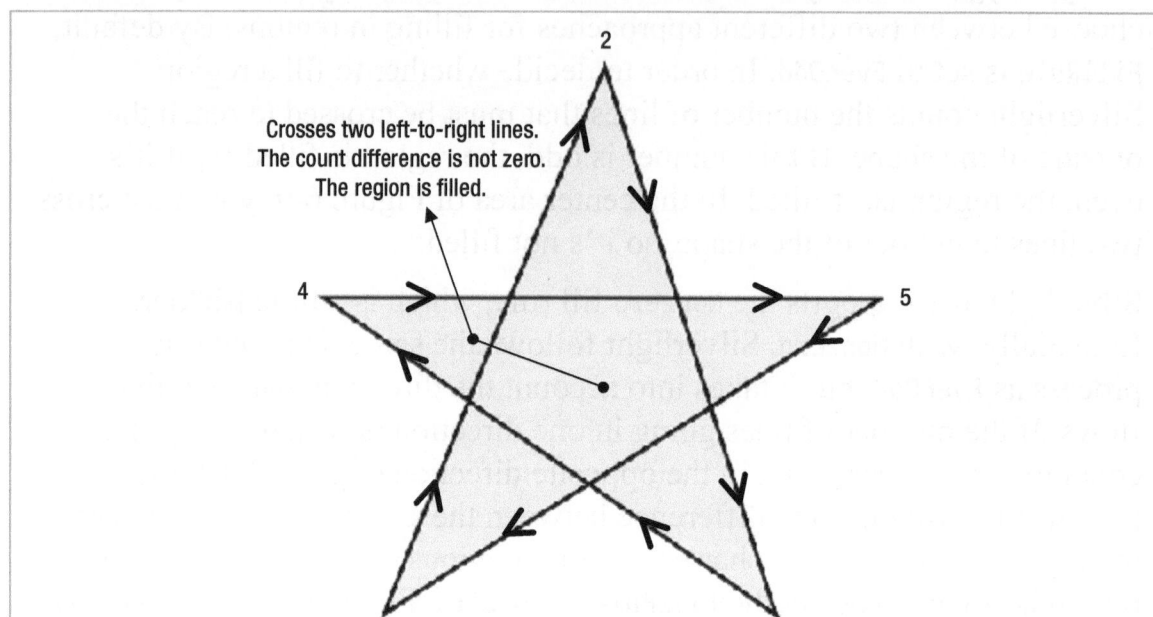

The tricky part about **Nonzero** is that its fill settings depend on *how* you draw the shape, not what the shape itself looks like. For example, you could draw the same shape in such a way that the center isn't filled (although it's much more awkward, you'd begin by drawing the inner region, and then draw the outside spikes in the reverse direction).

Here's the markup that draws the star shown in Figure 6-9:

```
<Polygon Stroke="Blue" StrokeThickness="1" Fill="Yellow"
 Canvas.Left="10" Canvas.Top="175" FillRule="Nonzero"
 Points="15,200 68,70 110,200 0,125 135,125">
</Polygon>
```

Line Caps and Line Joins

When drawing with the `Line` and `Polyline` shapes, you can choose how the starting and ending edge of the line is drawn using the `StartLineCap` and `EndLineCap` properties. (These properties have no effect on other shapes because they're closed.)

Ordinarily, both `StartLineCap` and `EndLineCap` are set to `Flat`, which means the line ends immediately at its final coordinate. Your other choices are `Round` (which rounds the corner off gently), `Triangle` (which draws the two sides of the line together in a point), and `Square` (which ends the line with a sharp edge). All of these values add length to the line—in other words, they take it beyond the position where it would otherwise end. The extra distance is half the thickness of the line.

Note   The only difference between `Flat` and `Square` is the fact that the `Square`-edged line extends this extra distance. In all other respects, the edge looks the same.

Figure 6-10 shows different line caps at the end of a line.

Figure 6-10. Line caps

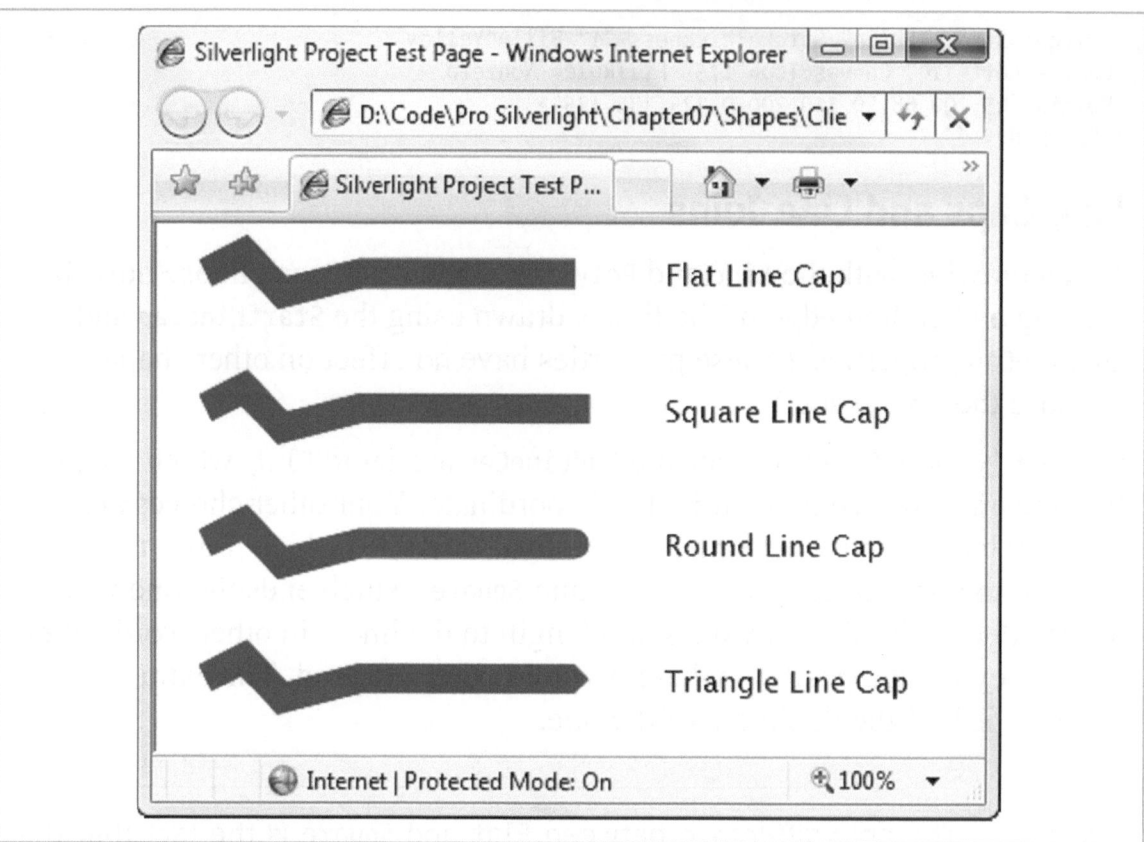

All shapes except Line allow you to tweak how their corners are shaped using the StrokeLineJoin property. You have three choices. The default value, Miter, uses sharp edges, while Bevel cuts off the point edge, and Round rounds it out gently. Figure 6-11 shows the difference.

Figure 6-11. Line joins

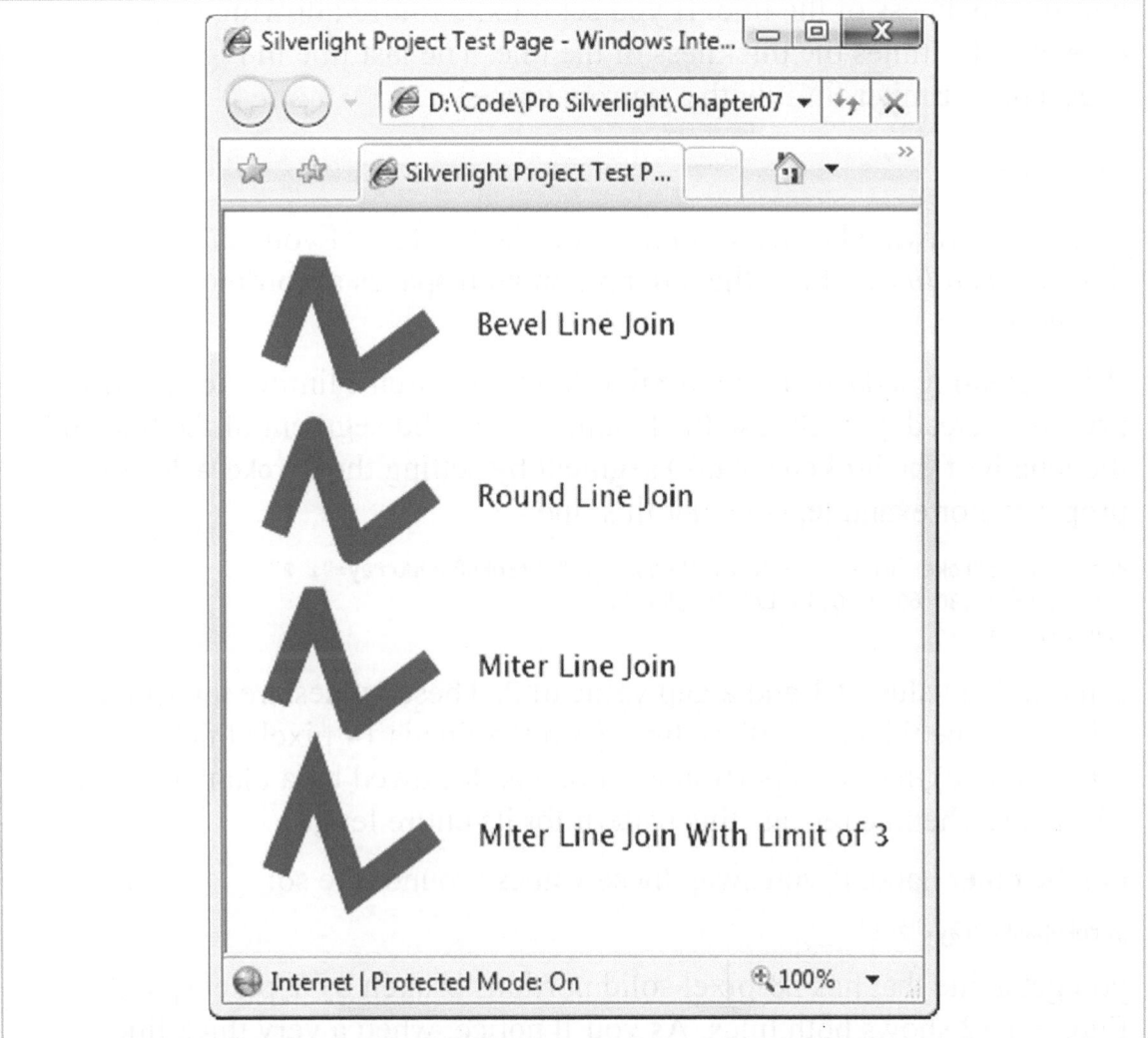

When using mitered edges with thick lines and very small angles, the sharp corner can extend an impractically long distance. In this case, you can use Bevel or Round to pare down the corner. Or you could use the StrokeMiterLimit, which automatically bevels the edge when it reaches a certain maximum length. The StrokeMiterLimit is a ratio that compares the length used to miter the corner to half the thickness of the line. If you set this to 1 (which is the default value), you're allowing the corner to extend half the thickness of the line. If you set it to 3, you're allowing the corner to extend to 1.5 times the thickness of the line. The last line in Figure 6-11 uses a higher miter limit with a narrow corner.

Dashes

Instead of drawing boring solid lines for the borders of your shape, you can draw *dashed lines*—lines that are broken with spaces according to a pattern you specify.

When creating a dashed line in Silverlight, you aren't limited to specific presets. Instead, you choose the length of the solid segment of the line and the length of the broken (blank) segment by setting the `StrokeDashArray` property. For example, consider this line:

```
<Polyline Stroke="Blue" StrokeThickness="14" StrokeDashArray="1 2"
  Points="10,30 60,0 90,40 120,10 350,10">
</Polyline>
```

It has a line value of 1 and a gap value of 2. These values are interpreted relative to the thickness of the line. So if the line is 14 pixels thick (as in this example), the solid portion is 14 pixels, followed by a blank portion of 28 pixels. The line repeats this pattern for its entire length.

On the other hand, if you swap these values around like so:

```
StrokeDashArray="2 1"
```

you get a line that has 28-pixel solid portions broken by 7-pixel spaces. Figure 6-12 shows both lines. As you'll notice, when a very thick line segment falls on a corner, it may be broken unevenly.

Figure 6-12. Dashed lines

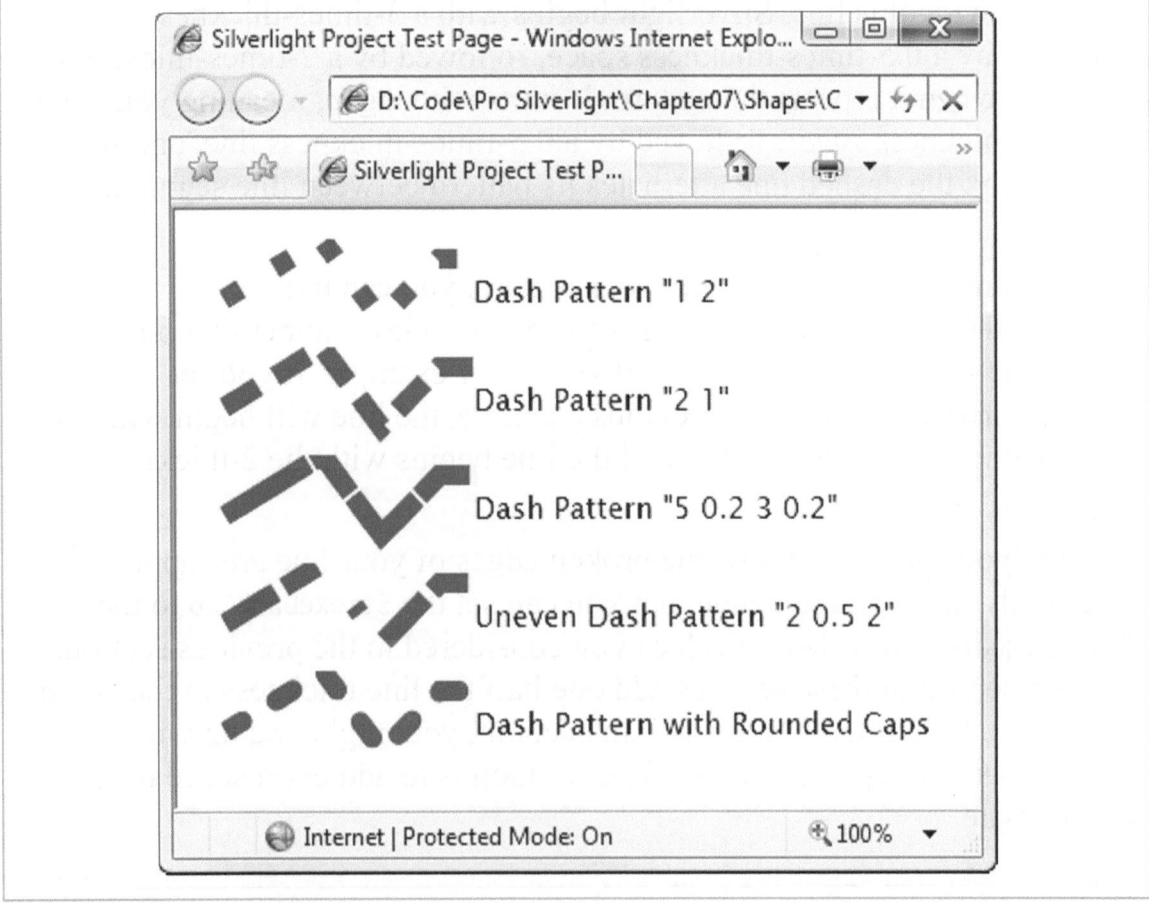

There's no reason that you need to stick with whole number values. For example, this **StrokeDashArray** is perfectly reasonable:

```
StrokeDashArray="5 0.2 3 0.2"
```

It supplies a more complex sequence—a dashed line that's 5×14 length, then a 0.2×15 break, followed by a 3×14 length and another 0.2×14 length. At the end of this sequence, the line repeats the pattern from the beginning.

An interesting thing happens if you supply an odd number of values for the **StrokeDashArray**. Take this one for example:

```
StrokeDashArray="3 0.5 2"
```

When drawing this line, Silverlight begins with a 3-times-thickness line, followed by a 0.5-times-thickness space, followed by a 2-times-thickness line. But when it repeats the pattern, it starts with a gap, meaning you get a 3-times-thickness *space*, followed by a 0.5-times-thickness line, and so on. Essentially, the dashed line alternates its pattern between line segments and spaces.

If you want to start midway into your pattern, you can use the StrokeDashOffset property, which is a 0-based index number that points to one of the values in your StrokeDashArray. For example, if you set StrokeDashOffset to 1 in the previous example, the line will begin with the 0.5-thickness space. Set it to 2, and the line begins with the 2-thickness segment.

Finally, you can control how the broken edges of your line are capped. Ordinarily, it's a straight edge, but you can set the StrokeDashCap to the Bevel, Square, and Triangle values you considered in the previous section. Remember, all of these settings add one half the line thickness to the end of your dash. If you don't take this into account, you might end up with dashes that overlap one another. The solution is to add extra space to compensate.

Tip   When using the StrokeDashCap property with a line (not a shape), it's often a good idea to set the StartLineCap and EndLineCap to the same values. This makes the line look consistent.

Paths and Geometries

Earlier in this chapter, you took a look at a number of classes that derive from Shape, including Rectangle, Ellipse, Polygon, and Polyline. However, there's one Shape-derived class that you haven't considered yet, and it's the most powerful by far. The Path class has the ability to encompass any simple shape, groups of shapes, and more complex ingredients such as curves.

The Path class includes a single property, named Data, that accepts a Geometry object that defines the shape (or shapes) the path includes. You can't create a Geometry object directly because it's an abstract class. Instead, you need to use one of the derived classes listed in Table 6-3.

Table 6-3. Geometry Classes

NAME	DESCRIPTION
LineGeometry	Represents a straight line. The geometry equivalent of the Line shape.
RectangleGeometry	Represents a rectangle (optionally with rounded corners). The geometry equivalent of the Rectangle shape.
EllipseGeometry	Represents an ellipse. The geometry equivalent of the Ellipse shape.
GeometryGroup	Adds any number of Geometry objects to a single path, using the EvenOdd or Nonzero fill rule to determine what regions to fill.
PathGeometry	Represents a more complex figure that's composed of arcs, curves, and lines, and can be open or closed.

Note   Silverlight does not include all the geometry classes that WPF supports. Notably absent is the `CombinedGeometry` class, which allows to geometries to be fused together (although the effect can be duplicated with the more powerful `PathGeometry` class). Also missing is `StreamGeometry`, which provides a lightweight read-only equivalent to `PathGeometry`.

At this point, you might be wondering what the difference is between a path and a geometry. The geometry *defines* a shape. A path allows you to *draw* the shape. Thus, the `Geometry` object defines details such as the coordinates and size of your shape, while the `Path` object supplies the `Stroke` and `Fill` brushes you'll use to paint it. The `Path` class also includes the features it inherits from the `UIElement` infrastructure, such as mouse and keyboard handling.

In the following sections, you'll explore all the classes that derive from `Geometry`.

Line, Rectangle, and Ellipse Geometries

The `LineGeometry`, `RectangleGeometry`, and `EllipseGeometry` classes map directly to the `Line`, `Rectangle`, and `Ellipse` shapes that you learned about in the first half of this chapter. For example, you can convert this markup that uses the `Rectangle` element:

```
<Rectangle Fill="Yellow" Stroke="Blue"
  Width="100" Height="50" ></Rectangle>
```

to this markup that uses the `Path` element:

```
<Path Fill="Yellow" Stroke="Blue">
  <Path.Data>
    <RectangleGeometry Rect="0,0 100,50"></RectangleGeometry>
  </Path.Data>
</Path>
```

The only real difference is that the `Rectangle` shape takes `Height` and `Width` values, while the `RectangleGeometry` takes four numbers that describe the size *and* location of the rectangle. The first two numbers describe the x and y coordinates where the top-left corner will be placed, while the last two numbers set the width and height of the rectangle. You can start the rectangle out at (0, 0) to get the same effect as an ordinary `Rectangle` element, or you can offset the rectangle using different values. The `RectangleGeometry` class also includes the `RadiusX` and `RadiusY` properties that let you round the corners (as described earlier).

Similarly, you can convert the following `Line`:

```
<Line Stroke="Blue" X1="0" Y1="0" X2="10" Y2="100"></Line>
```

to this `LineGeometry`:

```
<Path Fill="Yellow" Stroke="Blue">
  <Path.Data>
    <LineGeometry StartPoint="0,0" EndPoint="10,100"></LineGeometry>
  </Path.Data>
</Path>
```

and you can convert an `Ellipse` like this:

```
<Ellipse Fill="Yellow" Stroke="Blue"
  Width="100" Height="50" HorizontalAlignment="Left"></Ellipse>
```

to this `EllipseGeometry`:

```
<Path Fill="Yellow" Stroke="Blue">
  <Path.Data>
    <EllipseGeometry RadiusX="50" RadiusY="25" Center="50,25"></EllipseGeometry>
  </Path.Data>
</Path>
```

Notice that the two radius values are simply half of the width and height values. You can also use the `Center` property to offset the location of the ellipse. In this example, the center is placed in the exact middle of the ellipse bounding box, so that it's drawn in exactly the same way as the `Ellipse` shape.

Overall, these simple geometries work in exactly the same way as the corresponding shapes. You get the added ability to offset rectangles and ellipses, but that's not necessary if you're placing your shapes on a Canvas, which already gives you the ability to position your shapes at a specific location. In fact, if this were all you could do with geometries, you probably wouldn't bother to use the Path element. The difference appears when you decide to group more than one geometry in the same path and when you step up to more complex curves, as described in the following sections.

Combining Shapes with GeometryGroup

The simplest way to combine geometries is to use the GeometryGroup and nest the other Geometry-derived objects inside. Here's an example that places an ellipse next to a square:

```
<Path Fill="Yellow" Stroke="Blue" Margin="5" Canvas.Top="10" Canvas.Left="10" >
  <Path.Data>
    <GeometryGroup>
      <RectangleGeometry Rect="0,0 100,100"></RectangleGeometry>
      <EllipseGeometry Center="150,50" RadiusX="35" RadiusY="25"></EllipseGeometry>
    </GeometryGroup>
  </Path.Data>
</Path>
```

The effect of this markup is the same as if you supplied two Path elements, one with the RectangleGeometry and one with the EllipseGeometry (and that's the same as if you used a Rectangle and Ellipse shape instead). However, there's one advantage to this approach. You've replaced two elements with one, which means you've reduced the overhead of your user interface. In general, a page that uses a smaller number of elements with more complex geometries will perform faster than a page that has a large number of elements with simpler geometries. This effect won't be apparent in a page that has just a few dozen shapes, but it may become significant in one that requires hundreds or thousands.

Of course, there's also a drawback to combining geometries in a single Path element—namely, you won't be able to perform event handling of the different shapes separately. Instead, the Path element will fire all mouse events. However, you can still manipulate the nested RectangleGeometry and EllipseGeometry objects independently to change the overall path. For example, each geometry provides a Transform property that you can set to stretch, skew, or rotate that part of the path.

Another advantage of geometries is that you can reuse the same geometry in several separate Path elements. No code is necessary—you simply need to define the geometry in a Resources collection and refer to it in your path with the StaticExtension markup extensions. Here's an example that rewrites the markup shown previously to show instances of the CombinedGeometry, at two different locations on a Canvas and with two different fill colors:

```
<UserControl.Resources>
  <GeometryGroup x:Key="Geometry">
    <RectangleGeometry Rect="0 ,0 100 ,100"></RectangleGeometry>
    <EllipseGeometry Center="150, 50" RadiusX="35" RadiusY="25"></EllipseGeometry>
  </GeometryGroup>
</UserControl.Resources>

<Canvas>
  <Path Fill="Yellow" Stroke="Blue" Margin="5" Canvas.Top="10" Canvas.Left="10"
   Data="{StaticResource Geometry}">
  </Path>
  <Path Fill="Green" Stroke="Blue" Margin="5" Canvas.Top="150" Canvas.Left="10"
   Data="{StaticResource Geometry}">
  </Path>
</Canvas>
```

The GeometryGroup becomes more interesting when your shapes intersect. Rather than simply treating your drawing as a combination of solid shapes, the GeometryGroup uses its FillRule property (which can be EvenOdd or Nonzero, as described earlier) to decide what shapes to fill. Consider what happens if you alter the markup shown earlier like this, placing the ellipse over the square:

```
<Path Fill="Yellow" Stroke="Blue" Margin="5" Canvas.Top="10" Canvas.Left="10" >
  <Path.Data>
    <GeometryGroup>
      <RectangleGeometry Rect="0,0 100,100"></RectangleGeometry>
      <EllipseGeometry Center="50,50" RadiusX="35" RadiusY="25"></EllipseGeometry>
    </GeometryGroup>
  </Path.Data>
</Path>
```

Now this markup creates a square with an ellipse-shaped hole in it. If you change FillRule to Nonzero, you'll get a solid ellipse over a solid rectangle, both with the same yellow fill.

You could create the square-with-a-hole effect by simply superimposing a white-filled ellipse over your square. However, the GeometryGroup class becomes more useful if you have content underneath, which is typical in a complex drawing. Because the ellipse is treated as a hole in your shape (not another shape with a different fill), any content underneath shows through. For example, if you add this line of text:

```
<TextBlock Canvas.Top="50" Canvas.Left="20" FontSize="25" FontWeight="Bold">
  Hello There</TextBlock>
```

Curves and Lines with PathGeometry

PathGeometry is the superpower of geometries. It can draw anything that the other geometries can, and much more. The only drawback is a lengthier (and somewhat more complex) syntax.

Every PathGeometry object is built out of one or more PathFigure objects (which are stored in the PathGeometry.Figures collection). Each PathFigure is a continuous set of connected lines and curves that can be closed or open. The figure is closed if the end of the last line in the figure connects to the beginning of the first line.

The PathFigure class has four key properties, as described in Table 6-4.

Table 6-4. PathFigure Properties

NAME	DESCRIPTION
StartPoint	This is a Point that indicates where the line for the figure begins.
Segments	This is a collection of PathSegment objects that are used to draw the figure.
IsClosed	If true, Silverlight adds a straight line to connect the starting and ending points (if they aren't the same).
IsFilled	If true, the area inside the figure is filled in using the Path.Fill brush.

So far, this all sounds fairly straightforward. The PathFigure is a shape that's drawn using an unbroken line that consists of a number of segments. However, the trick is that there are several type of segments, all of which derive from the PathSegment class. Some are simple, like the LineSegment, which draws a straight line. Others, like the BezierSegment, draw curves and are correspondingly more complex.

You can mix and match different segments freely to build your figure. Table 6-5 lists the segment classes you can use.

Table 6-5. PathSegment Classes

NAME	DESCRIPTION
LineSegment	Creates a straight line between two points.
ArcSegment	Creates an elliptical arc between two points.
BezierSegment	Creates a Bézier curve between two points.
QuadraticBezierSegment	Creates a simpler form of Bézier curve that has one control point instead of two, and is faster to calculate.

Table 6-5. continued

NAME	DESCRIPTION
PolyLineSegment	Creates a series of straight lines. You can get the same effect using multiple LineSegment objects, but a single PolyLineSegment is more concise.
PolyBezierSegment	Creates a series of Bézier curves.
PolyQuadraticBezierSegment	Creates a series of simpler quadratic Bézier curves.

Straight Lines

It's easy enough to create simple lines using the LineSegment and PathGeometry classes. You simply set the StartPoint and add one LineSegment for each section of the line. The LineSegment.Point property identifies the end point of each segment.

For example, the following markup begins at (10, 100), draws a straight line to (100, 100), and then draws a line from that point to (100, 50). Because the PathFigure.IsClosed property is set to true, a final line segment connects (100, 50) to (0, 0). The final result is a right-angled triangle.

```
<Path Stroke="Blue">
  <Path.Data>
    <PathGeometry>
      <PathFigure IsClosed="True" StartPoint="10,100">
        <LineSegment Point="100,100" />
        <LineSegment Point="100,50" />
      </PathFigure>
    </PathGeometry>
  </Path.Data>
</Path>
```

Arcs

Arcs are a little more interesting than straight lines. You identify the end point of the line using the `ArcSegment.Point` property, just as you would with a `LineSegment`. However, the `PathFigure` draws a curved line from the starting point (or the end point of the previous segment) to the end point of your arc. This curved connecting line is actually a portion of the edge of an ellipse.

Obviously, the end point isn't enough information to draw the arc because there are many curves (some gentle, some more extreme) that could connect two points. You also need to indicate the size of the imaginary ellipse that's being used to draw the arc. You do this using the `ArcSegment.Size` property, which supplies the x radius and the y radius of the ellipse. The larger the ellipse size of the imaginary ellipse, the more gradually its edge curves.

Note   For any two points, there is a practical maximum and minimum size for the ellipse. The maximum occurs when you create an ellipse so large the line segment you're drawing appears straight. Increasing the size beyond this point has no effect. The minimum occurs when the ellipse is small enough that a full semicircle connects the two points. Shrinking the size beyond this point also has no effect.

Here's an example that creates the gentle arc shown in Figure 6-13:

```
<Path Stroke="Blue" StrokeThickness="3">
  <Path.Data>
    <PathGeometry>
      <PathFigure IsClosed="False" StartPoint="10,100" >
        <ArcSegment Point="250,150" Size="200,300" />
      </PathFigure>
    </PathGeometry>
  </Path.Data>
</Path>
```

Figure 6-13. A simple arc

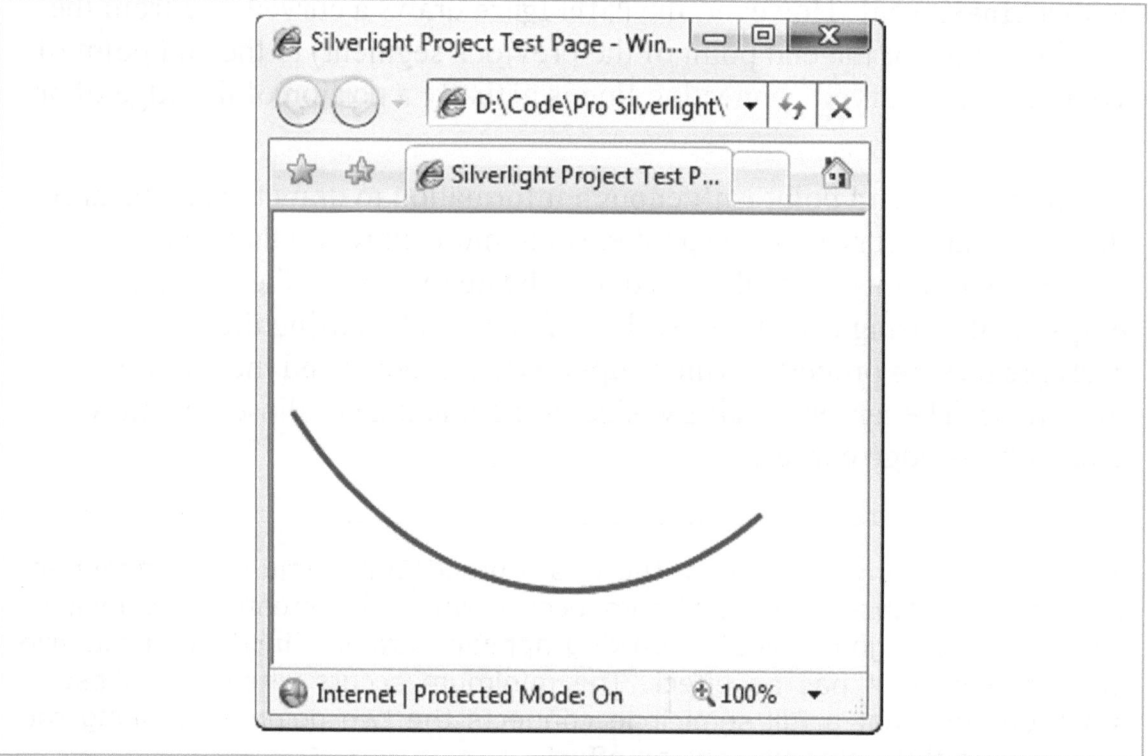

So far, arcs sound fairly straightforward. However, it turns out that even with the start and end point and the size of the ellipse, you still don't have all the information you need to draw your arc unambiguously. In the previous example, you're relying on two default values that may not be set to your liking.

To understand the problem, you need to consider the other ways that an arc can connect the same two points. If you picture two points on an ellipse, it's clear that you can connect them in two ways—by going around the short side or by going around the long side. Figure 6-14 illustrates.

Figure 6-14. Two ways to trace a curve along an ellipse

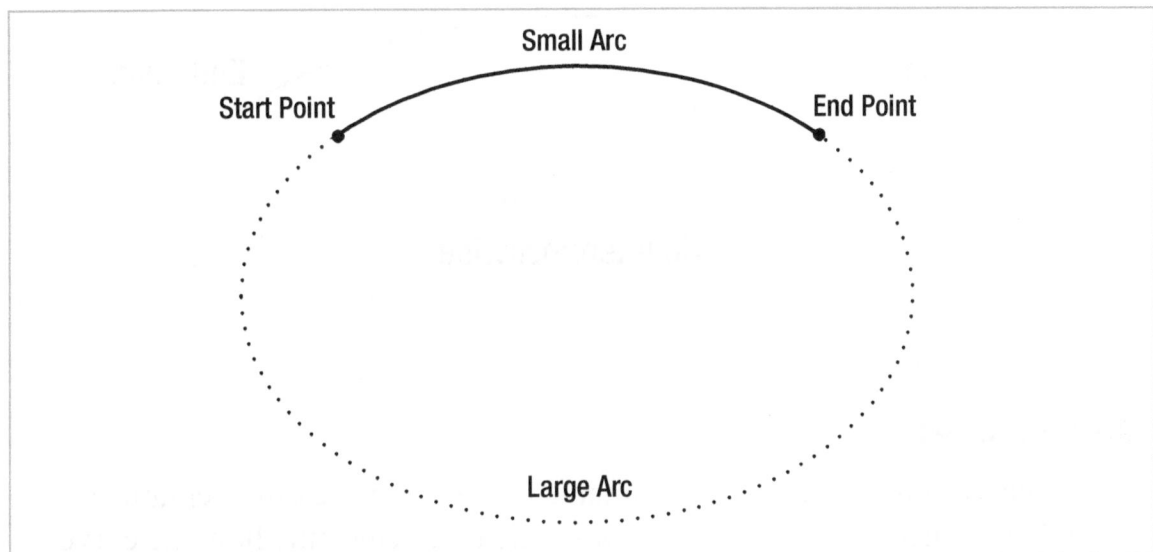

You set the direction using the `ArcSegment.IsLargeArc` property, which can be true or false. The default value is false, which means you get the shorter of the two arcs.

Even once you've set the direction, there is still one point of ambiguity— where the ellipse is placed. For example, imagine you draw an arc that connects a point on the left with a point on the right, using the shortest possible arc. The curve that connects these two points could be stretched down and then up (as it does in Figure 6-13), or it could be flipped so that it curves up and then down. The arc you get depends on the order in which you define the two points in the arc and the `ArcSegment.SweepDirection` property, which can be `Counterclockwise` (the default) or `Clockwise`. Figure 6-15 shows the difference.

Figure 6-15. Two ways to flip a curve

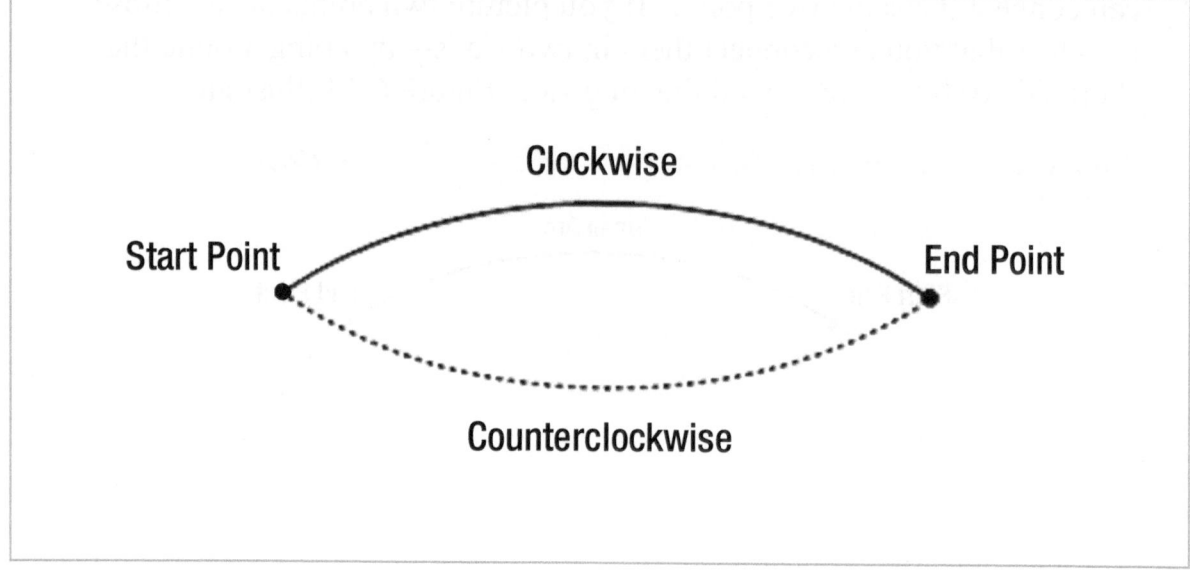

Bézier Curves

Bézier curves connect two line segments using a complex mathematical formula that incorporates two *control points* that determine how the curve is shaped. Bézier curves are an ingredient in virtually every vector drawing application ever created because they're remarkably flexible. Using nothing more than start point, end point, and two control points, you can create a surprisingly wide variety of smooth curves (including loops). Figure 6-16 shows a classic Bézier curve. Two small circles indicate the control points, and a dashed line connects each control point to the end of the line it affects the most.

Figure 6-16. A Bézier curve

Even without understanding the math underpinnings, it's fairly easy to get the "feel" of how Bézier curves work. Essentially, the two control points do all the magic. They influence the curve in two ways:

- At the starting point, a Bézier curve runs parallel with the line that connects it to the first control point. At the ending point, the curve runs parallel with the line that connects it to the end point. (In between, it curves.)

- The degree of curvature is determined by the distance to the two control points. If one control point is farther away, it exerts a stronger "pull."

To define a Bézier curve in markup, you supply three points. The first two points (**BezierSegment.Point1** and **BezierSegment.Point2**) are the control points. The third point (**BezierSegment.Point3**) is the end point of the curve.

As always, the starting point is that starting point of the path or wherever the previous segment leaves off.

The example shown in Figure 6-16 includes three separate components, each of which uses a different stroke and thus requires a separate Path element. The first path creates the curve, the second adds the dashed lines, and the third applies the circles that indicate the control points. Here's the complete markup:

```
<Canvas>
  <Path Stroke="Blue" StrokeThickness="5" Canvas.Top="20">
    <Path.Data>
      <PathGeometry>
        <PathFigure StartPoint="10,10">
          <BezierSegment Point1="130,30" Point2="40,140"
          Point3="150,150"></BezierSegment>
        </PathFigure>
      </PathGeometry>
    </Path.Data>
  </Path>
  <Path Stroke="Green" StrokeThickness="2" StrokeDashArray="5 2" Canvas.Top="20">
    <Path.Data>
      <GeometryGroup>
        <LineGeometry StartPoint="10,10" EndPoint="130,30"></LineGeometry>
        <LineGeometry StartPoint="40,140" EndPoint="150,150"></LineGeometry>
      </GeometryGroup>
    </Path.Data>
  </Path>
  <Path Fill="Red" Stroke="Red" StrokeThickness="8"  Canvas.Top="20">
    <Path.Data>
      <GeometryGroup>
        <EllipseGeometry Center="130,30"></EllipseGeometry>
        <EllipseGeometry Center="40,140"></EllipseGeometry>
      </GeometryGroup>
    </Path.Data>
  </Path>
</Canvas>
```

Trying to code Bézier paths is a recipe for many thankless hours of trial-and-error computer coding. You're much more likely to draw your curves (and many other graphical elements) in a dedicated drawing program that has an export-to-XAML feature or Microsoft Expression Blend.

Tip   To learn more about the algorithm that underlies the Bézier curve, you can read an informative Wikipedia article on the subject at http://en.wikipedia.org/wiki/Bezier_curve.

The Geometry Mini-Language

The geometries you've seen so far have been relatively concise, with only a few points. More complex geometries are conceptually the same but can easily require hundreds of segments. Defining each line, arc, and curve in a complex path is extremely verbose and unnecessary—after all, it's likely that complex paths will be generated by a design tool rather than written by hand, so the clarity of the markup isn't all that important. With this in mind, the creators of Silverlight added a more concise alternate syntax for defining geometries that allows you to represent detailed figures with much smaller amounts of markup. This syntax is often described as the *geometry mini-language* (and sometimes the *path mini-language* due to its application with the Path element).

To understand the mini-language, you need to realize that it is essentially a long string holding a series of commands. These commands are read by a type converter that then creates the corresponding geometry. Each command is a single letter and is optionally followed by a few bits of numeric information (such as x and y coordinates) separated by spaces. Each command is also separated from the previous command with a space.

For example, a bit earlier you created a basic triangle using a closed path with two line segments. Here's the markup that did the trick:

```
<Path Stroke="Blue">
  <Path.Data>
    <PathGeometry>
      <PathFigure IsClosed="True" StartPoint="10,100">
        <LineSegment Point="100,100" />
        <LineSegment Point="100,50" />
      </PathFigure>
    </PathGeometry>
  </Path.Data>
</Path>
```

To duplicate this figure using the mini-language, you'd write this:

```
<Path Stroke="Blue" Data="M 10,100 L 100,100 L 100,50 Z"/>
```

This path uses a sequence of four commands. The first command (M) creates the PathFigure and sets the starting point to (10, 100). The following two commands (L) create line segments. The final command (Z) ends the PathFigure and sets the IsClosed property to true. The commas in this string are optional, as are the spaces between the command and its parameters, but you must leave at least one space between adjacent parameters and commands. That means you can reduce the syntax even further to this less-readable form:

```
<Path Stroke="Blue" Data="M10 100 L100 100 L100 50 Z"/>
```

The geometry mini-language is easy to grasp. It uses a fairly small set of commands, which are detailed in Table 6-6. Parameters are shown in italics.

Table 6-6. Commands for the Geometry Mini-Language

COMMAND	DESCRIPTION
F value	Sets the Geometry.FillRule property. Use 0 for EvenOdd or 1 for Nonzero. This command must appear at the beginning of the string (if you decide to use it).
M x,y	Creates a new PathFigure for the geometry and sets its start point. This command must be used before any other commands except F. However, you can also use it during your drawing sequence to move the origin of your coordinate system. (The M stands for move.)
L x,y	Creates a LineSegment to the specified point.
H x	Creates a horizontal LineSegment using the specified x value and keeping the y value constant.
V y	Creates a vertical LineSegment using the specified y value and keeping the x value constant.
A radiusX, radiusY degrees isLargeArc, isClockwise x,y	Creates an ArcSegment to the indicated point. You specify the radii of the ellipse that describes the arc, the number of degrees the arc is rotated, and Boolean flags that set the IsLargeArc and SweepDirection properties described earlier.
C x1,y1 x2,y2 x,y	Creates a BezierSegment to the indicated point, using control points at (x1, y1) and (x2, y2).

Table 6-6. continued

COMMAND	DESCRIPTION
Q x1, y1 x,y	Creates a QuadraticBezierSegment to the indicated point, with one control point at (x1, y1).
S x2,y2 x,y	Creates a smooth BezierSegment by using the second control point from the previous BezierSegment as the first control point in the new BezierSegment.
Z	Ends the current PathFigure and sets IsClosed to true. You don't need to use this command if you don't want to set IsClosed to true —instead, simply use M if you want to start a new PathFigure or end the string.

Tip   There's one more trick in the geometry mini-language: you can use a command in lowercase if you want its parameters to be evaluated relative to the previous point rather than using absolute coordinates.

Clipping with Geometry

As you've seen, geometries are the most powerful way to create a shape. However, geometries aren't limited to the Path element. They're also used anywhere you need to supply the abstract definition of a shape (rather than draw a real, concrete shape in a page).

Another place geometries are used is to set the Clip property, which is provided by all elements. The Clip property allows you to constrain the outer bounds of an element to fit a specific geometry. You can use the Clip property to create a number of exotic effects. Although it's commonly used to trim down image content in an `Image` element, you can use the `Clip` property with any element. The only limitation is that you'll need a closed geometry if you actually want to see anything—individual curves and line segments aren't of much use.

Exporting Clip Art

In most cases, you won't create Silverlight art by hand. Instead, you (or a designer) will use a design tool to create vector art, and then export it to XAML. The exported XAML document you'll end up with is essentially a `Canvas` that contains a combination of shape elements. You can place that `Canvas` inside an existing `Canvas` to show your artwork.

Although many drawing programs don't have built-in support for XAML export, there are still many options for getting the graphics you need. The following sections outline the options you can use to get vector art out of virtually any application.

Expression Design

Expression Design, Microsoft's illustration and graphic design program, has a built-in XAML export. It can import a variety of vector art file formats, including Adobe Illustrator (`.ai`) files, and it can export to XAML.

When exporting to XAML, follow these steps:

1. Choose File ➤ Export from the menu.
2. In the Save As Type list of the Export dialog box, choose XAML. Then, enter a file name and click Save. The Export XAML window will appear (see Figure 6-17), which shows you the image you are exporting and a preview of the XAML content it will create (click the XAML tab to see it).

Figure 6-17. Creating a Silverlight-compatible XAML file

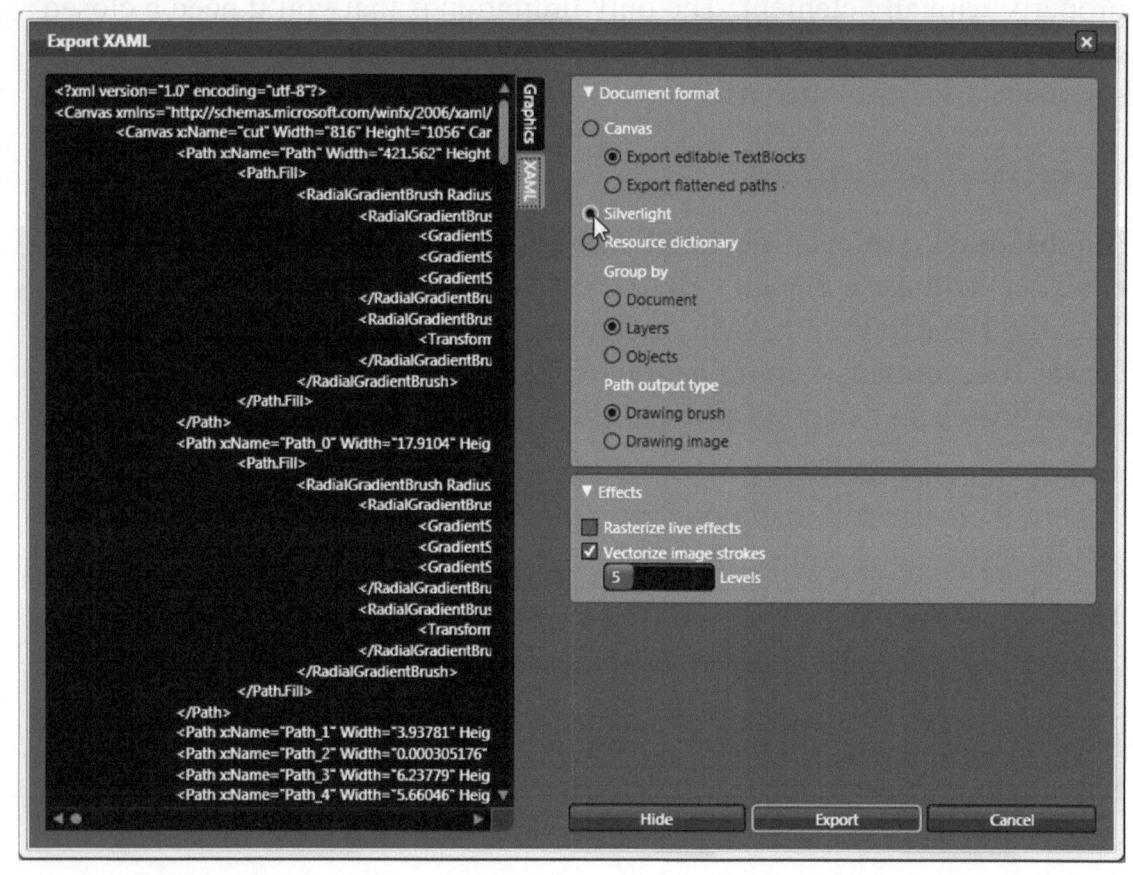

3. In the Document format group of settings, click Silverlight to ensure you're creating a Silverlight-compatible XAML file. This ensures that XAML features that are supported in WPF but not in Silverlight won't be used.

4. Click Export to save the file.

Note   Usually, the standard XAML export option (`Canvas`) will work with Silverlight applications, with minimal changes, such as manually removing a few unsupported attributes. However, the Resource Dictionary export option will create XAML files that won't work with Silverlight. That's because this option stores the graphic in a collection of `DrawingBrush` resources instead of a `Canvas`. This makes it easier to efficiently reuse the drawing in WPF, but it's useless in Silverlight, because Silverlight doesn't include the `Drawing` or `DrawingBrush` classes.

The generated XAML file includes a root-level `Canvas` element. Inside the `Canvas`, you'll find dozens of `Path` elements, each positioned at a specific place in the `Canvas`, and with its own data and brushes. You can cut and paste this entire block of markup into any Silverlight page to reproduce the graphic. However, it's more common for an application to have a variety of graphical resources, and it's often inconvenient to embed them all into your markup. A better idea is to store each drawing as an application resource in the root `App.xaml` file, and then draw on these resources to build your interface.

Conversion

Microsoft Expression Design is one example of a design tool that supports XAML natively. However, plug-ins and conversion tools are available for many other popular formats. Mike Swanson, a Microsoft evangelist, maintains a page at `http://blogs.msdn.com/mswanson/articles/WPFToolsAndControls.aspx` with links to many free converters, including

- An Adobe Illustrator (`.ai`) to XAML converter
- A Flash (`.swf`) to XAML converter
- A Visio plug-in for exporting XAML

You can also find more non-free XAML conversion tools on the Web. These tools won't necessarily create XAML content that is completely compatible with Silverlight. However, in most cases it will take only minor edits to fix markup errors.

Save or Print to XPS

The XML Paper Specification (XPS) is a Microsoft standard for creating fixed, print-ready documents. It's similar to the Adobe PDF standard, and support is included in Office 2007 and Windows Vista. However, the XPS standard is based on XAML, which makes it possible to transfer content from an XPS document to a Silverlight page. If you're using Windows Vista, this gives you a backdoor to get graphic output from virtually any application.

For example, Figure 6-18 shows a document in Word 2007 after performing a clip-art search and dragging a vector image (a stack of money) onto the page. The easiest way to save this graphic as an XPS document is to use the free Save As PDF or XPS add-in that Microsoft provides at `http://tinyurl.com/y69y7g`. Then, you can save the document simply by choosing File ➤ Save As ➤ PDF or XPS. If you're using Windows Vista, you have another option that works with other non-Office programs. You can choose to print your document to the Microsoft XPS Document Writer print device.

Figure 6-18. Exporting pictures to XAML through XPS

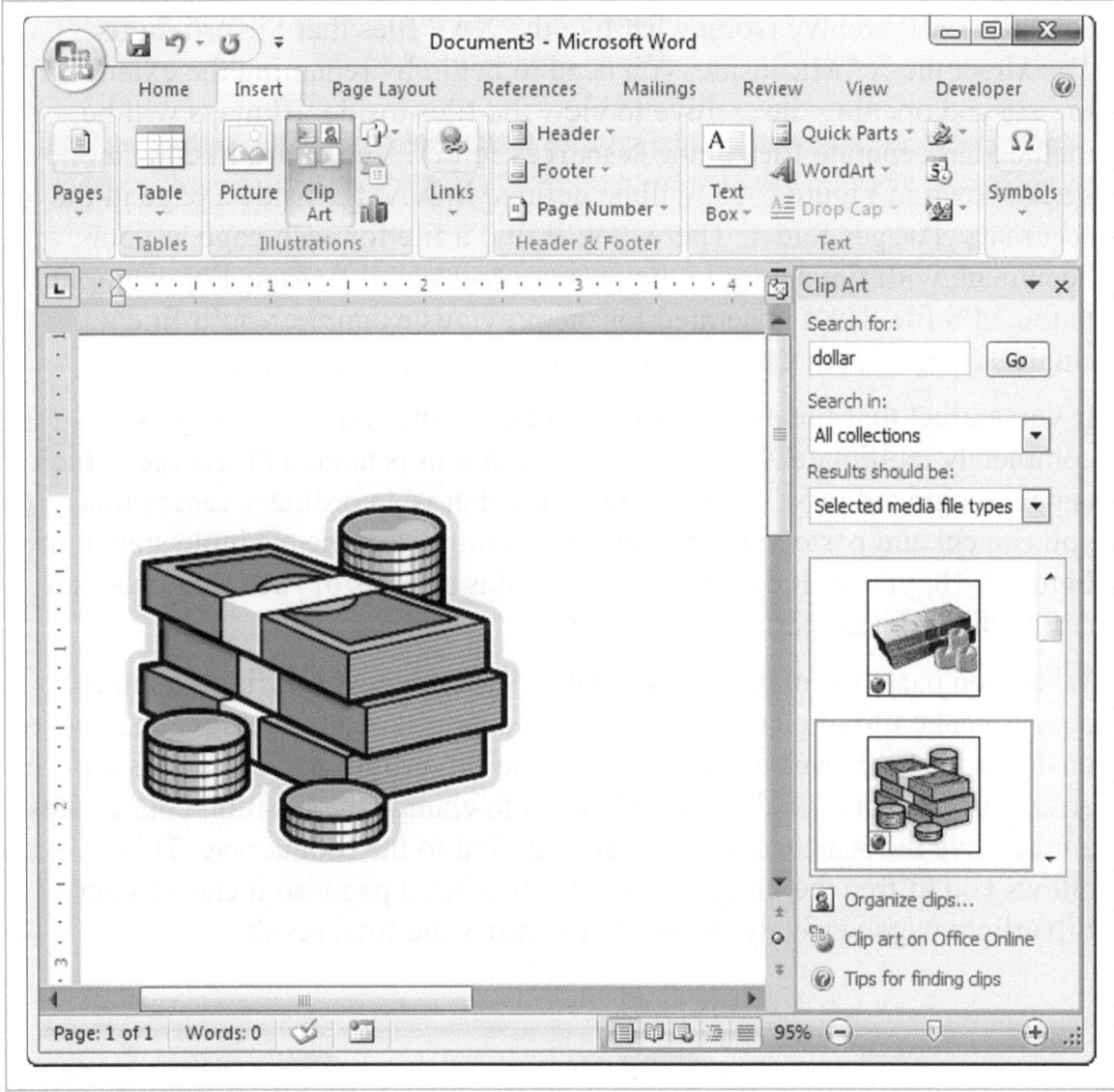

Either way, you'll end up with a file that has the extension `.xps`. This file is actually a ZIP archive (somewhat like the XAP files that Silverlight uses). To extract the XAML inside, you need to begin by renaming the extension to `.zip` and opening the archive to view the files inside. Bitmaps will be included as separate files in the `Resources` folder. Vector art, like the money stack shown in Figure 6-18, will be defined in XAML inside a page in the `Documents\1\Pages` folder. There, you'll find a file for each page in your document, with file names in the format `[PageNumber].fpage`. For example, in the XPS file that's generated for the previous example, you'll find a single `1.fpage` file that defines the page with the money graphic.

If you extract that file and open it in a text editor, you'll see that it's completely legitimate XAML. The root element is named `FixedPage`, which is not recognized in Silverlight, but inside that is an ordinary `Canvas` that you can cut and paste into a Silverlight window. For the example shown in Figure 6-18, you'll find that the `Canvas` holds a series of `Path` elements that define the different parts of the shape.

When you paste the markup into a Silverlight page, you'll find you may need to make minor changes. For example, you'll need to remove the unsupported `BidiLevel` attribute, which the Silverlight parser flags as an error. Furthermore, you'll probably want to change the position coordinates and remove the scale transform that's applied to the root `Canvas`. This allows you to free the image from the full printed page, so it can fit your Silverlight page perfectly. Figure 6-19 shows the final result.

Figure 6-19. Content from an XPS in Silverlight

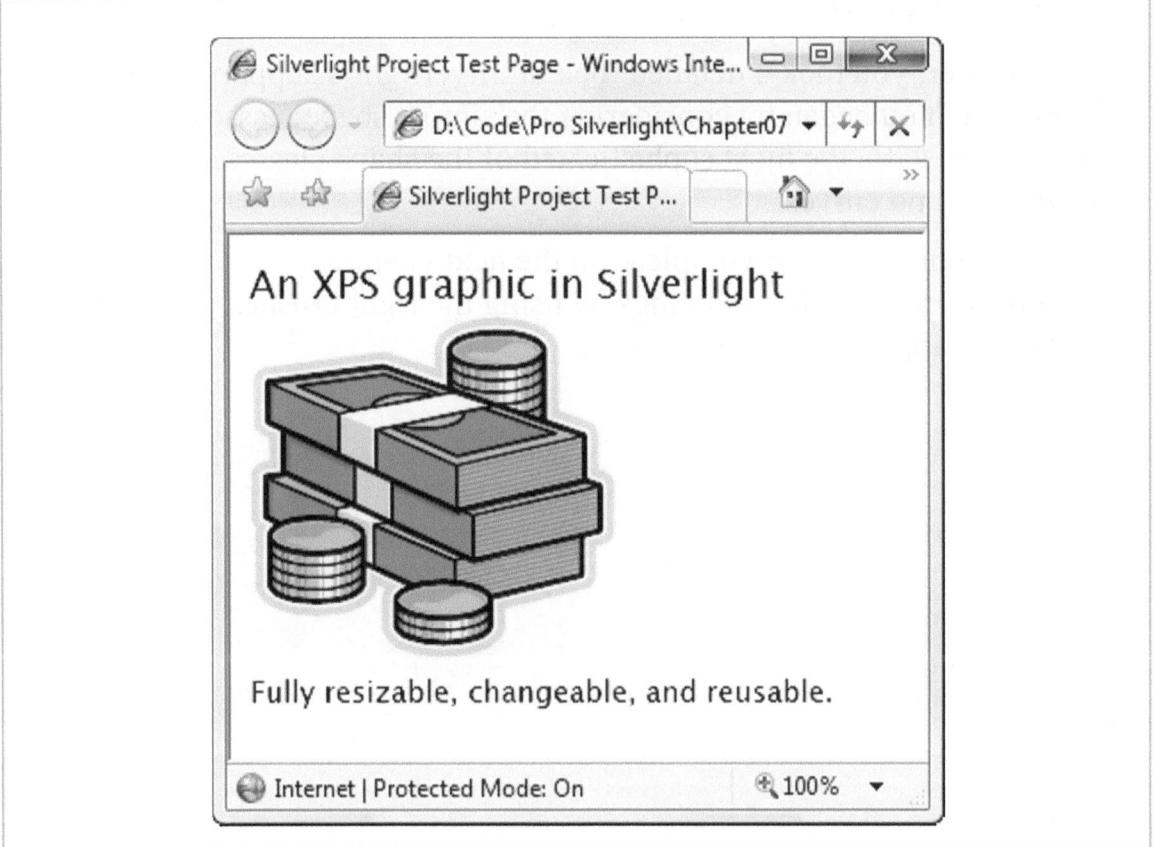

The Last Word

In this chapter, you took a detailed look at Silverlight's support for basic 2D drawing. You began by considering the simple shape classes and continued the `Path`, the most sophisticated of the shape classes, which lets you add arcs and curves.

However, your journey is complete. In the next chapter, you'll consider how you can create better drawings by using the right brushes, controlling opacity, and applying with transforms.

Chapter 7: Brushes and Transforms

In the previous chapter, you considered how you can use `Shape`-derived classes like the `Rectangle`, `Ellipse`, `Polygon`, `Polyline`, and `Path` to create a variety of different drawings into Silverlight's 2-D drawing model. However, shapes alone fall short of what you need to create detailed 2D vector art for a graphically rich application. There are more exotic Silverlight brushes that allow you to create gradients, tiled patterns, and bitmap fills in any shape. Silverlight's effortless support for transparency allows you to blend multiple images and elements together. *Transforms* are specialized objects that can change the visual appearance of any element by scaling, rotating, or skewing it. When you combine these features—for example, tossing together a dash of transparency with the warping effect of a transform—you can create popular effects, like reflections, glows, and shadows.

Brushes

As you know, brushes fill an area, whether it's the background, foreground, or border of an element, or the fill or stroke of a shape. For elements, you use brushes with the `Foreground`, `Background`, and `BorderBrush` properties. For shapes, you use the `Fill` and `Stroke` properties.

You've used brushes throughout this book, but so far you've done most of your work with the straightforward `SolidColorBrush`. Although `SolidColorBrush` is indisputably useful, several other classes that inherit from `System.Windows.Media.Brush` can give you more exotic effects. Table 7-1 lists them all.

Table 7-1. Brush Classes

NAME	DESCRIPTION
SolidColorBrush	Paints an area using a solid single-color fill.
LinearGradientBrush	Paints an area using a gradient fill, a gradually shaded fill that changes from one color to another (and, optionally, to another and then another, and so on).
RadialGradientBrush	Paints an area using a radial gradient fill, which is similar to a linear gradient except it radiates out in a circular pattern starting from a center point.
ImageBrush	Paints an area using an image that can be stretched, scaled, or tiled.
VideoBrush	Paints an area using a MediaElement (which gets its content from a video file). This allows you to play video in any shape or element.

Transparency

The shapes you've seen have been completely opaque. However, Silverlight supports true transparency. That means if you layer several elements on top of one another and give them all varying layers of transparency, you'll see exactly what you expect. At its simplest, this feature gives you the ability to create graphical backgrounds that "show through" the elements you place on top. At its most complex, this feature allows you to create multilayered animations and other effects.

There are several ways to make an element partly transparent:

- **Set the Opacity property**: Opacity is a fractional value from 0 to 1, where 1 is completely solid (the default) and 0 is completely transparent. The `Opacity` property is defined in the `UIElement` class, so it applies to all elements.

- **Use a semitransparent color**: Any color that has an alpha value less than 255 is semitransparent. You can use a semitransparent color when setting the foreground, background, or border of an element.

- **Set the OpacityMask property**: This allows you to make specific regions of an element transparent or partially transparent. For example, you can use it to fade a shape gradually into transparency.

Making the Silverlight Control Transparent

So far, you've seen how to make different elements in a Silverlight region transparent. But there's one more transparency trick you can use—making the background of the Silverlight content region completely transparent. The most common reason to use this technique is because you want nonrectangular Silverlight content to blend in seamlessly with the web page background underneath. However, you might also give the Silverlight control a transparent background in order to put HTML elements and Silverlight elements side by side, which is particularly useful if these elements interact.

Transforms

A great deal of drawing tasks can be made simpler with the use of a *transform*—an object that alters the way a shape or element is drawn by secretly shifting the coordinate system it uses. In Silverlight, transforms are represented by classes that derive from the abstract `System.Windows.Media.Transform` class, as listed in Table 7-3.

Table 7-3. Transform Classes

NAME	DESCRIPTION	IMPORTANT PROPERTIES
TranslateTransform	Displaces your coordinate system by some amount. This transform is useful if you want to draw the same shape in different places.	X, Y
RotateTransform	Rotates your coordinate system. The shapes you draw normally are turned around a center point you choose.	Angle, CenterX, CenterY
ScaleTransform	Scales your coordinate system up or down, so that your shapes are drawn smaller or larger. You can apply different degrees of scaling in the x and y dimensions, thereby stretching or compressing your shape. When a shape is resized, Silverlight resizes its inside area and its border proportionately. That means the larger your shape grows, the thicker its border will be.	ScaleX, ScaleY, CenterX, CenterY
SkewTransform	Warps your coordinate system by slanting it a number of degrees. For example, if you draw a square, it becomes a parallelogram.	AngleX, AngleY, CenterX, CenterY

NAME	DESCRIPTION	IMPORTANT PROPERTIES
MatrixTransform	Modifies your coordinate system using matrix multiplication with the matrix you supply. This is the most complex option—it requires some mathematical skill.	Matrix
TransformGroup	Combines multiple transforms so they can all be applied at once. The order in which you apply transformations is important—it affects the final result. For example, rotating a shape (with RotateTransform) and then moving it (with TranslateTransform) sends the shape off in a different direction than if you move it and *then* rotate it.	N/A

Technically, all transforms use matrix math to alter the coordinates of your shape. However, using the prebuilt transforms such as TranslateTransform, RotateTransform, ScaleTransform, and SkewTransform is far simpler than using the MatrixTransform and trying to work out the right matrix for the operation you want to perform. When you perform a series of transforms with the TransformGroup, Silverlight fuses your transforms together into a single MatrixTransform, ensuring optimal performance.

Note   All transforms have automatic change notification support. If you change a transform that's being used in a shape, the shape will redraw itself immediately.

Transforms are one of those quirky concepts that turn out to be extremely useful in a variety of different contexts. Some examples include the following:

- **Angling a shape**: Using the `RotateTransform`, you can turn your coordinate system to create certain shapes more easily.

- **Repeating a shape**: Many drawings are built using a similar shape in several different places. Using a transform, you can take a shape and then move it, rotate it, resize it, and so on.

Tip   In order to use the same shape in multiple places, you'll need to duplicate the shape in your markup (which isn't ideal), use code (to create the shape programmatically), or use the `Path` shape described in Chapter 6. The `Path` shape accepts `Geometry` objects, and you can store a geometry object as a resource so it can be reused throughout your markup.

- **Dynamic effects and animation**: You can create a number of sophisticated effects with the help of a transform, such as rotating a shape, moving it from one place to another, and warping it dynamically.

Note   Using the tools of Silverlight graphics, you can implement other effects, like glows and shadows, which use multiple layers of gradient fills. You   can   find   one   example   at `http://blogs.msdn.com/timrule/archive/2008/04/21/shadow-effect.aspx`.

The Last Word

It's important to understand the plumbing behind 2D graphics, because it makes it far easier for you to manipulate them. For example, you can alter a standard 2D graphic by modifying the brushes used to paint various shapes, applying transforms to individual geometries, or altering the opacity or transform of an entire layer of shapes. More dramatically, you can add, remove, or alter individual geometries. These techniques can be easily combined with the animation. For example, it's easy to rotate a `Geometry` object by modifying the `Angle` property of a `RotateTransform`, fade a layer of shapes into existence using `DrawingGroup.Opacity`, or create a swirling gradient effect by animating a `LinearGradientBrush` that paints the fill for a `GeometryDrawing`.

Chapter 8: Animation

Animation allows you to create truly *dynamic* user interfaces. It's often used to apply effects—for example, icons that grow when you move over them, logos that spin, text that scrolls into view, and so on. Sometimes these effects seem like excessive glitz. But used properly, animations can enhance an application in a number of ways. They can make an application seem more responsive, natural, and intuitive. (For example, a button that slides in when you click it feels like a real, physical button—not just another gray rectangle.) Animations can also draw attention to important elements and guide the user through transitions to new content. (For example, an application could advertise new content with a twinkling, blinking, or pulsing icon.)

Animations are a core part of the Silverlight model. That means you don't need to use timers and event handling code to put them into action. Instead, you can create them declaratively, configure them using one of a handful of classes, and put them into action without writing a single line of C# code. Animations also integrate themselves seamlessly into ordinary Silverlight pages. For example, if you animate a button so it drifts around the page, the button still behaves like a button. It can be styled, it can receive focus, and it can be clicked to fire off the typical event handling code. This is what separates animation from traditional media files, such as video. When you put a video page in your application, it's a completely separate region of your application—it's able to play video content, but it's not user interactive.

Note   Silverlight animation is a scaled-down version of the WPF animation system. It keeps the same conceptual framework, the same model for defining animations with animation classes, and the same storyboard system. However, WPF developers will find some key differences, particularly in the way that animations are created and started in code. (For example, Silverlight elements lack the built-in `BeginAnimation()` method that they have in WPF.)

Understanding Silverlight Animation

Often, an animation is thought of as a series of frames. To perform the animation, these frames are shown one after the other, like a stop-motion video.

Silverlight animations use a dramatically different model. Essentially, a Silverlight animation is simply a way to modify the value of a dependency property over an interval of time. For example, to make a button that grows and shrinks, you can modify its `Width` property in an animation. To make it shimmer, you could change the properties of the `LinearGradientBrush` that it uses for its background. The secret to creating the right animation is determining what properties you need to modify.

If you want to make other changes that can't be made by modifying a property, you're out of luck. For example, you can't add or remove elements as part of animation. Similarly, you can't ask Silverlight to perform a transition between a starting scene and an ending scene (although some crafty workarounds can simulate this effect). And finally, you can use animation only with a dependency property, because only dependency properties use the dynamic property resolution system that takes animations into account.

At first glance, the property-focused nature of Silverlight animations seems terribly limiting. However, as you work with Silverlight, you'll find that it's surprisingly capable. In fact, you can create a wide range of animated effects using common properties that every element supports.

The Rules of Animation

In order to understand Silverlight animation, you need to understand the following key rules:

- **Silverlight animations are time-based**: Thus, you set the initial state, the final state, and the duration of your animation. Silverlight calculates the frame rate.

- **Animations act on properties**: That means a Silverlight animation can do only one thing: modify the value of a property over an interval of time. This sounds like a significant limitation (and it many ways it is), but there's a surprisingly large range of effects you can create by simply modifying properties.

- **Every data type requires a different animation class**: For example, the `Button.Width` property uses the double data type. To animate it, you use the `DoubleAnimation` class. If you want to modify the color that's used to paint the background of your `Canvas`, you need to use the `ColorAnimation` class.

Silverlight has relatively few animation classes, so you're limited in the data types you can use. At present, you can use animations to modify properties with the following data types: double, object, `Color`, and `Point`. However, you can also craft your own animation classes that work for different data types—all you need to do is derive from `System.Windows.Media.Animation` and indicate how the value should change as time passes.

Many data types don't have a corresponding animation class because it wouldn't be practical. A prime example is enumerations. For example, you can control how an element is placed in a layout panel using the `HorizontalAlignment` property, which takes a value from the `HorizontalAlignment` enumeration. However, the `HorizontalAlignment` enumeration allows you to choose between only four values (`Left`, `Right`, `Center`, and `Stretch`), which greatly limits its use in an animation. Although you can swap between one orientation and another, you can't smoothly transition an element from one alignment to another. For that reason, there's no animation class for the `HorizontalAlignment` data type. You can build one yourself, but you're still constrained by the four values of the enumeration.

Reference types are not usually animated. However, their subproperties are. For example, all content controls sport a `Background` property that allows you to set a `Brush` object that's used to paint the background. It's rarely efficient to use animation to switch from one brush to another, but you can use animation to vary the properties of a brush. For example, you could vary the `Color` property of a `SolidColorBrush` (using the `ColorAnimation` class) or the `Offset` property of a `GradientStop` in a `LinearGradientBrush` (using the `DoubleAnimation` class). This extends the reach of Silverlight animation, allowing you to animate specific aspects of an element's appearance.

The Last Word

This chapter should have given you a basic understanding of Silverlight animation capabilities and the rules for animation. That pretty much wraps up this book. I hope you have gotten a feel for the visual elements of Silverlight and that this has been a helpful introduction.

Related Titles

Ghosh, Jit, Scherotter, Michael, *Silverlight 2 Recipes: A Problem-Solution Approach*, Berkeley, CA: Apress, 2008

MacDonald, Matthew, *Pro Silverlight 2*, Berkeley, CA: Apress, 2008

MacDonald, Matthew, *Pro WPF*: *Windows Presentation Foundation in .NET 3.0*, Berkeley, CA: Apress, 2007

Copyright

Silverlight 2 Visual Essentials

© 2008 by Matthew MacDonald

ISBN-13 (electronic): 978-1-4302-1583-7

ISBN-13 (paperback): 978-1-4302-1582-0

Distributed to the book trade in the United States by Springer-Verlag New York, Inc., 233 Spring Street, 6th Floor, New York, NY 10013, and outside the United States by Springer-Verlag GmbH & Co. KG, Tiergartenstr. 17, 69112 Heidelberg, Germany.

In the United States: phone 1-800-SPRINGER, fax 201-348-4505, e-mail orders@springer-ny.com, or visit http://www.springer-ny.com. Outside the United States: fax +49 6221 345229, e-mail orders@springer.de, or visit http://www.springer.de.

For information on translations, please contact Apress directly at 2855 Telegraph Ave, Suite 600, Berkeley, CA 94705. Phone 510-549-5930, fax 510-549-5939, e-mail info@apress.com, or visit http://www.apress.com.

Copyright